EVERYMAN,
I WILL GO WITH THEE,
AND BE THY GUIDE,
IN THY MOST NEED
TO GO BY THY SIDE

# ANNE FRANK

# THE DIARY
## OF A YOUNG
# GIRL

## THE DEFINITIVE EDITION

EDITED BY OTTO H. FRANK
AND MIRJAM PRESSLER

TRANSLATED BY SUSAN MASSOTTY

EVERYMAN'S LIBRARY
Alfred A. Knopf  New York  Toronto

333

THIS IS A BORZOI BOOK
PUBLISHED BY ALFRED A. KNOPF

First included in Everyman's Library, 2010
Copyright © 1991 by The Anne Frank-Fonds, Basel, Switzerland
English translation Copyright © by Doubleday, a division of
Random House, Inc.
Photographs Copyright © by the Anne Frank-Fonds, Basel, Switzerland
Anne Frank Stichting
Introduction Copyright © 2010 by Francine Prose
Bibliography and Chronology Copyright © 2010 by Everyman's Library
Typography by Peter B. Willberg

www.randomhouse.com/everymans

ISBN: 978-0-307-59400-6 (US)

*Book design by Barbara de Wilde and Carol Devine Carson*

Typeset in the UK by AccComputing, North Barrow, Somerset

Printed and bound in Germany by GGP Media GmbH, Pössneck

# C O N T E N T S

## THE DIARY OF A YOUNG GIRL

# INTRODUCTION

Every masterpiece is unique, but some are more anomalous than others. If we consider all the volumes that have appeared so far in the Everyman series, the cornerstones and classics of our cultural tradition, *The Diary of Anne Frank* is, we may notice, the only one to have been written by a girl between the ages of thirteen and fifteen. If it seems improbable that a person of that tender age should have produced a work not just of maturity but of genius, that improbability only increases the awe we feel, or ought to feel, in the presence of a book that possesses all the qualities we expect of great memoirs and spiritual autobiographies, and, to some extent, of great novels.

Varied and memorable characters are revealed in all their complexity and depth, summoned to life on the page complete with all their most admirable virtues and most maddening flaws, their engagingly and appallingly human quirks and contradictions. We find ourselves in the presence of a singular consciousness, a highly particular and utterly persuasive narrative voice, elastic and capacious enough to encompass the most day-to-day details of domestic life (how to peel potatoes!), incisive portrayals of the ways in which people behave under enormous stress, flights of speculative metaphysics, and passages of sophisticated inquiry into the mystery of human nature. Comparing Anne Frank's diary to the *Confessions* of Saint Augustine, the poet John Berryman pointed out that a diary allows its readers to watch the growth of a soul, the simultaneously quotidian and miraculous transformation that accompanies what Berryman termed "the conversion of a child into a person," a process that, in his view, had never been so brilliantly or even adequately described before Anne Frank tracked it in herself, and recorded it in her diary. "It took, I believe," wrote Berryman, "a special pressure forcing the child–adult conversion, and exceptional self-awareness and exceptional candour and exceptional powers of expression, to bring that strange or normal change into view."

The diary reminds us of what it is like to go through a stage of life – adolescence – that all readers past childhood have endured and still remember, or have tried to forget. It speaks to us about the universal experiences of first love, family entanglements, hope and despair, society and solitude, terror and even boredom, and at the same time it reports on an utterly specific and exceptionally ugly period in our history, an era that is receding from living memory with every second that passes. Like all great art, it reveals something about the individual hand that created it, and something about what it means to be a human being – in this case, what is required to maintain human decency and compassion in the most inhuman and dehumanizing circumstances.

*

*The Diary of Anne Frank* is among the most widely read and taught and (for a variety of reasons, most often its delicate but clear-eyed portrayal of adolescent sexuality) most frequently censored texts in the world; translated from the original Dutch into dozens of languages, it appears on the curriculum of schools everywhere. Viewing Laurent Cantet's 2008 French film, *The Class* (*Entre les murs*), set in a high school in the suburbs of Paris, we watch a group of teenagers, nearly all of them first-generation immigrants to France, studying and discussing the diary. In 2004, a segment of the CBS series *60 Minutes* reported that North Korean schoolchildren were being instructed to see themselves as Anne Frank, and George W. Bush as the modern equivalent of Hitler.

What most students learn is that Anne Frank began writing in the little book, with its checked cloth cover, soon after she received it as a gift from her parents on the occasion of her thirteenth birthday, in June 1942. Roughly a month after Anne commenced her giddy narrative of friends and boyfriends, childish allegiances and humorous experiences at school, her family went into hiding in a cramped attic (as it is often termed, though this common feature of Amsterdam canal-house construction more resembles what might be called a rear addition) above and behind the spice and pectin business that her father Otto ran until the Nazi racial laws made it illegal for Otto, a Jew, to conduct any business at all.

# INTRODUCTION

For the next twenty-five months, until August 1944, when the Frank family was arrested and deported, first to the Westerbork transit camp and afterwards to Auschwitz, the Franks – Otto, his wife Edith, their daughters Margot and Anne – shared the "secret annex" with the Van Pels family (Hermann, Auguste, and their son Peter) and a dentist named Fritz Pfeffer. As those months wore on, Anne's vivid account of their lives in hiding developed into a very different kind of book from anything that she, newly turned thirteen, could have imagined that she would be confiding in her journal.

By contrast, her parents had known all too well that the deceptively normal life they were leading in the spring of 1942 could not possibly last much longer. For Anne's birthday, they had arranged a party at which her friends watched a film of Rin Tin Tin, which they showed in their apartment, in Amsterdam's Merwedeplein neighborhood. By then the Jews of Holland had been forbidden to attend the public cinema, and an increasingly capricious and sadistic series of regulations had banned Jews from parks, pools, public transportation, and theaters, made it illegal for them to own radios or bicycles, or sit in their own gardens after eight in the evening, and had mandated that Jewish children attend separate schools from their Christian neighbors.

Born and raised in Frankfurt, Otto, the son of a banking family, had already fled Germany to escape the Nazi anti-Jewish laws, and he had hoped that Holland might provide a safe haven for him and his family. But those hopes were dashed when the Germans invaded the Netherlands in May 1940.

By 1942, the occupying forces, aided by the local police, had begun rounding up Dutch Jews and deporting them for forced labor "in the east." A small minority chose to remain and go underground, concealed in barns and attics and cellars, hidden and kept alive by members of the Dutch resistance and by brave Dutch citizens. The most famous of these was Miep Gies, who together with her husband Jan and a handful of Otto Frank's former employees, took on the dangerous and demanding responsibility of concealing and feeding the eight people in the annex behind the offices of the Opekta spice warehouse at 263 Prinsengracht, in central Amsterdam.

For some time, the Franks had been making arrangements to disappear, constructing and outfitting their hiding place for a stay of indefinite length. But their plans were drastically altered in early July 1942, when sixteen-year-old Margot received a call-up notice for deportation. As soon as Anne began to recover from her shock at having been compelled to trade a life that, however restricted, included sunshine and air and freedom, for an existence in which she was forbidden to make a sound during the hours when business was being conducted in the offices downstairs, she began to describe that constrained but nonetheless richly complex new world, in pages of her diary.

During the next two years, she recorded her observations of how she and her family and their neighbors lived, the terrifying break-ins, the perpetual fear of betrayal, the family squabbles, the shifting loyalties, the frayed nerves, and the moments of communal harmony. She fell in and out of love with Peter van Pels, formed and reformed her ideas about God, herself, and her fellow humans, all the while keeping her readers informed – with the aid of news brought by the helpers and the contraband radio on which the family listened to music and broadcasts from the Dutch government in exile – about the progress of the war and the increasingly horrific persecution of the Jews all over Holland, not only in the streets outside the attic.

In August 1944, someone (there has been much debate about the identity of the informer) betrayed the Franks. Led by an officer of the Dutch Gestapo, a group of armed men forced the Opekta employees, at gunpoint, to show them where the Jews were hiding. After the Franks and the Van Pelses and Fritz Pfeffer had been taken away, Miep Gies, with another of the helpers and a warehouse worker, collected the journals and the loose pages on which Anne had been writing. Miep's intention was to return Anne's diary to her when she came back – which of course she never did. After it had become clear that Anne had died of malnutrition and disease, at the age of fifteen, in the Bergen-Belsen concentration camp, Miep gave the diary to Otto Frank, the only one of the eight hidden Jews who had survived the war.

The diary ends before the Franks' arrest, and though published versions include an epilogue describing what happened to Anne and her family after they were taken from the attic, it has been observed that some of the book's readers (younger students, in particular) have been allowed to remain ignorant – or, as some see it, have been spared the shattering knowledge – of its author's tragic fate. But for most, their initial exposure to her book situates it firmly in its horrific historical context.

But what very few readers, of any age, seem to know is what sort of book they are holding in their hands. What they imagine, or have been told, is that they are reading the entries Anne made, every day or every few days, in the little checked book, which were then transcribed, more or less exactly as written, corrected by her father, and subsequently published. The unlikeliness of this should have been obvious, if only because the diminutive diary we see in photos could hardly have contained such a large quantity of text unless it had been written in microscopic script. More importantly, we might have been struck by the remarkable consistency in tone – by which I mean the narrative voice, the diction, the confident maturity of the authorial stance, the deftness with which that voice moves between narration and reflection – between the earliest and latest diary entries. Considering how far we watch Anne travel within the confines of that claustrophobic space, considering her astonishing change from a little girl to a young woman, how could it have been possible that the little girl wrote almost exactly as the young woman did, so that Anne's literary voice remained, in essence, the same?

The answer is that during her final months in the attic, Anne herself revised and edited the sections she had written throughout her years in hiding. This information was made readily available in 1986, for readers of Dutch, and three years later for anglophones, with the publication, by the Netherlands State Institute for War Documentation, of *The Critical Edition* of *The Diary of Anne Frank*. This massive volume includes – in horizontal parallel bands, printed across its pages – three versions of the diary: Anne's original draft, her revisions, and the text Otto Frank compiled using Anne's first and second drafts. Included in *The Critical Edition* are photographs of the manuscripts, facsimiles that allow us to see how Anne's handwriting changed from the childish block printing of the earliest entries to the practiced and confident cursive with which, by the end of her time in the attic, she was covering as much as eleven pages a day.

In March 1944, four months before the Franks' arrest, they heard, over their contraband radio, a broadcast in which the Dutch minister of culture in exile called for ordinary Dutch citizens to preserve their personal papers so their descendants would understand what they had endured during the war. Anne, a passionate reader who had long thought of herself as a writer – a childhood friend described Anne scribbling secretively in her notebook, and while in hiding she was working on a novel, essays and stories in addition to the diary – rapidly decided (with the concurrence of the others in the annex) that her journal was precisely what the minister had in mind.

Imagining that her account of life in hiding would eventually be published, she began to revise it, this time with the general reader in mind. She went back to the first entries – cutting, editing, explicating, rethinking her accounts of certain events, and adding sections (for example, the diagram of the living quarters at 263 Prinsengracht) that would not have been necessary if she were to be the sole audience for what she termed her "romance of the secret annex." Only in revision did she come up with the idea of writing the diary letters to the imaginary friend she called Kitty, a literary device that allowed her to address the reader more directly, in the intimate second person. In many cases, she predated entries, so that the famous diary letter in which she speaks to Kitty of the loneliness and alienation that haunts her despite her many friends and would-be boyfriends was in fact composed almost two years after that demanding social life had completely ceased to exist. The differences between the first and second versions are most marked in her revisions of the earliest diary letters, somewhat jumbled accounts of recent events that she was better able to explain by availing herself of the clarity and relative calm of retrospect. By the morning of her arrest, on August 4, 1944, Anne had not only filled the checked, cloth-covered journal, but also two exercise books that the Dutch helpers had brought her. Her revisions cover more than three hundred sheets of loose colored paper.

When, upon reading his daughter's diary, Otto Frank became convinced that she'd wanted it to be widely read, he combined her first and second drafts, most often respecting her editing decisions, though on occasion reversing the changes she had made. He restored the intensity that Anne had deleted from her account of her relationship with Peter; in her second draft, Anne, who had outgrown her obsession with the boy upstairs, had recast their romance as a more platonic friendship. Otto employed the pseudonyms that Anne had chosen to use for her neighbors in the event that her book was published, but he opted to keep his own family's real names, though Anne had specified that she and her parents and sister would be called the Robins. Overall, comparing Anne's two drafts, and Otto's compilation, we cannot help but applaud his editorial skills, his instincts for what was necessary or extraneous, illuminating or confusing, and for what would keep his daughter's narrative moving swiftly along.

But finally what impresses and moves us most is the quality of Anne's writing: her eye for detail and gesture, her instinct for pacing and rhythm, her skill at weaving together meditation and narration, reflection and drama, at knowing how to make her compelling story exert its unrelenting magnetic claim on the reader's attention. Throughout, the freshness and the apparent naivety of Anne's voice seduce us into considering, along with her, the extremes of human behavior, the heights and depths of what we are willing to do to – and for – one another.

And it can only deepen our admiration to know that this book, which has been universally read and admired, this intensely personal memoir which over time has become emblematic of the sufferings of so many millions, is not simply the spontaneous, accidental outpourings of a young girl's heart but rather a consciously crafted work of literature. Anne Frank's diary is as expertly written, as beautiful, and as powerful as she must have intended, when, in the final months of a life that would so soon be cut short, she labored, like any artist, to fashion something solid and enduring from her dream of what she so urgently wanted her book to be.

Francine Prose

# SELECT BIBLIOGRAPHY

WORKS BY ANNE FRANK:
*The Diary of a Young Girl,* translated by B. M. Mooyaart-Doubleday, introduction by Eleanor Roosevelt. Garden City: Doubleday, 1952.
*The Diary of Anne Frank: The Critical Edition.* Prepared by the Netherlands State Institute for War Documentation. Edited by David Barnouw and Gerrold van der Stroom, translated by Arnold J. Pomerans and B. M. Mooyaart-Doubleday. New York: Doubleday, 1989.
*The Diary of Anne Frank: The Revised Critical Edition.* Prepared by the Netherlands State Institute for War Documentation. Edited by David Barnouw and Gerrold van der Stroom, translated by Arnold J. Pomerans and B. M. Mooyaart-Doubleday. New York: Doubleday, 2003.
*The Diary of a Young Girl: The Definitive Edition,* Edited by Otto H. Frank and Mirjam Pressler, translated by Susan Masotty. New York: Doubleday, 1995.
*Anne Frank's Tales from the Secret Annex: Fables, Short Stories, Essays, and an Unfinished Novel by the Author of "The Diary of a Young Girl."* Translated by Michel Mok and Ralph Manheim. New York: Washington Square Press, 1983.

BIOGRAPHY AND CRITICISM:
*Anne Frank House: A Museum with a Story.* Amsterdam: Anne Frank House, 2001.
BLOOM, HAROLD, ed., *A Scholarly Look at* The Diary of Anne Frank. Philadelphia: Chelsea House, 1999.
ENZER, HYMAN A., and SANDRA SOLOTAROFF-ENZER, eds, *Anne Frank: Reflections on Her Life and Legacy.* Urbana and Chicago: University of Illinois Press, 2000.
GIES, MIEP, with ALISON LESLIE GOLD, *Anne Frank Remembered: The Story of the Woman Who Helped to Hide the Frank Family.* New York: Simon & Schuster, 1987.
GOODRICH, FRANCES, and ALBERT HACKETT, *The Diary of Anne Frank.* Based upon *The Diary of a Young Girl.* Newly adapted by Wendy Kesselman. New York: Dramatists Play Series, Inc., 2000.
KOPF, HEDDA ROSNER, *Understanding Anne Frank's "The Diary of a Young Girl." A Student Casebook to Issues, Sources, and Historical Documents.* Westport, Connecticut: Greenwood Press, 1997.
LINDWER, WILLY, *The Last Seven Months of Anne* Frank, translated by Alison Meersshaert. New York: Pantheon, 1991.

MÜLLER, MELISSA, *Anne Frank: The Biography*, translated by Rita and Robert Kimber. New York: Henry Holt, 1998.

PRESSLER, MIRJAM, *Anne Frank: A Hidden Life*. New York: Puffin Books, 1999.

PROSE, FRANCINE, *Anne Frank: The Book, the Life, the Afterlife*. New York: HarperCollins Publishers, 2009.

ROL, RUUD VAN DER, and RIAN VERHOEVEN, eds, *Anne Frank: Beyond the Diary*. New York: Viking Press, 1993.

SCHNABEL, ERNST, *Anne Frank: A Portrait in Courage*, translated by Richard Winston and Clara Winston. New York: Harcourt, Brace, 1958.

FRANCINE PROSE is a novelist and critic and the author of *Anne Frank: The Book, the Life, the Afterlife*.

# CHRONOLOGY

---

| DATE | AUTHOR'S LIFE | LITERARY CONTEXT |
|------|---------------|------------------|
| 1922 | | Mandelstam: *Tristia*. |
| | | Pasternak: *My Sister – Life*. |
| | | Mansfield: *The Garden Party*. |
| | | Eliot: *The Wasteland*. |
| | | Joyce: *Ulysses*. |
| | | Cummings: *The Enormous Room*. |
| 1923 | | Colette: *Le Blé en herbe*. |
| | | Radiguet: *Le Diable au corps*. |
| | | Slauerhoff: *Archipel (Archipelago)*. |
| 1924 | | Breton's Surrealist Manifesto. |
| | | Desnos: *Deuil pour deuil*. |
| | | Bulgakov: *The White Guard*. |
| | | Ehrenburg: *The Love of Jeanne Ney*. |
| | | Mann: *The Magic Mountain*. |
| | | Ford: *Parade's End* (to 1928). |
| 1925 | German-born Otto Frank, who fought in the German army in the First World War and afterwards reluctantly took over the family bank, marries Edith Holländer in a Jewish ceremony at the Aachen synagogue on May 12. They live in Frankfurt am Main, Germany, after a honeymoon in Italy. | Trotsky: *Literature and Revolution*. Morand: *L'Europe galante*. Forster: *A Passage to India*. Fitzgerald: *The Great Gatsby*. Kafka: *The Trial*. Woolf: *Mrs Dalloway*. |
| 1926 | Anne's older sister Margot Betti Frank is born, February 16. | Lawrence: *The Plumed Serpent*. Kafka: *The Castle*. Schreiner: *From Man to Man*. Nabokov: *Mary*. Tsvetaeva: *The Ratcatcher*. Hemingway: *The Sun Also Rises*. |
| 1927 | | Proust: *Le Temps retrouvé* (last volume of seven-novel sequence *A la recherche du temps perdu*, begun in 1913). Woolf: *To the Lighthouse*. Hesse: *Steppenwolf*. Heidegger: *Being and Time*. Zweig: *Confusion of Feelings*. Birth of Günter Grass. |

Stalin becomes Secretary of Communist Party Central Commitee; Russia becomes USSR. Mussolini's march on Rome; Mussolini appointed premier by King Victor Emmanuel III. British mandate in Palestine.

Hyper-inflation in Germany. Repeated German defaults on reparations lead Poincaré, French prime minister, to send troops into the Ruhr Valley. Hitler's Munich putsch fails.
Dawes Plan ends reparations crisis. Death of Lenin.

Period of Franco-German reconciliation; Locarno Conference guarantees Franco-German frontier. French troops evacuate the Ruhr. Hitler publishes *Mein Kampf*. Mussolini dismisses Italian parliament and assumes dictatorial powers. Qajar dynasty deposed in Persia; Reza Khan becomes shah.

France sponsors Germany's entry into the League of Nations. General strike in Britain.

Trotsky, co-founder with Lenin of modern Russia, expelled from Russian Communist Party. Stalin's struggle for power in Russia. Chiang Kai-shek, leader of the Kuomintang (KMT), the Chinese nationalist party, unleashes an anti-communist purge; beginning of Chinese Civil War (to 1949). Lindbergh flies the Atlantic.

| DATE | AUTHOR'S LIFE | LITERARY CONTEXT |
|------|---------------|------------------|
| 1928 | | Waugh: *Decline and Fall*. Lawrence: *Lady Chatterley's Lover* (not published in full in UK until 1960). Brecht/Weill: *Threepenny Opera*. Birth of Elie Wiesel. |
| 1929 | Annelies Marie Frank is born, June 12. | Schreiner: *Undine*. Hemingway: *A Farewell to Arms*. Shaw: *The Apple Cart*. Woolf: *A Room of One's Own*. Zweig: *Buchmendal*. Döblin: *Berlin Alexanderplatz*. Remarque: *All Quiet on the Western Front*. Mann: *Mario and the Magician*. Death of Hugo Hofmannsthal. |
| 1930 | | Stapledon: *Last and First Men*. Freud: *Civilization and its Discontents*. Musil: *The Man Without Qualities* (to 1932). Hesse: *Narziss and Goldmund*. Waugh: *Vile Bodies*. |
| 1931 | The Frank family move to a smaller house, 24 Ganghofer-strasse, due to the decline of the family bank and because their landlord is a member of the Nazi party. | Lawrence: *Apocalypse*. Woolf: *The Waves*. |
| 1932 | | Huxley: *Brave New World*. Broch: *The Sleepwalkers*. Roth: *The Radetzky March*. Slauerhoff: *Het verboden rijk* (*The Forbidden Realm*). |
| 1933 | In the summer, increasing discrimination against Jews and difficulties running the family business in the face of a German boycott lead the Franks to move to Amsterdam. Otto Frank sets up a company selling Opekta, a gelling preparation used for making jam, while Anne stays with her grandmother in Germany. Miep Santrouschitz begins working as Otto Frank's secretary. | Orwell: *Down and Out in Paris and London*. Hemingway: *Winner Take Nothing*. Wells: *The Shape of Things to Come*. Malraux: *La Condition humaine*. Asch: *Three Cities*. Slauerhoff: *Soleares*. |

# CHRONOLOGY

In Britain women over 21 are given right to vote. Stalin announces first Five-Year Plan to transform industry and agriculture in USSR. Chiang Kai-shek captures Peking; unification of Republic of China. Birth of the Dalai Lama. Fleming discovers penicillin.

Wall Street Crash: collapse of New York Stock Exchange; worldwide economic depression follows. Forcible collectivization of agriculture begins in USSR; around ten million peasants killed, exiled or sent to concentration camps. Term "apartheid" first used at Kroonstad to describe separate development of black and white cultures.

Nazis win seats from moderates in German elections. Gandhi begins civil disobedience campaign in India. Land Apportionment Act restricts land ownership rights of black farmers in Southern Rhodesia, exacerbating antipathy towards colonial rule.

Statue of Westminster establishes legal status of dominions of British Commonwealth. Japanese army invades Manchuria.

In July the Nazi party becomes the largest party in Germany with 37% of votes. SA troops march through streets singing anti-semitic songs. Germany suspends payment of war reparations. Oswald Mosley founds British Union of Fascists. Unemployed marchers clash with police in London. Landslide victory for Democrat F. D. Roosevelt in US presidential election.
Nazi party comes to power in Germany with Adolf Hitler as Chancellor and proclaims Third Reich in January; National Socialist Party declared only legal party. Freedom of speech and assembly is disallowed. The Gestapo – Nazi secret police – established. Boycotts of Jewish shops are organized as early as April. Books by Jews and other "undesirables" are burned in huge rallies in Germany in May. The Aryan declaration, the *Berufsverbote*, prevents Jews from working in important professions. Many Jewish Germans seek refugee status in neighboring countries. Germany leaves the League of Nations. First Nazi concentration camps in Germany. Roosevelt's "New Deal" strategies revealed. Japan withdraws from League of Nations.

| DATE | AUTHOR'S LIFE | LITERARY CONTEXT |
|------|---------------|------------------|
| 1934 | Anne arrives at her new home in Amsterdam in February as a surprise birthday present for her sister Margot. Anne starts attending a Montessori kindergarten in May. | Fitzgerald: *Tender is the Night.* Waugh: *A Handful of Dust.* Mann: *The Young Joseph.* Cain: *The Postman Always Rings Twice.* Vestdijk: *Terug tot Ina Damman (Back to Ina Damman).* |
| 1935 | | Compton-Burnett: *A House and its Head.* Vestdijk: *Else Böhler.* Slauerhoff: *Een eerlijk zeemansgraf (An Honourable Seaman's Grave).* |
| 1936 | | Huxley: *Eyeless in Gaza.* Sartre: *L'Imagination.* Vestdijk: *Meneer Visser's hellevaart (Mr Visser's Perdition).* |
| 1937 | Van Pels family emigrate from Osnabruck to Amsterdam in June. Hermann van Pels becomes Otto Frank's business partner. Bep Voskuijl comes to work for the company. | Steinbeck: *Of Mice and Men.* Orwell: *The Road to Wigan Pier.* Wells: *Star Begotten.* Stapledon: *Star Maker.* Blixen: *Out of Africa.* |
| 1938 | Otto Frank and Hermann van Pels set up the Petacon company making a spice mixture for use in the preparation of meats. Johannes Kleiman starts work as bookkeeper. | Sartre: *Nausea.* Greene: *Brighton Rock.* Orwell: *Homage to Catalonia.* Bowen: *The Death of the Heart.* Nabokov: *The Gift.* Vestdijk: *De nadagen van Pilatus (The Last Days of Pilate).* |
| 1939 | Anne's grandmother Holländer moves to Amsterdam and lives with the Franks. Van Pels family move to Rivierenbuurt, close by the Franks. Otto Frank and Hermann van Pels become close friends. Fritz Pfeffer enters the Netherlands in December by train as a refugee and is later joined by his Catholic girlfriend, Charlotte Kaletta. | Steinbeck: *The Grapes of Wrath.* Mann: *Lotte in Weimar.* Joyce: *Finnegans Wake.* |
| 1940 | On December 1 the Opekta/ Petacon companies relocate to 263 Prinsengracht. | Greene: *The Power and the Glory.* Hemingway: *For Whom the Bell Tolls.* Stead: *The Man Who Loved Children.* |

# CHRONOLOGY

New Dutch immigration laws to stop flow of Jewish refugees into the
country. Night of the Long Knives in Germany; Hitler orders assassination
of SA Chief Ernst Röhm. Unrest in Spain. Hitler becomes Führer. German
rearmament commences. Forced sterilization of Gypsies and African-
Germans begins. Mao Zedong's "Long March" across China (October
1934–October 1935).

Great Terror in USSR. Seventh and final congress of Comintern officially
endorses Popular Front against Fascism. Military conscription introduced in
Germany, violating the Versailles treaty. German government's Nuremberg
Laws, legitimizing persecution of Jews and debarring them from public life.
Italy invades Abyssinia; League of Nations applies economic sanctions.
Persian empire is renamed Iran.
German troops enter Rhineland. Spanish Civil War (to 1939). Stalinist
show trials (to 1938). Rome–Berlin Axis allies Hitler with Mussolini.
Anti-Comintern Pact agreed by Germany and Japan (Italy joins later).
Abdication of Edward VIII.
Basque village of Guernica destroyed by German bomber planes. Religious
persecution in Germany: arrests begin of Protestant pastors and Roman
Catholic priests. Chamberlain becomes prime minister in Britain. Stalin
begins purge of the Red Army. Sino-Japanese War (to 1945).

Germany annexes Austria on March 12 (*Anschluss*). Munich conference.
Germany occupies disputed areas of Czechoslovakia. November 9: "Night
of Broken Glass" (*Kristallnacht*); synagogues are attacked, over 100 Jews
killed and 30,000 male Jews deported to concentration camps and prisons.
All Jewish businesses are confiscated, Jews are banned from owning a
business. Manifesto of Fascist racialist ideology adopted by Mussolini's
government.
Nazi–Soviet Pact and "Pact of Steel" between Germany and Italy.
September 1: Hitler invades Poland, occupation of Danzig, France and
Britain declare war on Germany; outbreak of World War II. Soviet invasion
of Poland and Finland. Soviet Union expelled from League of Nations.
Spanish Civil War ends.

May 10: Hitler invades the Netherlands. More than 150 Jews commit suicide
when the Germans reach Amsterdam. Hitler's armies reach Paris on
June 14. Italy joins the war as Germany's ally after German invasion of
Norway and Denmark. Auschwitz concentration camp established and
Warsaw ghetto opened; by the end of 1941 almost all Polish Jews are in

| DATE | AUTHOR'S LIFE | LITERARY CONTEXT |
|------|---------------|------------------|
| 1940 *cont.* | | Koestler: *Darkness at Noon.*<br>Akhmatova: *From Six Books.* |
| 1941 | The Opekta business is registered in the name of Johannes Kleiman. Victor Kugler becomes the proxy director and the business is renamed Gies and Co. Miep and Jan Gies are married; Otto Frank holds a party in the office. Anne is forced to leave the Montessori school and attend the Jewish Lyceum with her sister Margot in accordance with new Nazi laws. Johannes Kleiman suggests the annex as a suitable hiding place to Otto Frank. | Fitzgerald: *The Last Tycoon.*<br>Brecht: *Mother Courage and Her Children.*<br>Vestdijk: *Aktaion onder de sterren* (*Aktaion Under the Stars*).<br>Death of Virginia Woolf. |
| 1942 | Anne's grandmother Holländer dies of cancer in January. Anne receives a diary as a present for her 13th birthday. Preparation of the secret annex begins.<br>On July 5, Anne's sister Margot receives a call-up for deportation to Germany. The Franks go into hiding in the annex the next day. The Van Pels family move into the annex July 13. On November 16 Fritz Pfeffer, Miep's dentist, joins them. | Eliot: *Four Quartets.*<br>Camus: *L'Etranger.*<br>Zweig: *The Royal Game.*<br>Klaus Mann's autobiography, *The Turning Point.*<br>Hesse: *The Glass Bead Game.*<br>Birth of Peter Handke. |
| 1943 | | Sartre: *L'Être et le néant.*<br>de Beauvoir: *L'Invitée.*<br>West: *Black Lamb and Grey Falcon.* |
| 1944 | After hearing the Bolkestein radio broadcast on March 29, Anne begins editing her diary for publication. August 1 is Anne's last diary entry. On August 4 an SS officer and three Dutch policemen raid the Opekta store. The Franks, Van Pelses, Fritz Pfeffer and two helpers (Kugler and Kleiman) are taken to a German jail for interrogation. | Borges: *Ficciones.*<br>Eliot: *Four Quartets.*<br>Bellow: *Dangling Man.* |

# CHRONOLOGY

ghettos or concentration camps. Churchill becomes prime minister in UK. British Expeditionary Force evacuated from Dunkirk. Battle of Britain. The Blitz. USSR annexes Baltic states.
All Dutch Jews forced to register with the state and banned from movie theaters. All Jewish children have to attend Jewish schools by autumn. Random street round-ups of Jews (*razzia*) are common as political violence increases in the Netherlands. Mass murders of Russian Jews in Kiev. Experiments in mass murder using Zyklon B at Auschwitz; 600 Soviet POWs are killed in the cellars of Block 11. Germans invade USSR; siege of Leningrad commences. Britain and the Soviet Union invade Iran; Reza Shah abdicates in favor of his son Mohammed Reza Pahlavi. Japanese attack Pearl Harbor; US enters war.

January: senior Nazi officials draft the "final solution" for the Jews at the Wannsee Conference. Every Jew over six years old must wear the yellow Star of David badge. Mass deportation of Jews begins; 6,000 Dutch Jews deported by July. Mass murder of Jews by gassing increases at Auschwitz with regular systematic selections carried out. Construction of four more gas chambers and crematoria at the camp begins where Germans estimate 1.6 million people a year could be killed. SS begin "liquidation" of the ghettos in Poland. Russian troops halt German advance at Stalingrad. Britain suspends convoys to Russia because of losses; Stalin accuses Allies of lack of support. North Africa campaign; battle of El Alamein.

Germans retreat in Russia, Africa and Italy. Churchill and Roosevelt agree to insist on the "unconditional surrender" of Germany. Meeting of the "Big Three" (Churchill, Roosevelt and Stalin) at Tehran, the first conference attended by Stalin, in November. "Liquidation" of the Warsaw ghetto. March 29: Gerrit Bolkestein, minister of education, art and science for exiled Dutch government, calls for national archive of "ordinary documents" by Dutch citizens on radio broadcast. Normandy landings. Polish Home Army begins Warsaw uprising which is later brutally crushed by the Nazis. Hitler survives assassination attempt. Liberation of France. Waffen SS executes 81 prisoners of war in Malmedy Massacre.

| DATE | AUTHOR'S LIFE | LITERARY CONTEXT |
|------|---------------|------------------|
| 1944 *cont.* | Miep Gies and Bep Voskuijl rescue Anne's diary papers. On August 8 the eight Jews are transported to Westerbork and put to work in the punishment block. On September 3 they are deported to Auschwitz-Birkenau where the men and women are separated. Unable to work due to exhaustion, Hermann van Pels is murdered in the gas chambers. Johannes Kleiman is released from Amersfoort labor camp on account of ill health after Red Cross intervention. In October Anne and Margot Frank are transported to Bergen-Belsen, along with Auguste van Pels. Fritz Pfeffer is moved to Sachsenhausen, and then Neuengamme where he dies from illness and exhaustion in December. | |
| 1945 | Edith Frank dies of disease and exhaustion at Auschwitz in January. Peter van Pels is forced to march to Mathausen camp in Austria. Otto Frank stays in Auschwitz and is liberated by the Communists on January 27. In March Margot and then Anne dies of typhus, a few weeks before Bergen-Belsen is liberated by the British army. Victor Kugler escapes during a forced march to Germany and goes into hiding. On May 5 Peter van Pels dies of exhaustion in Mathausen. Auguste van Pels dies on a forced march near Theresienstadt. Otto Frank receives word of Edith's death in June and returns to Amsterdam on June 3. On July 18 he learns of Anne and Margot's death. Miep Gies then hands him Anne's diary papers. | Sartre: *L'Age de raison.* Camus: *Caligula.* Broch: *The Death of Virgil.* Orwell: *Animal Farm.* Waugh: *Brideshead Revisited.* Wright: *Black Boy.* Frisch: *Now They Sing Again.* |

# CHRONOLOGY

January 27: Warsaw is liberated. 7,650 survivors are liberated from Auschwitz by the Communist army after at least 1.1 million people including 200,000 children and young people died. Approximately 1 million of the people who died were Jews. Mussolini hanged by Italian partisans; Venice falls to Allied forces. Hitler commits suicide; unconditional surrender of Germany. SS Reichsführer Heinrich Himmler commits suicide. Atomic bombs detonated over Hiroshima and Nagasaki; unconditional surrender of Japan. End of World War II. United Nations founded. Death of Roosevelt; Truman becomes US president. Churchill voted out as prime minister in UK. Yalta Conference: Germany to be divided into four zones of occupation and administered by Allied Control Commission; war criminals to be prosecuted Tito elected president of Yugoslavia.

| DATE | AUTHOR'S LIFE | LITERARY CONTEXT |
|---|---|---|
| 1946 | | Sartre: *L'existentialisme est un humanisme.*. Stead: *Letty Fox: Her Luck.* Hermann Hesse receives Nobel prize for literature. Alfred Andersch and Hans W. Richter publish the popular literary magazine *Der Ruf* until 1947 when it is banned by the American military government. Vestdijk: *Ierse nachten (Irish Nights).* Death of H. G. Wells. |
| 1947 | Anne Frank's diary *Het Achterhuis (The Secret Annex)* is first published in Dutch. The English translation *Anne Frank: The Diary of a Young Girl* is published later in the year. | Compton-Burnett: *Manservant and Maidservant.* Camus: *La Peste.* Levi: *If this is a Man.* Mann: *Doctor Faustus.* Sachs: *In the Houses of Death.* Stefan Zweig commits suicide with his wife in Brazil. |
| 1948 | | Greene: *The Heart of the Matter.* Paton: *Cry, the Beloved Country.* Vestdijk: *Pastorale 1943* and *De redding van Fré Bolderhey (Fré Bolderhey's Salvation).* |
| 1949 | | Orwell: *Nineteen Eighty-Four.* de Beauvoir: *La deuxième sexe.* Miller: *Death of a Salesman.* Frisch: *When the War Came to an End.* Sachs: *Eclipse of the Stars.* Vestdijk: *De kellner en de levenden (The Waiter and the Living).* |
| 1950 | Charlotte Kaletta marries Fritz Pfeffer posthumously. | Greene: *The Third Mann.* Ionesco: *The Bald Prima Donna.* Dürrenmatt: *The Judge and his Hangman.* Vestdijk: *De koperen tuin (The Copper Garden).* |
| 1951 | | Salinger: *The Catcher in the Rye.* Vestdijk: *Ivoren wachters (Ivory Guardians).* |
| 1952 | *The Diary of a Young Girl* published in the US. | Beckett: *Waiting for Godot.* Waugh: *Sword of Honour* (trilogy, to 1961). |

# CHRONOLOGY

Nuremberg trials; Hermann Göring commits suicide and 10 other war criminals are hanged. Trial of Nazi doctors involved in human experimentation; 7 are sentenced to death. "Iron Curtain" speech by Churchill. Start of the Cold War. King Victor Emmanuel of Italy abdicates; Italy becomes a republic.

The Marshall Plan to aid post-war Europe instituted but rejected by USSR as threat to Communism. Cominform (Communist Information Bureau) is created in USSR. Indian Independence Act.

Assassination of Gandhi in India. Jewish state of Israel comes into existence. National Party wins elections in South Africa; policy of apartheid adopted. Russian blockade of West Berlin.

North Atlantic Treaty (NATO) signed. Representatives of four occupying powers in Germany agree to end Berlin Blockade. Federal Republic of Germany (West Germany) and German Democratic Republic (East Germany) come into existence. Mao Zedong, leader of the Communist Party of China, proclaims a People's Republic of China; KMT forces retreat and set up a Nationalist government on the island of Formosa (Taiwan).

US proposes German re-armament, Polish–German frontier fixed on Oder-Neisse. Churchill returns as prime minister in Britain. Senator McCarthy launches unsubstantiated campaign against Communist infiltration of US federal government (to 1954). African National Congress (ANC), led by Nelson Mandela, institutes campaign of civil disobedience in response to apartheid. Korean War (to 1953).
Dr Mohammad Mossadeq nationalizes Iranian oil industry, formerly under control of British-owned Anglo-Iranian Oil Company.

Eisenhower elected US president. Accession of Elizabeth II in UK.

| DATE | AUTHOR'S LIFE | LITERARY CONTEXT |
|---|---|---|
| 1953 | Otto Frank retires from work and devotes more time to Anne's diary. Johannes Kleiman succeeds him as company director. Otto Frank remarries a former neighbor and Auschwitz survivor Elfriede (Fritzi) Markovits, and moves to Basel, Switzerland, in November. | |
| 1955 | Première of the Broadway adaptation of *The Diary of Anne Frank*. Otto Frank is unable to attend as it is too painful for him. | |
| 1959 | Death of Johannes Kleiman. | |
| 1960 | Anne Frank House opens on May 3. Otto Frank attends the opening. | Wiesel: *Night*. |
| 1975 | | Levi: *The Periodic Table*. Kertész: *Fateless*. |
| 1980 | Otto Frank dies in Switzerland on August 19, aged 91. | Améry: *At the Mind's Limits: Contemplations by a Survivor of Auschwitz and Its Realities*. Hersh: *Save the Children!* |
| 1981 | Death of Victor Kugler. | |
| 1983 | *Anne Frank's Tales from the Secret Annex: Fables, Short Stories, Essays, and an Unfinished Novel by the Author of "The Diary of a Young Girl"* published. Death of Bep Voskuijl. | |
| 1987 | Miep Gies publishes her story in *Anne Frank Remembered*. | Levi: *The Drowned and the Saved*. |
| 1988 | Five more pages of Anne's diary are discovered. | |
| 1989 | *The Diary of a Young Girl: The Critical Edition* published in the US. | |
| 1995 | *The Diary of a Young Girl: The Definitive Edition* published in the US. | Wiesel: *All Rivers Run to the Sea*. |
| 1996 | Jon Blair's *Anne Frank Remembered* wins an Academy Award for Documentary Feature. | |
| 2003 | *The Diary of Anne Frank: The Revised Critical Edition* published. | |
| 2010 | Miep Gies dies aged 100. | |

# CHRONOLOGY

Yad Vashem established in Jerusalem to commemorate victims of the Holocaust.

# ILLUSTRATIONS

*Between pages 34 and 35*

Brothers Robert and Otto Frank in the German Army, 1916.
Wedding of Edith and Otto Frank, Aachen, Germany, 1925.

Margot and Anne with their father, Frankfurt, Germany, 1930.
Anne and her friend Sanne Ledermann, Amsterdam, 1935.
Edith Frank, May 1935.
Anne, Aachen, Germany, 1934.
Otto Frank, May 1936.

Anne's tenth birthday, Amsterdam, June 12, 1939.
Margot, Anne and Grandma Holländer, Zandvoort, Holland, 1939.

Anne, Amsterdam, 1941.
Mrs van Daan, Mr van Daan and Victor Kugler, Amsterdam, 1941.
Otto, Anne and Margot Frank walking along with other guest to
the wedding of Jan and Miep Gies, Amsterdam, June 1941.

*Between pages 210 and 211*

The Frank family, Amsterdam, 1941.
Photographs of Anne in Amsterdam, 1935–42.

263 Prinsengracht, Amsterdam, front view.
263 Prinsengracht, Amsterdam, rear view.

Johannes Kleiman next to the bookcase, after the war.
Peter van Daan.
Albert Dussel.

Miep Gies and Bep Voskuijl, Amsterdam, 1945.
Johannes Kleiman and Victor Kugler, Amsterdam, 1945.

# THE DIARY OF A
# YOUNG GIRL

# FOREWORD

ANNE FRANK KEPT a diary from June 12, 1942, to August 1, 1944. Initially, she wrote it strictly for herself. Then, one day in 1944, Gerrit Bolkestein, a member of the Dutch government in exile, announced in a radio broadcast from London that after the war he hoped to collect eyewitness accounts of the suffering of the Dutch people under the German occupation, which could be made available to the public. As an example, he specifically mentioned letters and diaries.

Impressed by this speech, Anne Frank decided that when the war was over she would publish a book based on her diary. She began rewriting and editing her diary, improving on the text, omitting passages she didn't think were interesting enough and adding others from memory. At the same time, she kept up her original diary. In the scholarly work *The Diary of Anne Frank: The Critical Edition* (1989), Anne's first, unedited diary is referred to as version *a*, to distinguish it from her second, edited diary, which is known as version *b*.

The last entry in Anne's diary is dated August 1, 1944. On August 4, 1944, the eight people hiding in the Secret Annex were arrested. Miep Gies and Bep Voskuijl, the two secretaries working in the building, found Anne's diaries strewn all over the floor. Miep Gies tucked them away in a desk drawer for safekeeping. After the war, when it became clear that Anne was dead, she gave the diaries, unread, to Anne's father, Otto Frank.

After long deliberation, Otto Frank decided to fulfill his daughter's wish and publish her diary. He selected material from versions *a* and *b*, editing them into a shorter version later referred to as version *c*. Readers all over the world know this as *The Diary of a Young Girl*.

In making his choice, Otto Frank had to bear several points in mind. To begin with, the book had to be kept short so that it would fit in with a series put out by the Dutch publisher. In addition, several passages dealing with Anne's sexuality were omitted; at the time of the diary's initial publication, in 1947, it was not customary to write openly about sex, and certainly not in books for young adults. Out of respect for the dead, Otto Frank also omitted a number of unflattering passages about his wife and the other residents of the Secret Annex. Anne Frank, who was thirteen when she began her diary and fifteen when she was forced to stop, wrote without reserve about her likes and dislikes.

When Otto Frank died in 1980, he willed his daughter's manuscripts to the Netherlands State Institute for War Documentation in Amsterdam. Because the authenticity of the diary had been challenged ever since its publication, the Institute for War Documentation ordered a thorough investigation. Once the diary was proved, beyond a shadow of a doubt, to be genuine, it was published in its entirety, along with the results of an exhaustive study. *The Critical Edition* contains not only versions *a*, *b* and *c*, but also articles on the background of the Frank family, the circumstances surrounding their arrest and deportation, and the examination into Anne's handwriting, the document and the materials used.

The Anne Frank–Fonds (Anne Frank Foundation) in Basel (Switzerland), which as Otto Frank's legal heir had inherited his daughter's copyrights, then decided to have a new, expanded edition of the diary published for general readers. This new edition in no way affects the integrity of the old one originally edited by Otto Frank, which brought the diary and its message to millions of people. The task of compiling the expanded edition was given to the writer and translator Mirjam Pressler. Otto Frank's original selection has now been supplemented with passages from Anne's *a* and *b* versions. Mirjam Pressler's definitive edition, approved by the Anne Frank–Fonds, contains approximately 30 percent more material and is intended to give the reader more insight into the world of Anne Frank.

In 1998 the existence of five previously unknown pages of the diary came to light. Now, with the permission of the Anne Frank–Fonds in Basel, a long passage dated February 8, 1944, has been added to the end of the already-existing entry of that date.

A short alternative to the entry of June 20, 1942, has not been included here because a more detailed version of it is already part of the diary. Furthermore, in line with recent findings, the entry of November 7, 1942, has been moved to October 30, 1943. For more information, the reader is referred to the revised *Critical Edition.*

In writing her second version (*b*), Anne invented pseudonyms for the people who would appear in her book. She initially wanted to call herself Anne Aulis, and later Anne Robin. Otto Frank opted to call his family by their own names and to follow Anne's wishes with regard to the others. Over the years, the identity of the people who helped the families in the Secret Annex has become common knowledge. In this edition, the helpers are now referred to by their real names, as they so justly deserve to be. All other persons are named in accordance with the pseudonyms in *The Critical Edition*. The Institute for War Documentation has arbitrarily assigned initials to those persons wishing to remain anonymous.

The real names of the other people hiding in the Secret Annex are:

THE VAN PELS FAMILY
(from Osnabrück, Germany):

Auguste van Pels (born September 9, 1900)
Hermann van Pels (born March 31, 1898)
Peter van Pels (born November 8, 1926)

Called by Anne, in her manuscript: Petronella,
Hans and Alfred van Daan; and in the book:
Petronella, Hermann and Peter van Daan.

FRITZ PFEFFER
(born April 30, 1889, in Giessen, Germany):

Called by Anne, in her manuscript and in the book:
Albert Dussel.

The reader may wish to bear in mind that much of this edition is based on the *b* version of Anne's diary, which she wrote when she was around fifteen years old. Occasionally, Anne went back and commented on a passage she had written earlier. These comments are clearly marked in this edition. Naturally, Anne's spelling and linguistic errors have been corrected. Otherwise, the text has basically been left as she wrote it, since any attempts at editing and clarification would be inappropriate in a historical document.

*Ik zal hoop ik een jou alles kunnen toevertrouwen, zoals ik het nog aan niemand gekund heb, en ik hoop dat je een grote steun voor me zult zijn.*

*Anne Frank. 12 Juni 1942.*

*I hope I will be able to confide everything to you, as I have never been able to confide in anyone, and I hope you will be a great source of comfort and support.*

I hope I will be able to confide everything to you, as I have never been able to confide in anyone, and I hope you will be a great source of comfort and support.

COMMENT ADDED BY ANNE ON SEPTEMBER 28, 1942:
*So far you truly have been a great source of comfort to me, and so has Kitty, whom I now write to regularly. This way of keeping a diary is much nicer, and now I can hardly wait for those moments when I'm able to write in you.*

*Oh, I'm so glad I brought you along!*

SUNDAY, JUNE 14, 1942
I'll begin from the moment I got you, the moment I saw you lying on the table among my other birthday presents. (I went along when you were bought, but that doesn't count.)

On Friday, June 12, I was awake at six o'clock, which isn't surprising, since it was my birthday. But I'm not allowed to get up at that hour, so I had to control my curiosity until quarter to seven. When I couldn't wait any longer, I went to the dining room, where Moortje (the cat) welcomed me by rubbing against my legs.

A little after seven I went to Daddy and Mama and then to the living room to open my presents, and *you* were the first thing I saw, maybe one of my nicest presents. Then a bouquet of roses, some peonies and a potted plant. From Daddy and Mama I got a blue blouse, a game, a bottle of grape juice, which to my mind tastes a bit like wine (after all, wine is made from grapes), a puzzle, a jar of cold cream, 2.50 guilders and a gift certificate for two books. I got another book as well, *Camera Obscura* (but Margot already has it, so I exchanged mine for something else), a platter of homemade cookies (which I made myself, of course, since I've become quite an expert at baking cookies), lots of candy and a strawberry tart from Mother. And a letter from Grammy, right on time, but of course that was just a coincidence.

Then Hanneli came to pick me up, and we went to school. During recess I passed out cookies to my teachers and my class, and then it was time to get back to work. I didn't arrive home until five, since I went to gym with the rest of the class. (I'm not allowed to take part because my shoulders and hips tend to get dislocated.) As it was my birthday, I got to decide which game my classmates would play, and I chose volleyball. Afterward they all danced around me in a circle and sang "Happy Birthday." When I got home, Sanne Ledermann was already there. Ilse Wagner, Hanneli Goslar and Jacqueline van Maarsen came home with me after gym, since we're in the same class. Hanneli and Sanne used to be my two best friends. People who saw us together used to say, "There goes Anne, Hanne and Sanne." I only met Jacqueline van Maarsen when I started at the Jewish Lyceum, and now she's my best friend. Ilse is Hanneli's best friend, and Sanne goes to another school and has friends there.

They gave me a beautiful book, *Dutch Sagas and Legends*, but they gave me Volume II by mistake, so I exchanged two other books for Volume 1. Aunt Helene brought me a puzzle, Aunt Stephanie a darling brooch and Aunt Leny a terrific book: *Daisy Goes to the Mountains*.

This morning I lay in the bathtub thinking how wonderful it would be if I had a dog like Rin Tin Tin. I'd call him Rin Tin Tin too, and I'd take him to school with me, where he could stay in the janitor's room or by the bicycle racks when the weather was good.

MONDAY, JUNE 15, 1942

I had my birthday party on Sunday afternoon. The Rin Tin Tin movie was a big hit with my classmates. I got two brooches, a bookmark and two books.

I'll start by saying a few things about my school and my class, beginning with the students.

Betty Bloemendaal looks kind of poor, and I think she

probably is. She lives on some obscure street in West Amsterdam, and none of us know where it is. She does very well at school, but that's because she works so hard, not because she's so smart. She's pretty quiet.

Jacqueline van Maarsen is supposedly my best friend, but I've never had a real friend. At first I thought Jacque would be one, but I was badly mistaken.

D.Q.* is a very nervous girl who's always forgetting things, so the teachers keep assigning her extra homework as punishment. She's very kind, especially to G.Z.

E.S. talks so much it isn't funny. She's always touching your hair or fiddling with your buttons when she asks you something. They say she can't stand me, but I don't care, since I don't like her much either.

Henny Mets is a nice girl with a cheerful disposition, except that she talks in a loud voice and is really childish when we're playing outdoors. Unfortunately, Henny has a girlfriend named Beppy who's a bad influence on her because she's dirty and vulgar.

J.R. – I could write a whole book about her. J. is a detestable, sneaky, stuck-up, two-faced gossip who thinks she's so grown-up. She's really got Jacque under her spell, and that's a shame. J. is easily offended, bursts into tears at the slightest thing and, to top it all off, is a terrible show-off. Miss J. always has to be right. She's very rich, and has a closet full of the most adorable dresses that are way too old for her. She thinks she's gorgeous, but she's not. J. and I can't stand each other.

Ilse Wagner is a nice girl with a cheerful disposition, but she's extremely finicky and can spend hours moaning and groaning about something. Ilse likes me a lot. She's very smart, but lazy.

Hanneli Goslar, or Lies as she's called at school, is a bit on the strange side. She's usually shy – outspoken at home, but reserved around other people. She blabs whatever you tell her to her mother. But she says what she thinks, and lately I've come to appreciate her a great deal.

*Initials have been assigned at random to those persons who prefer to remain anonymous.

Nannie van Praag-Sigaar is small, funny and sensible. I think she's nice. She's pretty smart. There isn't much else you can say about Nannie.

Eefje de Jong is, in my opinion, terrific. Though she's only twelve, she's quite the lady. She acts as if I were a baby. She's also very helpful, and I like her.

G.Z. is the prettiest girl in our class. She has a nice face, but is kind of dumb. I think they're going to hold her back a year, but of course I haven't told her that.

COMMENT ADDED BY ANNE AT A LATER DATE:
*To my great surprise, G.Z. wasn't held back a year after all.*

And sitting next to G.Z. is the last of us twelve girls, me.

There's a lot to be said about the boys, or maybe not so much after all.

Maurice Coster is one of my many admirers, but pretty much of a pest.

Sallie Springer has a filthy mind, and rumor has it that he's gone all the way. Still, I think he's terrific, because he's very funny.

Emiel Bonewit is G.Z.'s admirer, but she doesn't care. He's pretty boring.

Rob Cohen used to be in love with me too, but I can't stand him anymore. He's an obnoxious, two-faced, lying, sniveling little goof who has an awfully high opinion of himself.

Max van de Velde is a farm boy from Medemblik, but a decent sort, as Margot would say.

Herman Koopman also has a filthy mind, just like Jopie de Beer, who's a terrible flirt and absolutely girl-crazy.

Leo Blom is Jopie de Beer's best friend, but has been ruined by his dirty mind.

Albert de Mesquita came from the Montessori School and skipped a grade. He's really smart.

Leo Slager came from the same school, but isn't as smart.

Ru Stoppelmon is a short, goofy boy from Almelo who transferred to this school in the middle of the year.

C.N. does whatever he's not supposed to.

Jacques Kocernoot sits behind us, next to C., and we (G. and I) laugh ourselves silly.

Harry Schaap is the most decent boy in our class. He's nice.

Werner Joseph is nice too, but all the changes taking place lately have made him too quiet, so he seems boring.

Sam Salomon is one of those tough guys from across the tracks. A real brat. (Admirer!)

Appie Riem is pretty Orthodox, but a brat too.

SATURDAY, JUNE 20, 1942

Writing in a diary is a really strange experience for someone like me. Not only because I've never written anything before, but also because it seems to me that later on neither I nor anyone else will be interested in the musings of a thirteen-year-old schoolgirl. Oh well, it doesn't matter. I feel like writing, and I have an even greater need to get all kinds of things off my chest.

"Paper has more patience than people." I thought of this saying on one of those days when I was feeling a little depressed and was sitting at home with my chin in my hands, bored and listless, wondering whether to stay in or go out. I finally stayed where I was, brooding. Yes, paper *does* have more patience, and since I'm not planning to let anyone else read this stiff-backed notebook grandly referred to as a "diary," unless I should ever find a real friend, it probably won't make a bit of difference.

Now I'm back to the point that prompted me to keep a diary in the first place: I don't have a friend.

Let me put it more clearly, since no one will believe that a thirteen-year-old girl is completely alone in the world. And I'm not. I have loving parents and a sixteen-year-old sister, and there are about thirty people I can call friends. I have a throng of admirers who can't keep their adoring eyes off me and who sometimes have to resort to using a broken pocket mirror to try and catch a glimpse of me in the classroom. I have a family, loving aunts and a good home. No, on the surface I seem to have everything, except my one true friend. All I think about when I'm with friends is having a good time. I can't bring myself to talk about anything but ordinary everyday things. We don't seem to be able to get any closer, and that's the problem. Maybe it's my fault that we don't confide in each other. In any case, that's just how things are, and unfortunately they're not liable to change. This is why I've started the diary.

To enhance the image of this long-awaited friend in my imagination, I don't want to jot down the facts in this diary the way most people would do, but I want the diary to be my friend, and I'm going to call this friend *Kitty*.

Since no one would understand a word of my stories to Kitty if I were to plunge right in, I'd better provide a brief sketch of my life, much as I dislike doing so.

My father, the most adorable father I've ever seen, didn't marry my mother until he was thirty-six and she was twenty-five. My sister Margot was born in Frankfurt am Main in Germany in 1926. I was born on June 12, 1929. I lived in Frankfurt until I was four. Because we're Jewish, my father immigrated to Holland in 1933, when he became the Managing Director of the Dutch Opekta Company, which manufactures products used in making jam. My mother, Edith Holländer Frank, went with him to Holland in September, while Margot and I were sent to Aachen to stay with our grandmother. Margot went to Holland in December, and I followed in February, when I was plunked down on the table as a birthday present for Margot.

I started right away at the Montessori nursery school. I stayed there until I was six, at which time I started first grade. In sixth grade my teacher was Mrs. Kuperus, the principal. At the end of the year we were both in tears as we said a heartbreaking farewell, because I'd been accepted at the Jewish Lyceum, where Margot also went to school.

Our lives were not without anxiety, since our relatives in Germany were suffering under Hitler's anti-Jewish laws. After the pogroms in 1938 my two uncles (my mother's brothers) fled Germany, finding safe refuge in North America. My elderly grandmother came to live with us. She was seventy-three years old at the time.

After May 1940 the good times were few and far between: first there was the war, then the capitulation and then the arrival of the Germans, which is when the trouble started for the Jews. Our freedom was severely restricted by a series of anti-Jewish decrees:

Jews were required to wear a yellow star; Jews were required
to turn in their bicycles; Jews were forbidden to use streetcars;
Jews were forbidden to ride in cars, even their own; Jews were
required to do their shopping between 3 and 5 p.m.; Jews
were required to frequent only Jewish-owned barbershops and
beauty parlors; Jews were forbidden to be out on the streets
between 8 p.m. and 6 a.m.; Jews were forbidden to go to theaters,
movies or any other forms of entertainment; Jews were forbidden to use swimming pools, tennis courts, hockey fields or any
other athletic fields; Jews were forbidden to go rowing; Jews were
forbidden to take part in any athletic activity in public; Jews
were forbidden to sit in their gardens or those of their friends
after 8 p.m.; Jews were forbidden to visit Christians in their
homes; Jews were required to attend Jewish schools, etc. You
couldn't do this and you couldn't do that, but life went on.
Jacque always said to me, "I don't dare do anything anymore,
'cause I'm afraid it's not allowed."

In the summer of 1941 Grandma got sick and had to have an
operation, so my birthday passed with little celebration. In the
summer of 1940 we didn't do much for my birthday either, since
the fighting had just ended in Holland. Grandma died in January
1942. No one knows how often I think of her and still love her.
This birthday celebration in 1942 was intended to make up for
the others, and Grandma's candle was lit along with the rest.

The four of us are still doing well, and that brings me to the
present date of June 20, 1942, and the solemn dedication of
my diary.

*Dearest Kitty!*                              SATURDAY, JUNE 20, 1942

Let me get started right away; it's nice and quiet now. Father
and Mother are out and Margot has gone to play Ping-Pong with
some other young people at her friend Trees's. I've been playing
a lot of Ping-Pong myself lately. So much that five of us girls
have formed a club. It's called "The Little Dipper Minus Two."
A really silly name, but it's based on a mistake. We wanted to give
our club a special name; and because there were five of us, we
came up with the idea of the Little Dipper. We thought it consisted of five stars, but we turned out to be wrong. It has seven,

like the Big Dipper, which explains the "Minus Two." Ilse
Wagner has a Ping-Pong set, and the Wagners let us play in their
big dining room whenever we want. Since we five Ping-Pong
players like ice cream, especially in the summer, and since you
get hot playing Ping-Pong, our games usually end with a visit
to the nearest ice-cream parlor that allows Jews: either Oasis or
Delphi. We've long since stopped hunting around for our purses
or money – most of the time it's so busy in Oasis that we manage
to find a few generous young men of our acquaintance or an
admirer to offer us more ice cream than we could eat in a week.

You're probably a little surprised to hear me talking about
admirers at such a tender age. Unfortunately, or not, as the case
may be, this vice seems to be rampant at our school. As soon as
a boy asks if he can bicycle home with me and we get to talking,
nine times out of ten I can be sure he'll become enamored on
the spot and won't let me out of his sight for a second. His ardor
eventually cools, especially since I ignore his passionate glances
and pedal blithely on my way. If it gets so bad that they start
rambling on about "asking Father's permission," I swerve
slightly on my bike, my schoolbag falls, and the young man feels
obliged to get off his bike and hand it to me, by which time I've
switched the conversation to another topic. These are the most
innocent types. Of course, there are those who blow you kisses
or try to take hold of your arm, but they're definitely knocking
on the wrong door. I get off my bike and either refuse to make
further use of their company or act as if I'm insulted and tell them
in no uncertain terms to go on home without me.

There you are. We've now laid the basis for our friendship.
Until tomorrow.

Yours, Anne

SUNDAY, JUNE 21, 1942

*Dearest Kitty,*

Our entire class is quaking in its boots. The reason, of course,
is the upcoming meeting in which the teachers decide who'll be
promoted to the next grade and who'll be kept back. Half the
class is making bets. G.Z. and I laugh ourselves sick at the two
boys behind us, C.N. and Jacques Kocernoot, who have staked
their entire vacation savings on their bet. From morning to night,

it's "You're going to pass," "No, I'm not," "Yes, you are," "No, I'm not." Even G.'s pleading glances and my angry outbursts can't calm them down. If you ask me, there are so many dummies that about a quarter of the class should be kept back, but teachers are the most unpredictable creatures on earth. Maybe this time they'll be unpredictable in the right direction for a change.

I'm not so worried about my girlfriends and myself. We'll make it. The only subject I'm not sure about is math. Anyway, all we can do is wait. Until then, we keep telling each other not to lose heart.

I get along pretty well with all my teachers. There are nine of them, seven men and two women. Mr. Keesing, the old fogey who teaches math, was mad at me for the longest time because I talked so much. After several warnings, he assigned me extra homework. An essay on the subject "A Chatterbox." A chatterbox, what can you write about that? I'd worry about that later, I decided. I jotted down the assignment in my notebook, tucked it in my bag and tried to keep quiet.

That evening, after I'd finished the rest of my homework, the note about the essay caught my eye. I began thinking about the subject while chewing the tip of my fountain pen. Anyone could ramble on and leave big spaces between the words, but the trick was to come up with convincing arguments to prove the necessity of talking. I thought and thought, and suddenly I had an idea. I wrote the three pages Mr. Keesing had assigned me and was satisfied. I argued that talking is a female trait and that I would do my best to keep it under control, but that I would never be able to break myself of the habit, since my mother talked as much as I did, if not more, and that there's not much you can do about inherited traits.

Mr. Keesing had a good laugh at my arguments, but when I proceeded to talk my way through the next class, he assigned me a second essay. This time it was supposed to be on "An Incorrigible Chatterbox." I handed it in, and Mr. Keesing had nothing to complain about for two whole classes. However, during the third class he'd finally had enough. "Anne Frank, as punishment for talking in class, write an essay entitled ' "Quack, Quack, Quack," Said Mistress Chatterback.' "

The class roared. I had to laugh too, though I'd nearly exhausted my ingenuity on the topic of chatterboxes. It was time to come up with something else, something original. My friend Sanne, who's good at poetry, offered to help me write the essay from beginning to end in verse. I jumped for joy. Keesing was trying to play a joke on me with this ridiculous subject, but I'd make sure the joke was on him.

I finished my poem, and it was beautiful! It was about a mother duck and a father swan with three baby ducklings who were bitten to death by the father because they quacked too much. Luckily, Keesing took the joke the right way. He read the poem to the class, adding his own comments, and to several other classes as well. Since then I've been allowed to talk and haven't been assigned any extra homework. On the contrary, Keesing's always making jokes these days.

Yours, Anne

Dearest Kitty,                          WEDNESDAY, JUNE 24, 1942

It's sweltering. Everyone is huffing and puffing, and in this heat I have to walk everywhere. Only now do I realize how pleasant a streetcar is, but we Jews are no longer allowed to make use of this luxury; our own two feet are good enough for us. Yesterday at lunchtime I had an appointment with the dentist on Jan Luykenstraat. It's a long way from our school on Stadstimmertuinen. That afternoon I nearly fell asleep at my desk. Fortunately, people automatically offer you something to drink. The dental assistant is really kind.

The only mode of transportation left to us is the ferry. The ferryman at Josef Israëlkade took us across when we asked him to. It's not the fault of the Dutch that we Jews are having such a bad time.

I wish I didn't have to go to school. My bike was stolen during Easter vacation, and Father gave Mother's bike to some Christian friends for safekeeping. Thank goodness summer vacation is almost here; one more week and our torment will be over.

Something unexpected happened yesterday morning. As I was passing the bicycle racks, I heard my name being called. I turned around and there was the nice boy I'd met the evening before at my friend Wilma's. He's Wilma's second cousin. I used to think Wilma was nice, which she is, but all she ever talks about is boys, and that gets to be a bore. He came toward me, somewhat shyly, and introduced himself as Hello Silberberg. I was a little surprised and wasn't sure what he wanted, but it didn't take me long to find out. He asked if I would allow him to accompany me to school. "As long as you're headed that way, I'll go with you," I said. And so we walked together. Hello is sixteen and good at telling all kinds of funny stories.

He was waiting for me again this morning, and I expect he will be from now on.

*Anne*

WEDNESDAY, JULY 1, 1942

*Dearest Kitty,*

Until today I honestly couldn't find the time to write you. I was with friends all day Thursday, we had company on Friday, and that's how it went until today.

Hello and I have gotten to know each other very well this past week, and he's told me a lot about his life. He comes from Gelsenkirchen and is living with his grandparents. His parents are in Belgium, but there's no way he can get there. Hello used to have a girlfriend named Ursula. I know her too. She's perfectly sweet and perfectly boring. Ever since he met me, Hello has realized that he's been falling asleep at Ursul's side. So I'm kind of a pep tonic. You never know what you're good for!

Jacque spent Saturday night here. Sunday afternoon she was at Hanneli's, and I was bored stiff.

Hello was supposed to come over that evening, but he called around six. I answered the phone, and he said, "This is Helmuth Silberberg. May I please speak to Anne?"

"Oh, Hello. This is Anne."

"Oh, hi, Anne. How are you?"

"Fine, thanks."

"I just wanted to say I'm sorry but I can't come tonight, though I would like to have a word with you. Is it all right if I come by and pick you up in about ten minutes?"

"Yes, that's fine. Bye-bye!"

"Okay, I'll be right over. Bye-bye!"

I hung up, quickly changed my clothes and fixed my hair. I was so nervous I leaned out the window to watch for him. He finally showed up. Miracle of miracles, I didn't rush down the stairs, but waited quietly until he rang the bell. I went down to open the door, and he got right to the point.

"Anne, my grandmother thinks you're too young for me to be seeing you on a regular basis. She says I should be going to the Lowenbachs', but you probably know that I'm not going out with Ursul anymore."

"No, I didn't know. What happened? Did you two have a fight?"

"No, nothing like that. I told Ursul that we weren't suited to each other and so it was better for us not to go together anymore, but that she was welcome at my house and I hoped I would be welcome at hers. Actually, I thought Ursul was hanging around with another boy, and I treated her as if she were. But that wasn't true. And then my uncle said I should apologize to her, but of course I didn't feel like it, and that's why I broke up with her. But that was just one of the reasons.

"Now my grandmother wants me to see Ursul and not you, but I don't agree and I'm not going to. Sometimes old people have really old-fashioned ideas, but that doesn't mean I have to go along with them. I need my grandparents, but in a certain sense they need me too. From now on I'll be free on Wednesday evenings. You see, my grandparents made me sign up for a wood-carving class, but actually I go to a club organized by the Zionists. My grandparents don't want me to go, because they're anti-Zionists. I'm not a fanatic Zionist, but it interests me. Anyway, it's been such a mess lately that I'm planning to quit. So next Wednesday will be my last meeting. That means I can see you Wednesday evening, Saturday afternoon, Saturday evening, Sunday afternoon and maybe even more."

"But if your grandparents don't want you to, you shouldn't go behind their backs."

"All's fair in love and war."

Just then we passed Blankevoort's Bookstore and there was Peter Schiff with two other boys; it was the first time he'd said hello to me in ages, and it really made me feel good.

Monday evening Hello came over to meet Father and Mother. I had bought a cake and some candy, and we had tea and cookies, the works, but neither Hello nor I felt like sitting stiffly on our chairs. So we went out for a walk, and he didn't deliver me to my door until ten past eight. Father was furious. He said it was very wrong of me not to get home on time. I had to promise to be home by ten to eight in the future. I've been asked to Hello's on Saturday.

Wilma told me that one night when Hello was at her house, she asked him, "Who do you like best, Ursul or Anne?"

He said, "It's none of your business."

But as he was leaving (they hadn't talked to each other the rest of the evening), he said, "Well, I like Anne better, but don't tell anyone. Bye!" And whoosh . . . he was out the door.

In everything he says or does, I can see that Hello is in love with me, and it's kind of nice for a change. Margot would say that Hello is a decent sort. I think so too, but he's more than that. Mother is also full of praise: "A good-looking boy. Nice and polite." I'm glad he's so popular with everyone. Except with my girlfriends. He thinks they're very childish, and he's right about that. Jacque still teases me about him, but I'm not in love with him. Not really. It's all right for me to have boys as friends. Nobody minds.

Mother is always asking me who I'm going to marry when I grow up, but I bet she'll never guess it's Peter, because I talked her out of that idea myself, without batting an eyelash. I love Peter as I've never loved anyone, and I tell myself he's only going around with all those other girls to hide his feelings for me. Maybe he thinks Hello and I are in love with each other, which we're not. He's just a friend, or as Mother puts it, a beau. *Yours, Anne*

*Dear Kitty,*

SUNDAY, JULY 5, 1942

The graduation ceremony in the Jewish Theater on Friday went as expected. My report card wasn't too bad. I got one D, a C− in algebra and all the rest B's, except for two B +'s and two B −'s. My parents are pleased, but they're not like other parents when it comes to grades. They never worry about report cards, good or bad. As long as I'm healthy and happy and don't talk back too much, they're satisfied. If these three things are all right, everything else will take care of itself.

I'm just the opposite. I don't want to be a poor student. I was accepted to the Jewish Lyceum on a conditional basis. I was supposed to stay in the seventh grade at the Montessori School, but when Jewish children were required to go to Jewish schools, Mr. Elte finally agreed, after a great deal of persuasion, to accept Lies Goslar and me. Lies also passed this year, though she has to repeat her geometry exam.

Poor Lies. It isn't easy for her to study at home; her baby sister, a spoiled little two-year-old, plays in her room all day. If Gabi doesn't get her way, she starts screaming, and if Lies doesn't look after her, Mrs. Goslar starts screaming. So Lies has a hard time doing her homework, and as long as that's the case, the tutoring she's been getting won't help much. The Goslar household is really a sight. Mrs. Goslar's parents live next door, but eat with the family. Then there's a hired girl, the baby, the always absentminded and absent Mr. Goslar and the always nervous and irritable Mrs. Goslar, who's expectmg another baby. Lies, who's all thumbs, gets lost in the mayhem.

My sister Margot has also gotten her report card. Brilliant, as usual. If we had such a thing as "cum laude," she would have passed with honors, she's so smart.

Father has been home a lot lately. There's nothing for him to do at the office; it must be awful to feel you're not needed. Mr. Kleiman has taken over Opekta, and Mr. Kugler, Gies & Co., the company dealing in spices and spice substitutes that was set up in 1941.

A few days ago, as we were taking a stroll around our neighborhood square, Father began to talk about going into hiding. He said it would be very hard for us to live cut off from the rest of the world. I asked him why he was bringing this up now.

"Well, Anne," he replied, "you know that for more than a year we've been bringing clothes, food and furniture to other people. We don't want our belongings to be seized by the Germans. Nor do we want to fall into their clutches ourselves. So we'll leave of our own accord and not wait to be hauled away."

"But when, Father?" He sounded so serious that I felt scared.

"Don't you worry. We'll take care of everything. Just enjoy your carefree life while you can."

That was it. Oh, may these somber words not come true for as long as possible.

The doorbell's ringing, Hello's here, time to stop.

*Yours, Anne*

*Dearest Kitty,* WEDNESDAY, JULY 8, 1942

It seems like years since Sunday morning. So much has happened it's as if the whole world had suddenly turned upside down. But as you can see, Kitty, I'm still alive, and that's the main thing, Father says. I'm alive all right, but don't ask where or how. You probably don't understand a word I'm saying today, so I'll begin by telling you what happened Sunday afternoon.

At three o'clock (Hello had left but was supposed to come back later), the doorbell rang. I didn't hear it, since I was out on the balcony, lazily reading in the sun. A little while later Margot appeared in the kitchen doorway looking very agitated. "Father has received a call-up notice from the SS," she whispered. "Mother has gone to see Mr. van Daan." (Mr. van Daan is Father's business partner and a good friend.)

I was stunned. A call-up: everyone knows what that means. Visions of concentration camps and lonely cells raced through my head. How could we let Father go to such a fate? "Of course he's not going," declared Margot as we waited for Mother in the living room. "Mother's gone to Mr. van Daan to ask whether we can move to our hiding place tomorrow. The van Daans are going with us. There will be seven of us altogether." Silence. We couldn't speak. The thought of Father off visiting someone in the Jewish Hospital and completely unaware of what was happening, the long wait for Mother, the heat, the suspense – all this reduced us to silence.

Suddenly the doorbell rang again. "That's Hello," I said.

"Don't open the door!" exclaimed Margot to stop me. But it wasn't necessary, since we heard Mother and Mr. van Daan downstairs talking to Hello, and then the two of them came inside and shut the door behind them. Every time the bell rang, either Margot or I had to tiptoe downstairs to see if it was Father, and we didn't let anyone else in. Margot and I were sent from the room, as Mr. van Daan wanted to talk to Mother alone.

When she and I were sitting in our bedroom, Margot told me that the call-up was not for Father, but for her. At this second shock, I began to cry. Margot is sixteen – apparently they want to send girls her age away on their own. But thank goodness she won't be going; Mother had said so herself, which must be what Father had meant when he talked to me about our going into hiding. Hiding ... where would we hide? In the city? In the country? In a house? In a shack? When, where, how ... ? These were questions I wasn't allowed to ask, but they still kept running through my mind.

Margot and I started packing our most important belongings into a schoolbag. The first thing I stuck in was this diary, and then curlers, handkerchiefs, schoolbooks, a comb and some old letters. Preoccupied by the thought of going into hiding, I stuck the craziest things in the bag, but I'm not sorry. Memories mean more to me than dresses.

Father finally came home around five o'clock, and we called Mr. Kleiman to ask if he could come by that evening. Mr. van Daan left and went to get Miep. Miep arrived and promised to return later that night, taking with her a bag full of shoes, dresses, jackets, underwear and stockings. After that it was quiet in our apartment; none of us felt like eating. It was still hot, and everything was very strange.

We had rented our big upstairs room to a Mr. Goldschmidt, a divorced man in his thirties, who apparently had nothing to do that evening, since despite all our polite hints he hung around until ten o'clock.

Miep and Jan Gies came at eleven. Miep, who's worked for Father's company since 1933, has become a close friend, and so has her husband Jan. Once again, shoes, stockings, books and underwear disappeared into Miep's bag and Jan's deep pockets. At eleven-thirty they too disappeared.

I was exhausted, and even though I knew it'd be my last night in my own bed, I fell asleep right away and didn't wake up until Mother called me at five-thirty the next morning. Fortunately, it wasn't as hot as Sunday; a warm rain fell throughout the day. The four of us were wrapped in so many layers of clothes it looked as if we were going off to spend the night in a refrigerator, and all that just so we could take more clothes with us. No Jew in our situation would dare leave the house with a suitcase full of clothes. I was wearing two undershirts, three pairs of underpants, a dress, and over that a skirt, a jacket, a raincoat, two pairs of stockings, heavy shoes, a cap, a scarf and lots more. I was suffocating even before we left the house, but no one bothered to ask me how I felt.

Margot stuffed her schoolbag with schoolbooks, went to get her bicycle and, with Miep leading the way, rode off into the great unknown. At any rate, that's how I thought of it, since I still didn't know where our hiding place was.

At seven-thirty we too closed the door behind us; Moortje, my cat, was the only living creature I said goodbye to. According to a note we left for Mr. Goldschmidt, she was to be taken to the neighbors, who would give her a good home.

The stripped beds, the breakfast things on the table, the pound of meat for the cat in the kitchen – all of these created the impression that we'd left in a hurry. But we weren't interested in impressions. We just wanted to get out of there, to get away and reach our destination in safety. Nothing else mattered.

More tomorrow.

Yours, Anne

THURSDAY, JULY 9, 1942

*Dearest Kitty,*

So there we were, Father, Mother and I, walking in the pouring rain, each of us with a schoolbag and a shopping bag filled to the brim with the most varied assortment of items. The people on their way to work at that early hour gave us sympathetic looks; you could tell by their faces that they were sorry they couldn't offer us some kind of transportation; the conspicuous yellow star spoke for itself.

Only when we were walking down the street did Father and Mother reveal, little by little, what the plan was. For months we'd been moving as much of our furniture and apparel out of the apartment as we could. It was agreed that we'd go into hiding on

July 16. Because of Margot's call-up notice, the plan had to be moved up ten days, which meant we'd have to make do with less orderly rooms.

The hiding place was located in Father's office building. That's a little hard for outsiders to understand, so I'll explain. Father didn't have a lot of people working in his office, just Mr. Kugler, Mr. Kleiman, Miep and a twenty-three-year-old typist named Bep Voskuijl, all of whom were informed of our coming. Mr. Voskuijl, Bep's father, works in the warehouse, along with two assistants, none of whom were told anything.

Here's a description of the building. The large warehouse on the ground floor is used as a workroom and storeroom and is divided into several different sections, such as the stockroom and the milling room, where cinnamon, cloves and a pepper substitute are ground.

Next to the warehouse doors is another outside door, a separate entrance to the office. Just inside the office door is a second door, and beyond that a stairway. At the top of the stairs is another door, with a frosted window on which the word "Office" is written in black letters. This is the big front office — very large, very light and very full. Bep, Miep and Mr. Kleiman work there during the day. After passing through an alcove containing a safe, a wardrobe and a big supply cupboard, you come to the small, dark, stuffy back office. This used to be shared by Mr. Kugler and Mr. van Daan, but now Mr. Kugler is its only occupant. Mr. Kugler's office can also be reached from the hallway, but only through a glass door that can be opened from the inside but not easily from the outside. If you leave Mr. Kugler's office and proceed through the long, narrow hallway past the coal bin and go up four steps, you find yourself in the private office, the showpiece of the entire building. Elegant mahogany furniture, a linoleum floor covered with throw rugs, a radio, a fancy lamp, everything first class. Next door is a spacious kitchen with a hot-water heater and two gas burners, and beside that a bathroom. That's the second floor.

A wooden staircase leads from the downstairs hallway to the third floor. At the top of the stairs is a landing, with doors on either side. The door on the left takes you up to the spice storage area, attic and loft in the front part of the house. A typically Dutch, very steep, ankle-twisting flight of stairs also runs from the front part of the house to another door opening onto the street.

The door to the right of the landing leads to the "Secret Annex" at the back of the house. No one would ever suspect there were so many rooms behind that plain gray door. There's just one small step in front of the door, and then you're inside. Straight ahead of you is a steep flight of stairs. To the left is a narrow hallway opening onto a room that serves as the Frank family's living room and bedroom. Next door is a smaller room, the bedroom and study of the two young ladies of the family.

2nd Floor            3rd Floor            4th Floor

To the right of the stairs is a windowless washroom with a sink. The door in the corner leads to the toilet and another one to Margot's and my room. If you go up the stairs and open the door at the top, you're surprised to see such a large, light and spacious room in an old canal-side house like this. It contains a stove (thanks to the fact that it used to be Mr. Kugler's laboratory) and a sink. This will be the kitchen and bedroom of Mr. and Mrs. van Daan, as well as the general living room, dining room and study for us all. A tiny side room is to be Peter van Daan's bedroom. Then, just as in the front part of the building, there's an attic and a loft. So there you are. Now I've introduced you to the whole of our lovely Annex!

Yours, Anne

*Dearest Kitty,*                          FRIDAY, JULY 10, 1942

I've probably bored you with my long description of our house, but I still think you should know where I've ended up; how I ended up here is something you'll figure out from my next letters.

But first, let me continue my story, because, as you know, I wasn't finished. After we arrived at 263 Prinsengracht, Miep quickly led us through the long hallway and up the wooden staircase to the next floor and into the Annex. She shut the door behind us, leaving us alone. Margot had arrived much earlier on her bike and was waiting for us.

Our living room and all the other rooms were so full of stuff that I can't find the words to describe it. All the cardboard boxes that had been sent to the office in the last few months were piled on the floors and beds. The small room was filled from floor to ceiling with linens. If we wanted to sleep in properly made beds that night, we had to get going and straighten up the mess. Mother and Margot were unable to move a muscle. They lay down on their bare mattresses, tired, miserable and I don't know what else. But Father and I, the two cleaner-uppers in the family, started in right away.

All day long we unpacked boxes, filled cupboards, hammered nails and straightened up the mess, until we fell exhausted into our clean beds at night. We hadn't eaten a hot meal all day, but we didn't care; Mother and Margot were too tired and keyed up to eat, and Father and I were too busy.

Tuesday morning we started where we left off the night before. Bep and Miep went grocery shopping with our ration coupons, Father worked on our blackout screens, we scrubbed the kitchen floor, and were once again busy from sunup to sundown. Until Wednesday, I didn't have a chance to think about the enormous change in my life. Then for the first time since our arrival in the Secret Annex, I found a moment to tell you all about it and to realize what had happened to me and what was yet to happen.

*Yours, Anne*

SATURDAY, JULY 11, 1942

*Dearest Kitty,*

Father, Mother and Margot still can't get used to the chiming of the Westertoren clock, which tells us the time every quarter of an hour. Not me, I liked it from the start; it sounds so reassuring, especially at night. You no doubt want to hear what I think of being in hiding. Well, all I can say is that I don't really know yet. I don't think I'll ever feel at home in this house, but that doesn't mean I hate it. It's more like being on vacation in some strange pension. Kind of an odd way to look at life in hiding, but that's how things are. The Annex is an ideal place to hide in. It may be damp and lopsided, but there's probably not a more comfortable hiding place in all of Amsterdam. No, in all of Holland.

Up to now our bedroom, with its blank walls, was very bare. Thanks to Father – who brought my entire postcard and movie-star collection here beforehand – and to a brush and a pot of glue, I was able to plaster the walls with pictures. It looks much more cheerful. When the van Daans arrive, we'll be able to build cupboards and other odds and ends out of the wood piled in the attic.

Margot and Mother have recovered somewhat. Yesterday Mother felt well enough to cook split-pea soup for the first time, but then she was downstairs talking and forgot all about it. The beans were scorched black, and no amount of scraping could get them out of the pan.

Last night the four of us went down to the private office and listened to England on the radio. I was so scared someone might hear it that I literally begged Father to take me back upstairs. Mother understood my anxiety and went with me. Whatever we do, we're very afraid the neighbors might hear or see us. We started off immediately the first day sewing curtains. Actually, you can hardly call them that, since they're nothing but scraps of fabric, varying greatly in shape, quality and pattern, which Father and I stitched crookedly together with unskilled fingers. These works of art were tacked to the windows, where they'll stay until we come out of hiding.

The building on our right is a branch of the Keg Company, a firm from Zaandam, and on the left is a furniture workshop. Though the people who work there are not on the premises after hours, any sound we make might travel through the walls. We've forbidden Margot to cough at night, even though she has a bad cold, and are giving her large doses of codeine.

I'm looking forward to the arrival of the van Daans, which is set for Tuesday. It will be much more fun and also not as quiet. You see, it's the silence that makes me so nervous during the evenings and nights, and I'd give anything to have one of our helpers sleep here.

It's really not that bad here, since we can do our own cooking and can listen to the radio in Daddy's office. Mr. Kleiman and Miep, and Bep Voskuijl too, have helped us so much. We've already canned loads of rhubarb, strawberries and cherries, so for the time being I doubt we'll be bored. We also have a supply of reading material, and we're going to buy lots of games. Of course, we can't ever look out the window or go outside. And we have to be quiet so the people downstairs can't hear us.

Yesterday we had our hands full. We had to pit two crates of cherries for Mr. Kugler to can. We're going to use the empty crates to make bookshelves.

Someone's calling me.

*Yours, Anne*

COMMENT ADDED BY ANNE ON SEPTEMBER 28, 1942:
*Not being able to go outside upsets me more than I can say, and I'm terrified our hiding place will be discovered and that we'll be shot. That, of course, is a fairly dismal prospect.*

SUNDAY, JULY 12, 1942

They were all so nice to me a month ago because of my birthday, and yet every day I feel myself drifting further away from Mother and Margot. I worked hard today and they praised me, only to start picking on me again five minutes later.

You can easily see the difference between the way they deal with Margot and the way they deal with me. For example, Margot broke the vacuum cleaner, and because of that we've been without light for the rest of the day. Mother said, "Well, Margot, it's easy to see you're not used to working; otherwise, you'd have known better than to yank the plug out by the cord." Margot made some reply, and that was the end of the story.

But this afternoon, when I wanted to rewrite something on Mother's shopping list because her handwriting is so hard to read, she wouldn't let me. She bawled me out again, and the whole family wound up getting involved.

I don't fit in with them, and I've felt that clearly in the last few weeks. They're so sentimental together, but I'd rather be sentimental on my own. They're always saying how nice it is with the four of us, and that we get along so well, without giving a moment's thought to the fact that I don't feel that way.

Daddy's the only one who understands me, now and again, though he usually sides with Mother and Margot. Another thing I can't stand is having them talk about me in front of outsiders, telling them how I cried or how sensibly I'm behaving. It's horrible. And sometimes they talk about Moortje and I can't take that at all. Moortje is my weak spot. I miss her every minute of the day, and no one knows how often I think of her; whenever I do, my eyes fill with tears. Moortje is so sweet, and I love her so much that I keep dreaming she'll come back to us.

I have plenty of dreams, but the reality is that we'll have to stay here until the war is over. We can't ever go outside, and the only visitors we can have are Miep, her husband Jan, Bep Voskuijl, Mr. Voskuijl, Mr. Kugler, Mr. Kleiman and Mrs. Kleiman, though she hasn't come because she thinks it's too dangerous.

COMMENT ADDED BY ANNE IN SEPTEMBER 1942:
*Daddy's always so nice. He understands me perfectly, and I wish we could have a heart-to-heart talk sometime without my bursting instantly into tears. But apparently that has to do with my age. I'd like to spend all my time writing, but that would probably get boring.*

*Up to now I've only confided my thoughts to my diary. I still haven't gotten around to writing amusing sketches that I could read aloud at a later date. In the future I'm going to devote less time to sentimentality and more time to reality.*

*Dear Kitty,*                       FRIDAY, AUGUST 14, 1942

I've deserted you for an entire month, but so little has happened that I can't find a newsworthy item to relate every single day. The van Daans arrived on July 13. We thought they were coming on the fourteenth, but from the thirteenth to sixteenth the Germans were sending out call-up notices right and left and causing a lot of unrest, so they decided it would be safer to leave a day too early than a day too late.

Peter van Daan arrived at nine-thirty in the morning (while we were still at breakfast). Peter's going on sixteen, a shy, awkward boy whose company won't amount to much. Mr. and Mrs. van Daan came half an hour later. Much to our amusement, Mrs. van Daan was carrying a hatbox with a large chamber pot inside. "I just don't feel at home without my chamber pot," she exclaimed, and it was the first item to find a permanent place under the divan. Instead of a chamber pot, Mr. van D. was lugging a collapsible tea table under his arm.

From the first, we ate our meals together, and after three days it felt as if the seven of us had become one big family. Naturally, the van Daans had much to tell about the week we'd been away from civilization. We were especially interested in what had happened to our apartment and to Mr. Goldschmidt.

Mr. van Daan filled us in: "Monday morning at nine, Mr. Goldschmidt phoned and asked if I could come over. I went straightaway and found a very distraught Mr. Goldschmidt. He showed me a note that the Frank family had left behind. As instructed, he was planning to bring the cat to the neighbors, which I agreed was a good idea. He was afraid the house was going to be searched, so we went through all the rooms, straightening up here and there and clearing the breakfast things off the table. Suddenly I saw a notepad on Mrs. Frank's desk, with an address in Maastricht written on it. Even though I knew Mrs. Frank had left it on purpose, I pretended to be surprised and horrified and begged Mr. Goldschmidt to burn this incriminating piece of paper. I swore up and down that I knew nothing about your disappearance, but that the note had given me an idea. 'Mr. Goldschmidt,' I said, 'I bet I know what this address refers to. About six months ago a high-ranking officer came to the office. It seems he and Mr. Frank grew up together. He promised to help Mr. Frank if it was ever necessary. As I recall, he was stationed in Maastricht. I think this officer has kept his word and is somehow planning to help them cross over to Belgium and then to Switzerland. There's no harm in telling this to any friends of the Franks who come asking about them. Of course, you don't need to mention the part about Maastricht.' And after that I left. This is the story most of your friends have been told, because I heard it later from several other people."

We thought it was extremely funny, but we laughed even harder when Mr. van Daan told us that certain people have vivid imaginations. For example, one family living on our square claimed they saw all four of us riding by on our bikes early in the morning, and another woman was absolutely positive we'd been loaded into some kind of military vehicle in the middle of the night.

*Yours, Anne*

*Dear Kitty,*

FRIDAY, AUGUST 21, 1942

Now our Secret Annex has truly become secret. Because so many houses are being searched for hidden bicycles, Mr. Kugler thought it would be better to have a bookcase built in front of the entrance to our hiding place. It swings out on its hinges and opens like a door. Mr. Voskuijl did the carpentry work. (Mr. Voskuijl has been told that the seven of us are in hiding, and he's been most helpful.)

Now whenever we want to go downstairs we have to duck and then jump. After the first three days we were all walking around with bumps on our foreheads from banging our heads against the low doorway. Then Peter cushioned it by nailing a towel stuffed with wood shavings to the doorframe. Let's see if it helps!

I'm not doing much schoolwork. I've given myself a vacation until September. Father wants to start tutoring me then, but we have to buy all the books first.

There's little change in our lives here. Peter's hair was washed today, but that's nothing special. Mr. van Daan and I are always at loggerheads with each other. Mama always treats me like a baby, which I can't stand. For the rest, things are going better. I don't think Peter's gotten any nicer. He's an obnoxious boy who lies around on his bed all day, only rousing himself to do a little carpentry work before returning to his nap. What a dope!

Mama gave me another one of her dreadful sermons this morning. We take the opposite view of everything. Daddy's a sweetheart; he may get mad at me, but it never lasts longer than five minutes.

It's a beautiful day outside, nice and hot, and in spite of everything, we make the most of the weather by lounging on the folding bed in the attic.

                                                        *Yours, Anne*

COMMENT ADDED BY ANNE ON SEPTEMBER 21, 1942:
*Mr. van Daan has been as nice as pie to me recently. I've said nothing, but have been enjoying it while it lasts.*

*Dearest Kitty,*          WEDNESDAY, SEPTEMBER 2, 1942

Mr. and Mrs. van Daan have had a terrible fight. I've never seen anything like it, since Mother and Father wouldn't dream of shouting at each other like that. The argument was based on something so trivial it didn't seem worth wasting a single word on it. Oh well, to each his own.

Of course, it's very difficult for Peter, who gets caught in the middle, but no one takes Peter seriously anymore, since he's hypersensitive and lazy. Yesterday he was beside himself with worry because his tongue was blue instead of pink. This rare phenomenon disappeared as quickly as it came. Today he's walking around with a thick scarf on because he's got a stiff neck. His

Highness has been complaining of lumbago too. Aches and pains in his heart, kidneys and lungs are also par for the course. He's an absolute hypochondriac! (That's the right word, isn't it?)

Mother and Mrs. van Daan aren't getting along very well. There are enough reasons for the friction. To give you one small example, Mrs. van D. has removed all but three of her sheets from our communal linen closet. She's assuming that Mother's can be used for both families. She'll be in for a nasty surprise when she discovers that Mother has followed her lead.

Furthermore, Mrs. van D. is ticked off because we're using her china instead of ours. She's still trying to find out what we've done with our plates; they're a lot closer than she thinks, since they're packed in cardboard boxes in the attic, behind a load of Opekta advertising material. As long as we're in hiding, the plates will remain out of her reach. Since I'm always having accidents, it's just as well! Yesterday I broke one of Mrs. van D.'s soup bowls.

"Oh!" she angrily exclaimed. "Can't you be more careful? That was my last one."

Please bear in mind, Kitty, that the two ladies speak abominable Dutch (I don't dare comment on the gentlemen: they'd be highly insulted). If you were to hear their bungled attempts, you'd laugh your head off. We've given up pointing out their errors, since correcting them doesn't help anyway. Whenever I quote Mother or Mrs. van Daan, I'll write proper Dutch instead of trying to duplicate their speech.

Last week there was a brief interruption in our monotonous routine. This was provided by Peter – and a book about women. I should explain that Margot and Peter are allowed to read nearly all the books Mr. Kleiman lends us. But the adults preferred to keep this special book to themselves. This immediately piqued Peter's curiosity. What forbidden fruit did it contain? He snuck off with it when his mother was downstairs talking, and took himself and his booty to the loft. For two days all was well. Mrs. van Daan knew what he was up to, but kept mum until Mr. van Daan found out about it. He threw a fit, took the book away and assumed that would be the end of the business. However, he'd neglected to take his son's curiosity into account. Peter, not in the least fazed by his father's swift action, began thinking up ways to read the rest of this vastly interesting book.

In the meantime, Mrs. van D. asked Mother for her opinion. Mother didn't think this particular book was suitable for Margot, but she saw no harm in letting her read most other books.

"You see, Mrs. van Daan," Mother said, "there's a big difference between Margot and Peter. To begin with, Margot's a girl, and girls are always more mature than boys. Second, she's already read many serious books and doesn't go looking for those which are no longer forbidden. Third, Margot's much more sensible and intellectually advanced, as a result of her four years at an excellent school."

Mrs. van Daan agreed with her, but felt it was wrong as a matter of principle to let youngsters read books written for adults.

Meanwhile, Peter had thought of a suitable time when no one would be interested in either him or the book. At seven-thirty in the evening, when the entire family was listening to the radio in the private office, he took his treasure and stole off to the loft again. He should have been back by eight-thirty, but he was so engrossed in the book that he forgot the time and was just coming down the stairs when his father entered the room. The scene that followed was not surprising: after a slap, a whack and a tug-of-war, the book lay on the table and Peter was in the loft.

This is how matters stood when it was time for the family to eat. Peter stayed upstairs. No one gave him a moment's thought; he'd have to go to bed without his dinner. We continued eating, chatting merrily away, when suddenly we heard a piercing whistle. We lay down our forks and stared at each other, the shock clearly visible on our pale faces.

Then we heard Peter's voice through the chimney: "I won't come down!"

Mr. van Daan leapt up, his napkin falling to the floor, and shouted, with the blood rushing to his face, "I've had enough!"

Father, afraid of what might happen, grabbed him by the arm and the two men went to the attic. After much struggling and kicking, Peter wound up in his room with the door shut, and we went on eating.

Mrs. van Daan wanted to save a piece of bread for her darling son, but Mr. van D. was adamant. "If he doesn't apologize this minute, he'll have to sleep in the loft."

We protested that going without dinner was enough punishment. What if Peter were to catch cold? We wouldn't be able to call a doctor.

Peter didn't apologize, and returned to the loft. Mr. van Daan decided to leave well enough alone, though he did note the next morning that Peter's bed had been slept in. At seven Peter went to the attic again, but was persuaded to come downstairs when Father spoke a few friendly words to him. After three days of sullen looks and stubborn silence, everything was back to normal.

*Yours, Anne*

MONDAY, SEPTEMBER 21, 1942

*Dearest Kitty,*

Today I'll tell you the general news here in the Annex. A lamp has been mounted above my divan bed so that in the future, when I hear the guns going off, I'll be able to pull a cord and switch on the light. I can't use it at the moment because we're keeping our window open a little, day and night.

The male members of the van Daan contingent have built a very handy wood-stained food safe, with real screens. Up to now this glorious cupboard has been located in Peter's room, but in the interests of fresh air it's been moved to the attic. Where it once stood, there's now a shelf. I advised Peter to put his table underneath the shelf, add a nice rug and hang his own cupboard where the table now stands. That might make his little cubbyhole more comfy, though I certainly wouldn't like to sleep there.

Mrs. van Daan is unbearable. I'm continually being scolded for my incessant chatter when I'm upstairs. I simply let the words bounce right off me! Madame now has a new trick up her sleeve: trying to get out of washing the pots and pans. If there's a bit of food left at the bottom of the pan, she leaves it to spoil instead of transferring it to a glass dish. Then in the afternoon when Margot is stuck with cleaning all the pots and pans, Madame exclaims, "Oh, poor Margot, you have so much work to do!"

Every other week Mr. Kleiman brings me a couple of books written for girls my age. I'm enthusiastic about the *Joop ter Heul* series. I've enjoyed all of Cissy van Marxveldt's books very much.

I've read *The Zaniest Summer* four times, and the ludicrous situations still make me laugh.

Father and I are currently working on our family tree, and he tells me something about each person as we go along.

I've begun my schoolwork. I'm working hard at French, cramming five irregular verbs into my head every day. But I've forgotten much too much of what I learned in school.

Peter has taken up his English with great reluctance. A few schoolbooks have just arrived, and I brought a large supply of notebooks, pencils, erasers and labels from home. Pim (that's our pet name for Father) wants me to help him with his Dutch lessons. I'm perfectly willing to tutor him in exchange for his assistance with French and other subjects. But he makes the most unbelievable mistakes!

I sometimes listen to the Dutch broadcasts from London. Prince Bernhard recently announced that Princess Juliana is expecting a baby in January, which I think is wonderful. No one here understands why I take such an interest in the Royal Family.

A few nights ago I was the topic of discussion, and we all decided I was an ignoramus. As a result, I threw myself into my schoolwork the next day, since I have little desire to still be a freshman when I'm fourteen or fifteen. The fact that I'm hardly allowed to read anything was also discussed. At the moment, Mother's reading *The House of Tavelinck*, and of course I'm not allowed to read it (though Margot is!). First I have to be more intellectually developed, like my genius of a sister. Then we discussed my ignorance of philosophy, psychology and physiology (I immediately looked up these big words in the dictionary!). It's true, I don't know anything about these subjects. But maybe I'll be smarter next year!

I've come to the shocking conclusion that I have only one long-sleeved dress and three cardigans to wear in the winter. Father's given me permission to knit a white wool sweater; the yarn isn't very pretty, but it'll be warm, and that's what counts. Some of our clothing was left with friends, but unfortunately we won't be able to get to it until after the war. Provided it's still there, of course.

I'd just finished writing something about Mrs. van Daan when she walked into the room. Thump, I slammed the book shut.

"Hey, Anne, can't I even take a peek?"

"No, Mrs. van Daan."

"Just the last page then?"

"No, not even the last page, Mrs. van Daan."

Of course, I nearly died, since that particular page contained a rather unflattering description of her.

There's something happening every day, but I'm too tired and lazy to write it all down.

*Yours, Anne*

*Dearest Kitty,* FRIDAY, SEPTEMBER 25, 1942

Father has a friend, a man in his mid-seventies named Mr. Dreher, who's sick, poor and deaf as a post. At his side, like a useless appendage, is his wife, twenty-seven years younger and equally poor, whose arms and legs are loaded with real and fake bracelets and rings left over from more prosperous days. This Mr. Dreher has already been a great nuisance to Father, and I've always admired the saintly patience with which he handled this pathetic old man on the phone. When we were still living at home, Mother used to advise him to put a gramophone in front of the receiver, one that would repeat every three minutes, "Yes, Mr. Dreher" and "No, Mr. Dreher," since the old man never understood a word of Father's lengthy replies anyway.

Today Mr. Dreher phoned the office and asked Mr. Kugler to come and see him. Mr. Kugler wasn't in the mood and said he would send Miep, but Miep canceled the appointment. Mrs. Dreher called the office three times, but since Miep was reportedly out the entire afternoon, she had to imitate Bep's voice. Downstairs in the office as well as upstairs in the Annex, there was great hilarity. Now each time the phone rings, Bep says "That's Mrs. Dreher!" and Miep has to laugh, so that the people on the other end of the line are greeted with an impolite giggle. Can't you just picture it? This has got to be the greatest office in the whole wide world. The bosses and the office girls have such fun together!

Some evenings I go to the van Daans for a little chat. We eat "mothball cookies" (molasses cookies that were stored in a closet that was mothproofed) and have a good time. Recently the conversation was about Peter. I said that he often pats me on the cheek, which I don't like. They asked me in a typically grown-up way whether I could ever learn to love Peter like a brother, since he loves me like a sister. "Oh, no!" I said, but what I was thinking was, "Oh, ugh!" Just imagine! I added that Peter's a bit stiff, perhaps because he's shy. Boys who aren't used to being around girls are like that.

I must say that the Annex Committee (the men's section) is very creative. Listen to the scheme they've come up with to get a message to Mr. Broks, an Opekta Co. sales representative and friend who's surreptitiously hidden some of our things for us! They're going to type a letter to a store owner in southern Zeeland who is, indirectly, one of Opekta's customers and ask him to fill out a form and send it back in the enclosed self-addressed envelope. Father will write the address on the envelope himself. Once the letter is returned from Zeeland, the form can be removed and a handwritten message confirming that Father is alive can be inserted in the envelope. This way Mr. Broks can read the letter without suspecting a ruse. They chose the province of Zeeland because it's close to Belgium (a letter can easily be smuggled across the border) and because no one is allowed to travel there without a special permit. An ordinary salesman like Mr. Broks would never be granted a permit.

Yesterday Father put on another act. Groggy with sleep, he stumbled off to bed. His feet were cold, so I lent him my bed socks. Five minutes later he flung them to the floor. Then he pulled the blankets over his head because the light bothered him. The lamp was switched off, and he gingerly poked his head out from under the covers. It was all very amusing. We started talking about the fact that Peter says Margot is a "buttinsky." Suddenly Daddy's voice was heard from the depths: "Sits on her butt, you mean."

Mouschi, the cat, is becoming nicer to me as time goes by, but I'm still somewhat afraid of her.

*Yours, Anne*

*Dearest Kitty,*

Mother and I had a so-called "discussion" today, but the annoying part is that I burst into tears. I can't help it. Daddy is *always* nice to me, and he also understands me much better. At moments like these I can't stand Mother. It's obvious that I'm a stranger to her; she doesn't even know what I think about the most ordinary things.

We were talking about maids and the fact that you're supposed to refer to them as "domestic help" these days. She claimed that when the war is over, that's what they'll want to be called. I didn't quite see it that way. Then she added that I talk about "later" so often and that I act as if I were such a lady, even though I'm not, but I don't think building sand castles in the air is such a terrible thing to do, as long as you don't take it too seriously. At any rate, Daddy usually comes to my defense. Without him I wouldn't be able to stick it out here.

I don't get along with Margot very well either. Even though our family never has the same kind of outbursts they have upstairs, I find it far from pleasant. Margot's and Mother's personalities are so alien to me. I understand my girlfriends better than my own mother. Isn't that a shame?

For the umpteenth time, Mrs. van Daan is sulking. She's very moody and has been removing more and more of her belongings and locking them up. It's too bad Mother doesn't repay every van Daan "disappearing act" with a Frank "disappearing act."

Some people, like the van Daans, seem to take special delight not only in raising their own children but in helping others raise theirs. Margot doesn't need it, since she's naturally good, kind and clever, perfection itself, but I seem to have enough mischief for the two of us. More than once the air has been filled with the van Daans' admonitions and my saucy replies. Father and Mother always defend me fiercely. Without them I wouldn't be able to jump back into the fray with my usual composure. They keep telling me I should talk less, mind my own business and be more modest, but I seem doomed to failure. If Father weren't so patient, I'd have long ago given up hope of ever meeting my parents' quite moderate expectations.

If I take a small helping of a vegetable I loathe and eat potatoes instead, the van Daans, especially Mrs. van Daan, can't get over how spoiled I am. "Come on, Anne, eat some more vegetables," she says.

"No, thank you, ma'am," I reply. "The potatoes are more than enough."

"Vegetables are good for you; your mother says so too. Have some more," she insists, until Father intervenes and upholds my right to refuse a dish I don't like.

Then Mrs. van D. really flies off the handle: "You should have been at our house, where children were brought up the way they should be. I don't call this a proper upbringing. Anne is terribly spoiled. I'd never allow that. If Anne were my daughter . . ."

This is always how her tirades begin and end: "If Anne were my daughter . . ." Thank goodness I'm not.

But to get back to the subject of raising children, yesterday a silence fell after Mrs. van D. finished her little speech. Father then replied, "I think Anne is very well brought up. At least she's learned not to respond to your interminable sermons. As far as the vegetables are concerned, all I have to say is look who's calling the kettle black. "

Mrs. van D. was soundly defeated. The pot calling the kettle black refers of course to Madame herself, since she can't tolerate beans or any kind of cabbage in the evening because they give her "gas." But I could say the same. What a dope, don't you think? In any case, let's hope she stops talking about me.

It's so funny to see how quickly Mrs. van Daan flushes. I don't, and it secretly annoys her no end.

*Yours, Anne*

MONDAY, SEPTEMBER 28, 1942

*Dearest Kitty,*

I had to stop yesterday, though I was nowhere near finished. I'm dying to tell you about another one of our clashes, but before I do I'd like to say this: I think it's odd that grown-ups quarrel so easily and so often and about such petty matters. Up to now I always thought bickering was just something children did and that they outgrew it. Of course, there's sometimes a reason to have a "real" quarrel, but the verbal exchanges that take place here are just plain bickering. I should be used to the fact that these squabbles are daily occurrences, but I'm not and never will be as long as I'm the subject of nearly every discussion. (They refer to these as "discussions" instead of "quarrels," but Germans don't know the difference!) They criticize everything, and I mean everything, about me: my behavior, my personality, my manners; every inch of me, from head to toe and back again, is the subject of gossip and debate. Harsh words and shouts are constantly being flung at my head, though I'm absolutely not used to it. According to the powers that be, I'm supposed to grin and bear it. But I can't! I have no intention of taking their insults lying down. I'll show them that Anne Frank wasn't born yesterday. They'll sit up and take notice and keep their big mouths shut when I make them see they ought to attend to their own manners instead of mine. How dare they act that way! It's simply barbaric. I've been astonished, time and again, at such rudeness and most of all ... at such stupidity (Mrs. van Daan). But as soon as I've gotten used to the idea, and that shouldn't take long, I'll give them a taste of their own medicine, and then they'll change their tune! Am I really as bad-mannered, headstrong, stubborn, pushy, stupid, lazy, etc., etc., as the van Daans say I am? No, of course not. I know I have my faults and shortcomings, but they blow them all out of proportion! If you only knew, Kitty, how I seethe when they scold and mock me. It won't take long before I explode with pent-up rage.

But enough of that. I've bored you long enough with my quarrels, and yet I can't resist adding a highly interesting dinner conversation.

Somehow we landed on the subject of Pim's extreme diffidence. His modesty is a well-known fact, which even the stupidest person wouldn't dream of questioning. All of a sudden Mrs. van Daan, who feels the need to bring herself into every conversation, remarked, "I'm very modest and retiring too, much more so than my husband!"

Have you ever heard anything so ridiculous? This sentence clearly illustrates that she's not exactly what you'd call modest!

Mr. van Daan, who felt obliged to explain the "much more so than my husband," answered calmly, "I have no desire to be modest and retiring. In my experience, you get a lot further by being pushy!" And turning to me, he added, "Don't be modest and retiring, Anne. It will get you nowhere."

Mother agreed completely with this viewpoint. But, as usual, Mrs. van Daan had to add her two cents. This time, however, instead of addressing me directly, she turned to my parents and said, "You must have a strange outlook on life to be able to say that to Anne. Things were different when I was growing up. Though they probably haven't changed much since then, except in your modern household!"

This was a direct hit at Mother's modern child-rearing methods, which she's defended on many occasions. Mrs. van Daan was so upset her face turned bright red. People who flush easily become even more agitated when they feel themselves getting hot under the collar, and they quickly lose to their opponents.

The nonflushed mother, who now wanted to have the matter over and done with as quickly as possible, paused for a moment to think before she replied. "Well, Mrs. van Daan, I agree that it's much better if a person isn't overmodest. My husband, Margot and Peter are all exceptionally modest. Your husband, Anne and I, though not exactly the opposite, don't let ourselves be pushed around."

Mrs. van Daan: "Oh, but Mrs. Frank, I don't understand what you mean! Honestly, I'm extremely modest and retiring. How can you say that I'm pushy?"

Mother: "I didn't say you were pushy, but no one would describe you as having a retiring disposition."

Mrs. van D.: "I'd like to know in what way I'm pushy! If I didn't look out for myself here, no one else would, and I'd soon starve, but that doesn't mean I'm not as modest and retiring as your husband."

Mother had no choice but to laugh at this ridiculous self-defense, which irritated Mrs. van Daan. Not exactly a born debater, she continued her magnificent account in a mixture of German and Dutch, until she got so tangled up in her own words that she finally rose from her chair and was just about to leave the room when her eye fell on me. You should have seen her!

As luck would have it, the moment Mrs. van D. turned around I was shaking my head in a combination of compassion and irony. I wasn't doing it on purpose, but I'd followed her tirade so intently that my reaction was completely involuntary. Mrs. van D. wheeled around and gave me a tongue-lashing: hard, Germanic, mean and vulgar, exactly like some fat, red-faced fishwife. It was a joy to behold. If I could draw, I'd like to have sketched her as she was then. She struck me as so comical, that silly little scatterbrain! I've learned one thing: you only really get to know a person after a fight. Only then can you judge their true character!

Yours, Anne

TUESDAY, SEPTEMBER 29, 1942

*Dearest Kitty,*

The strangest things happen to you when you're in hiding! Try to picture this. Because we don't have a bathtub, we wash ourselves in a washtub, and because there's only hot water in the office (by which I mean the entire lower floor), the seven of us take turns making the most of this great opportunity. But since none of us are alike and are all plagued by varying degrees of modesty, each member of the family has selected a different place to wash. Peter takes a bath in the office kitchen, even though it has a glass door. When it's time for his bath, he goes around to each of us in turn and announces that we shouldn't walk past the kitchen for the next half hour. He considers this measure to be sufficient. Mr. van D. takes his bath upstairs, figuring that the safety of his own room outweighs the difficulty of having to carry the hot water up all those stairs. Mrs. van D. has yet to take a bath; she's waiting to see which is the best place. Father bathes in the private office and Mother in the kitchen behind a fire screen, while Margot and I have declared the front office to be our bathing grounds. Since the curtains are drawn on Saturday afternoon, we scrub ourselves in the dark, while the one who isn't in the bath looks out the window through a chink in the curtains and gazes in wonder at the endlessly amusing people.

A week ago I decided I didn't like this spot and have been on the lookout for more comfortable bathing quarters. It was Peter who gave me the idea of setting my washtub in the spacious office bathroom. I can sit down, turn on the light, lock the door, pour out the water without anyone's help, and all without the fear of being seen. I used my lovely bathroom for the first time on Sunday and, strange as it may seem, I like it better than any other place.

The plumber was at work downstairs on Wednesday, moving the water pipes and drains from the office bathroom to the hallway so the pipes won't freeze during a cold winter. The plumber's visit was far from pleasant. Not only were we not allowed to run water during the day, but the bathroom was also off-limits. I'll tell you how we handled this problem; you may find it unseemly of me to bring it up, but I'm not so prudish about matters of this kind. On the day of our arrival, Father and I improvised a chamber pot, sacrificing a canning jar for this purpose. For the duration of the plumber's visit, canning jars were put into service during the daytime to hold our calls of nature. As far as I was concerned, this wasn't half as difficult as having to sit still all day and not say a word. You can imagine how hard that was for Miss Quack, Quack, Quack. On ordinary days we have to speak in a whisper; not being able to talk or move at all is ten times worse.

After three days of constant sitting, my backside was stiff and sore. Nightly calisthenics helped.

*Yours, Anne*

THURSDAY, OCTOBER 1, 1942

*Dear Kitty,*

Yesterday I had a horrible fright. At eight o'clock the doorbell suddenly rang. All I could think of was that someone was coming to get us, you know who I mean. But I calmed down when everybody swore it must have been either pranksters or the mailman.

The days here are very quiet. Mr. Levinsohn, a little Jewish pharmacist and chemist, is working for Mr. Kugler in the kitchen. Since he's familiar with the entire building, we're in constant dread that he'll take it into his head to go have a look at what used to be the laboratory. We're as still as baby mice. Who would have guessed three months ago that quicksilver Anne would have to sit so quietly for hours on end, and what's more, that she could?

Mrs. van Daan's birthday was the twenty-ninth. Though we didn't have a large celebration, she was showered with flowers, simple gifts and good food. Apparently the red carnations from her spouse are a family tradition.

Let me pause a moment on the subject of Mrs. van Daan and tell you that her attempts to flirt with Father are a constant source of irritation to me. She pats him on the cheek and head, hikes up her skirt and makes so-called witty remarks in an effort to get Pim's attention. Fortunately, he finds her neither pretty nor charming, so he doesn't respond to her flirtations. As you know, I'm quite the jealous type, and I can't abide her behavior. After all, Mother doesn't act that way toward Mr. van D., which is what I told Mrs. van D. right to her face.

From time to time Peter can be very amusing. He and I have one thing in common: we like to dress up, which makes everyone laugh. One evening we made our appearance, with Peter in one of his mother's skin-tight dresses and me in his suit. He wore a hat; I had a cap on. The grown-ups split their sides laughing, and we enjoyed ourselves every bit as much.

Bep bought new skirts for Margot and me at The Bijenkorf. The fabric is hideous, like the burlap bag potatoes come in. Just the kind of thing the department stores wouldn't dare sell in the olden days, now costing 24.00 guilders (Margot's) and 7.75 guilders (mine).

We have a nice treat in store: Bep's ordered a correspondence course in shorthand for Margot, Peter and me. Just you wait, by this time next year we'll be able to take perfect shorthand. In any case, learning to write a secret code like that is really interesting.

I have a terrible pain in my index finger (on my left hand), so I can't do any ironing. What luck!

Mr. van Daan wants me to sit next to him at the table, since Margot doesn't eat enough to suit him. Fine with me, I like changes. There's always a tiny black cat roaming around the yard, and it reminds me of my dear sweet Moortje. Another reason I welcome the change is that Mama's always carping at me, especially at the table. Now Margot will have to bear the brunt of it. Or rather, won't, since Mother doesn't make such sarcastic remarks to her. Not to that paragon of virtue! I'm always teasing

Margot about being a paragon of virtue these days, and she hates it. Maybe it'll teach her not to be such a goody-goody. High time she learned.

To end this hodgepodge of news, a particularly amusing joke told by Mr. van Daan:

What goes click ninety-nine times and clack once?
A centipede with a clubfoot.

*Bye-bye, Anne*

SATURDAY, OCTOBER 3, 1942
*Dear Kitty,*

Everybody teased me quite a bit yesterday because I lay down on the bed next to Mr. van Daan. "At your age! Shocking!" and other remarks along those lines. Silly, of course. I'd never want to sleep with Mr. van Daan the way they mean.

Yesterday Mother and I had another run-in and she really kicked up a fuss. She told Daddy all my sins and started to cry, which made me cry too, and I already had such an awful headache. I finally told Daddy that I love "him" more than I do Mother, to which he replied that it was just a passing phase, but I don't think so. I simply can't stand Mother, and I have to force myself not to snap at her all the time, and to stay calm, when I'd rather slap her across the face. I don't know why I've taken such a terrible dislike to her. Daddy says that if Mother isn't feeling well or has a headache, I should volunteer to help her, but I'm not going to because I don't love her and don't enjoy doing it. I can imagine Mother dying someday, but Daddy's death seems inconceivable. It's very mean of me, but that's how I feel. I hope Mother will *never* read this or anything else I've written.

I've been allowed to read more grown-up books lately. *Eva's Youth* by Nico van Suchtelen is currently keeping me busy. I don't think there's much of a difference between this and books for teenage girls. Eva thought that children grew on trees, like apples, and that the stork plucked them off the tree when they were ripe and brought them to the mothers. But her girlfriend's cat had kittens and Eva saw them coming out of the cat, so she thought cats laid eggs and hatched them like chickens, and that mothers who wanted a child also went upstairs a few days before their time to lay an egg and brood on it. After the babies arrived, the mothers were pretty weak from all that squatting. At some point, Eva wanted a baby too. She took a wool scarf and spread it on the ground so the egg could fall into it, and then she squatted down and began to push. She clucked as she waited, but no egg came out. Finally, after she'd been sitting for a long time, something did come, but it was a sausage instead of an egg. Eva was embarrassed. She thought she was sick. Funny, isn't it? There are also parts of *Eva's Youth* that talk about women selling their bodies on the street and asking loads of money. I'd be mortified in front of a man like that. In addition, it mentions Eva's menstruation. Oh, I long to get my period – then I'll really be grown up.

Daddy is grumbling again and threatening to take away my diary. Oh, horror of horrors! From now on, I'm going to hide it.

*Anne Frank*

WEDNESDAY, OCTOBER 7, 1942

I imagine that . . .

I've gone to Switzerland. Daddy and I sleep in one room, while the boys'\* study is turned into a sitting room, where I can receive visitors. As a surprise, they've bought new furniture for me, including a tea table, a desk, armchairs and a divan. Everything's simply wonderful. After a few days Daddy gives me 150 guilders – converted into Swiss money, of course, but I'll call them guilders – and tells me to buy everything I think I'll need, all for myself. (Later on, I get a guilder a week, which I can also use to buy whatever I want.) I set off with Bernd and buy:

    3 cotton undershirts @ 0.50 = 1.50
    3 cotton underpants @ 0.50 = 1.50
    3 wool undershirts @ 0.75 = 2.25
    3 wool underpants @ 0.75 = 2.25
    2 petticoats @ 0.50 = 1.00
    2 bras (smallest size) @ 0.50 = 1.00
    5 pajamas @ 1.00 = 5.00
    1 summer robe @ 2.50 = 2.50
    1 winter robe @ 3.00 = 3.00

\* Anne's cousins Bernhard (Bernd) and Stephan Elias.

2 bed jackets @ 0.75 = 1.50
1 small pillow @ 1.00 = 1.00
1 pair of lightweight slippers @ 1.00 = 1.00
1 pair of warm slippers @ 1.50 = 1.50
1 pair of summer shoes (school) @ 1.50 = 1.50
1 pair of summer shoes (dressy) @ 2.00 = 2.00
1 pair of winter shoes (school) @ 2.50 = 2.50
1 pair of winter shoes (dressy) @ 3.00 = 3.00
2 aprons @ 0.50 = 1.00
25 handkerchiefs @ 0.05 = 1.25
4 pairs of silk stockings @ 0.75 = 3.00
4 pairs of kneesocks @ 0.50 = 2.00
4 pairs of socks @ 0.25 = 1.00
2 pairs of thick stockings @ 1.00 = 2.00
3 skeins of white yarn (underwear, cap) = 1.50
3 skeins of blue yarn (sweater, skirt) = 1.50
3 skeins of variegated yarn (cap, scarf) = 1.50
Scarves, belts, collars, buttons = 1.25

Plus 2 school dresses (summer), 2 school dresses (winter),
2 good dresses (summer), 2 good dresses (winter),
1 summer skirt, 1 good winter skirt, 1 school winter skirt,
1 raincoat, 1 summer coat, 1 winter coat, 2 hats, 2 caps.
For a total of 108.00 guilders.

2 purses, 1 ice-skating outfit, 1 pair of skates, 1 case
(containing powder, skin cream, foundation cream,
cleansing cream, suntan lotion, cotton, first-aid kit, rouge,
lipstick, eyebrow pencil, bath salts, bath powder, eau de
cologne, soap, powder puff).

Plus 4 sweaters @ 1.50, 4 blouses @ 1.00, miscellaneous
items @ 10.00 and books, presents @ 4.50.

*Dearest Kitty,*                    FRIDAY, OCTOBER 9, 1942

Today I have nothing but dismal and depressing news to
report. Our many Jewish friends and acquaintances are being
taken away in droves. The Gestapo is treating them very roughly
and transporting them in cattle cars to Westerbork, the big camp

in Drenthe to which they're sending all the Jews. Miep told us about someone who'd managed to escape from there. It must be terrible in Westerbork. The people get almost nothing to eat, much less to drink, as water is available only one hour a day, and there's only one toilet and sink for several thousand people. Men and women sleep in the same room, and women and children often have their heads shaved. Escape is almost impossible; many people look Jewish, and they're branded by their shorn heads.

If it's that bad in Holland, what must it be like in those faraway and uncivilized places where the Germans are sending them? We assume that most of them are being murdered. The English radio says they're being gassed. Perhaps that's the quickest way to die.

I feel terrible. Miep's accounts of these horrors are so heart-rending, and Miep is also very distraught. The other day, for instance, the Gestapo deposited an elderly, crippled Jewish woman on Miep's doorstep while they set off to find a car. The old woman was terrified of the glaring searchlights and the guns firing at the English planes overhead. Yet Miep didn't dare let her in. Nobody would. The Germans are generous enough when it comes to punishment.

Bep is also very subdued. Her boyfriend is being sent to Germany. Every time the planes fly over, she's afraid they're going to drop their entire bomb load on Bertus's head. Jokes like "Oh, don't worry, they can't all fall on him" or "One bomb is all it takes" are hardly appropriate in this situation. Bertus is not the only one being forced to work in Germany. Trainloads of young men depart daily. Some of them try to sneak off the train when it stops at a small station, but only a few manage to escape unnoticed and find a place to hide.

But that's not the end of my lamentations. Have you ever heard the term "hostages"? That's the latest punishment for saboteurs. It's the most horrible thing you can imagine. Leading citizens − innocent people − are taken prisoner to await their execution. If the Gestapo can't find the saboteur, they simply grab five hostages and line them up against the wall. You read the announcements of their death in the paper, where they're referred to as "fatal accidents."

Fine specimens of humanity, those Germans, and to think I'm actually one of them! No, that's not true, Hitler took away our nationality long ago. And besides, there are no greater enemies on earth than the Germans and the Jews.

*Yours, Anne*

*Dear Kitty,*                    WEDNESDAY, OCTOBER 14, 1942

I'm terribly busy. Yesterday I began by translating a chapter from *La Belle Nivernaise* and writing down vocabulary words. Then I worked on an *awful* math problem and translated three pages of French grammar besides. Today, French grammar and history. I simply refuse to do that wretched math every day. Daddy thinks it's awful too. I'm almost better at it than he is, though in fact neither of us is any good, so we always have to call on Margot's help. I'm also working away at my shorthand, which I enjoy. Of the three of us, I've made the most progress.

I've read *The Storm Family*. It's quite good, but doesn't compare to *Joop ter Heul*. Anyway, the same words can be found in both books, which makes sense because they're written by the same author. Cissy van Marxveldt is a terrific writer. I'm definitely going to let my own children read her books too.

Moreover, I've read a lot of Körner plays. I like the way he writes. For example, *Hedwig*, *The Cousin from Bremen*, *The Governess*, *The Green Domino*, etc.

Mother, Margot and I are once again the best of buddies. It's actually a lot nicer that way. Last night Margot and I were lying side by side in my bed. It was incredibly cramped, but that's what made it fun. She asked if she could read my diary once in a while.

"Parts of it," I said, and asked about hers. She gave me permission to read her diary as well.

The conversation turned to the future, and I asked what she wanted to be when she was older. But she wouldn't say and was quite mysterious about it. I gathered it had something to do with teaching; of course, I'm not absolutely sure, but I suspect it's something along those lines. I really shouldn't be so nosy.

This morning I lay on Peter's bed, after first having chased him off it. He was furious, but I didn't care. He might consider being a little more friendly to me from time to time. After all, I did give him an apple last night.

I once asked Margot if she thought I was ugly. She said that I was cute and had nice eyes. A little vague, don't you think?

Well, until next time!

*Anne Frank*

PS. This morning we all took turns on the scale. Margot now weighs 132 pounds, Mother 136, Father 155, Anne 96, Peter 148, Mrs. van Daan 117, Mr. van Daan 165. In the three months since I've been here, I've gained 19 pounds. A lot, huh?

TUESDAY, OCTOBER 20, 1942

*Dearest Kitty,*

My hand's still shaking, though it's been two hours since we had the scare. I should explain that there are five fire extinguishers in the building. The office staff stupidly forgot to warn us that the carpenter, or whatever he's called, was coming to fill the extinguishers. As a result, we didn't bother to be quiet until I heard the sound of hammering on the landing (across from the bookcase). I immediately assumed it was the carpenter and went to warn Bep, who was eating lunch, that she couldn't go back downstairs. Father and I stationed ourselves at the door so we could hear when the man had left. After working for about fifteen minutes, he laid his hammer and some other tools on our bookcase (or so we thought!) and banged on our door. We turned white with fear. Had he heard something after all and now wanted to check out this mysterious-looking bookcase? It seemed so, since he kept knocking, pulling, pushing and jerking on it.

I was so scared I nearly fainted at the thought of this total stranger managing to discover our wonderful hiding place. Just when I thought my days were numbered, we heard Mr. Kleiman's voice saying, "Open up, it's me."

We opened the door at once. What had happened? The hook fastening the bookcase had gotten stuck, which is why no one had been able to warn us about the carpenter. After the man had left, Mr. Kleiman came to get Bep, but couldn't open the bookcase. I can't tell you how relieved I was. In my imagination, the man I thought was trying to get inside the Secret Annex had kept growing and growing until he'd become not only a giant but also the cruelest Fascist in the world. Whew. Fortunately, everything worked out all right, at least this time.

We had lots of fun on Monday. Miep and Jan spent the night with us. Margot and I slept in Father and Mother's room for the night so the Gieses could have our beds. The menu was drawn up in their honor, and the meal was delicious. The festivities were briefly interrupted when Father's lamp caused a short circuit and we were suddenly plunged into darkness. What were we to do? We did have fuses, but the fuse box was at the rear of the dark warehouse, which made this a particularly unpleasant job at night. Still, the men ventured forth, and ten minutes later we were able to put away the candles.

I was up early this morning. Jan was already dressed. Since he had to leave at eight-thirty, he was upstairs eating breakfast by eight. Miep was busy getting dressed, and I found her in her undershirt when I came in. She wears the same kind of long underwear I do when she bicycles. Margot and I threw on our clothes as well and were upstairs earlier than usual. After a pleasant breakfast, Miep headed downstairs. It was pouring outside and she was glad she didn't have to bicycle to work. Daddy and I made the beds, and afterward I learned five irregular French verbs. Quite industrious, don't you think?

Margot and Peter were reading in our room, with Mouschi curled up beside Margot on the divan. After my irregular French verbs, I joined them and read *Beyond Sing the Woods*. It's quite a beautiful book, but very unusual. I'm almost finished.

Next week it's Bep's turn to spend the night.

*Yours, Anne*

*My dearest Kitty,*           THURSDAY, OCTOBER 29, 1942

I'm very worried. Father's sick. He's covered with spots and has a high temperature. It looks like measles. Just think, we can't even call a doctor! Mother is making him perspire in hopes of sweating out the fever.

This morning Miep told us that the furniture has been removed from the van Daans' apartment on Zuider Amstellaan.

We haven't told Mrs. van D. yet. She's been so *"nervenmässig"* * lately, and we don't feel like hearing her moan and groan again about all the beautiful china and lovely chairs she had to leave behind. We had to abandon most of our nice things too. What's the good of grumbling about it now?

Father wants me to start reading books by Hebbel and other well-known German writers. I can read German fairly well by now, except that I usually mumble the words instead of reading them silently to myself. But that'll pass. Father has taken the plays of Goethe and Schiller down from the big bookcase and is planning to read to me every evening. We've started off with *Don Carlos*. Encouraged by Father's good example, Mother pressed her prayer book into my hands. I read a few prayers in German, just to be polite. They certainly sound beautiful, but they mean very little to me. Why is she making me act so religious and devout?

Tomorrow we're going to light the stove for the first time. The chimney hasn't been swept in ages, so the room is bound to fill with smoke. Let's hope the thing draws!

*Yours, Anne*

MONDAY, NOVEMBER 2, 1942

*Dear Kitty,*

Bep stayed with us Friday evening. It was fun, but she didn't sleep very well because she'd drunk some wine. For the rest, there's nothing special to report. I had an awful headache yesterday and went to bed early. Margot's being exasperating again.

This morning I began sorting out an index card file from the office, because it'd fallen over and gotten all mixed up. Before long I was going nuts. I asked Margot and Peter to help, but they were too lazy, so I put it away. I'm not crazy enough to do it all by myself!

*Anne Frank*

PS. I forgot to mention the important news that I'm probably going to get my period soon. I can tell because I keep finding a whitish smear in my panties, and Mother predicted it would start soon. I can hardly wait. It's such a momentous event. Too bad

* Nervous.

I can't use sanitary napkins, but you can't get them anymore, and Mama's tampons can be used only by women who've had a baby.

COMMENT ADDED BY ANNE ON JANUARY 22, 1944:
*I wouldn't be able to write that kind of thing anymore.*

*Now that I'm rereading my diary after a year and a half I'm surprised at my childish innocence. Deep down I know I could never be that innocent again, however much I'd like to be. I can understand the mood changes and the comments about Margot, Mother and Father as if I'd written them only yesterday, but I can't imagine writing so openly about other matters. It embarrasses me greatly to read the pages dealing with subjects that I remembered as being nicer than they actually were. My descriptions are so indelicate. But enough of that.*

*I can also understand my homesickness and yearning for Moortje. The whole time I've been here I've longed unconsciously – and at times consciously – for trust, love and physical affection. This longing may change in intensity, but it's always there.*

THURSDAY, NOVEMBER 5, 1942
*Dear Kitty,*

The British have finally scored a few successes in Africa and Stalingrad hasn't fallen yet, so the men are happy and we had coffee and tea this morning. For the rest, nothing special to report.

This week I've been reading a lot and doing little work. That's the way things ought to be. That's surely the road to success.

Mother and I are getting along better lately, but we're *never* close. Father's not very open about his feelings, but he's the same sweetheart he's always been. We lit the stove a few days ago and the entire room is still filled with smoke. I prefer central heating, and I'm probably not the only one. Margot's a stinker (there's no other word for it), a constant source of irritation, morning, noon and night.

*Anne Frank*

MONDAY, NOVEMBER 9, 1942
*Dearest Kitty,*

Yesterday was Peter's birthday, his sixteenth. I was upstairs by eight, and Peter and I looked at his presents. He received a game of Monopoly, a razor and a cigarette lighter. Not that he smokes so much, not at all; it just looks so distinguished.

The biggest surprise came from Mr. van Daan, who reported at one that the English had landed in Tunis, Algiers, Casablanca and Oran.

"This is the beginning of the end," everyone was saying, but Churchill, the British Prime Minister, who must have heard the same thing being repeated in England, declared, "This is not the end. It is not even the beginning of the end. But it is, perhaps, the end of the beginning." Do you see the difference? However, there's reason for optimism. Stalingrad, the Russian city that has been under attack for three months, still hasn't fallen into German hands.

In the true spirit of the Annex, I should talk to you about food. (I should explain that they're real gluttons up on the top floor.)

Bread is delivered daily by a very nice baker, a friend of Mr. Kleiman's. Of course, we don't have as much as we did at home, but it's enough. We also purchase ration books on the black market. The price keeps going up; it's already risen from 27 to 33 guilders. And that for mere sheets of printed paper!

To provide ourselves with a source of nutrition that will keep, aside from the hundred cans of food we've stored here, we bought three hundred pounds of beans. Not just for us, but for the office staff as well. We'd hung the sacks of beans on hooks in the hallway, just inside our secret entrance, but a few seams split under the weight. So we decided to move them to the attic, and Peter was entrusted with the heavy lifting. He managed to get five of the six sacks upstairs intact and was busy with the last one when the sack broke and a flood, or rather a hailstorm, of brown beans went flying through the air and down the stairs. Since there were about fifty pounds of beans in that sack, it made enough noise to raise the dead. Downstairs they were sure the house was falling down around their heads. Peter was stunned, but then burst into peals of laughter when he saw me standing at the bottom of the stairs, like an island in a sea of brown, with waves of beans lapping at my ankles. We promptly began picking them up, but beans are so small and slippery that they roll into every conceivable corner and hole. Now each time we go upstairs, we bend over and hunt around so we can present Mrs. van Daan with a handful of beans.

I almost forgot to mention that Father has recovered from his illness.

*Yours, Anne*

PS. The radio has just announced that Algiers has fallen. Morocco, Casablanca and Oran have been in English hands for several days. We're now waiting for Tunis.

*Dearest Kitty,*                    TUESDAY, NOVEMBER 10, 1942

Great news! We're planning to take an eighth person into hiding with us!

Yes, really. We always thought there was enough room and food for one more person, but we were afraid of placing an even greater burden on Mr. Kugler and Mr. Kleiman. But since reports of the dreadful things being done to the Jews are getting worse by the day, Father decided to sound out these two gentlemen, and they thought it was an excellent plan. "It's just as dangerous, whether there are seven or eight," they noted rightly. Once this was settled, we sat down and mentally went through our circle of acquaintances, trying to come up with a single person who would blend in well with our extended family. This wasn't difficult. After Father had rejected all the van Daan relatives, we chose a dentist named Albert Dussel. He lives with a charming Christian lady who's quite a bit younger than he is. They're probably not married, but that's beside the point. He's known to be quiet and refined, and he seemed, from our superficial acquaintance with him, to be nice. Miep knows him as well, so she'll be able to make the necessary arrangements. If he comes, Mr. Dussel will have to sleep in my room instead of Margot, who will have to make do with the folding bed.* We'll ask him to bring along something to fill cavities with.

*Yours, Anne*

*Dearest Kitty,*                   THURSDAY, NOVEMBER 12, 1942

Miep came to tell us that she'd been to see Dr. Dussel. He asked her the moment she entered the room if she knew of

---

*After Dussel arrived, Margot slept in her parents' bedroom.

a hiding place and was enormously pleased when Miep said she had something in mind. She added that he'd need to go into hiding as soon as possible, preferably Saturday, but he thought this was highly improbable, since he wanted to bring his records up to date, settle his accounts and attend to a couple of patients. Miep relayed the message to us this morning. We didn't think it was wise to wait so long. All these preparations require explanations to various people who we feel ought to be kept in the dark. Miep went to ask if Dr. Dussel couldn't manage to come on Saturday after all, but he said no, and now he's scheduled to arrive on Monday.

I think it's odd that he doesn't jump at our proposal. If they pick him up on the street, it won't help either his records or his patients, so why the delay? If you ask me, it's stupid of Father to humor him.

Otherwise, no news.

*Yours, Anne*

*Dearest Kitty!* TUESDAY, NOVEMBER 17, 1942

Mr. Dussel has arrived. Everything went smoothly. Miep told him to be at a certain place in front of the post office at 11 a.m., when a man would meet him, and he was at the appointed place at the appointed time. Mr. Kleiman went up to him, announced that the man he was expecting to meet was unable to come and asked him to drop by the office to see Miep. Mr. Kleiman took a streetcar back to the office while Mr. Dussel followed on foot.

It was eleven-twenty when Mr. Dussel tapped on the office door. Miep asked him to remove his coat, so the yellow star couldn't be seen, and brought him to the private office, where Mr. Kleiman kept him occupied until the cleaning lady had gone. On the pretext that the private office was needed for something else, Miep took Mr. Dussel upstairs, opened the bookcase and stepped inside, while Mr. Dussel looked on in amazement.

In the meantime, the seven of us had seated ourselves around the dining table to await the latest addition to our family with coffee and cognac. Miep first led him into the Frank family's room. He immediately recognized our furniture, but had no idea we were upstairs, just above his head. When Miep told him, he was so astonished he nearly fainted. Thank goodness she didn't leave him in suspense any longer, but brought him upstairs. Mr. Dussel sank into a chair and stared at us in dumbstruck silence, as though he thought he could read the truth on our faces. Then he stuttered, "*Aber* . . . but are you *nicht* in Belgium? The officer, the auto, they were not coming? Your escape was not working?"

We explained the whole thing to him, about how we'd deliberately spread the rumor of the officer and the car to throw the Germans and anyone else who might come looking for us off the track. Mr. Dussel was speechless in the face of such ingenuity, and could do nothing but gaze around in surprise as he explored the rest of our lovely and ultrapractical Annex. We all had lunch together. Then he took a short nap, joined us for tea, put away the few belongings Miep had been able to bring here in advance and began to feel much more at home. Especially when we handed him the following typewritten rules and regulations for the Secret Annex (a van Daan production):

### PROSPECTUS AND GUIDE TO THE SECRET ANNEX

A Unique Facility for the Temporary
Accommodation of Jews and Other
Dispossessed Persons

*Open all year round:* Located in beautiful, quiet, wooded surroundings in the heart of Amsterdam. No private residences in the vicinity. Can be reached by streetcar 13 or 17 and also by car and bicycle. For those to whom such transportation has been forbidden by the German authorities, it can also be reached on foot. Furnished and unfurnished rooms and apartments are available at all times, with or without meals.

*Price:* Free.

*Diet:* Low-fat.

*Running water* in the bathroom (sorry, no bath) and on various inside and outside walls. Cozy wood stoves for heating.

*Ample storage space* for a variety of goods. Two large, modern safes.

*Private radio* with a direct line to London, New York, Tel Aviv and many other stations. Available to all residents after 6 p.m. No listening to forbidden broadcasts, with certain exceptions, i.e., German stations may only be tuned in to listen to classical music. It is absolutely forbidden to listen to German news bulletins (regardless of where they are transmitted from) and to pass them on to others.

*Rest hours:* From 10 p.m. to 7:30 a.m.; 10:15 a.m. on Sundays. Owing to circumstances, residents are required to observe rest hours during the daytime when instructed to do so by the Management. To ensure the safety of all, rest hours must be strictly observed!!!

*Free-time activities:* None allowed outside the house until further notice.

*Use of language:* It is necessary to speak softly at all times. Only the language of civilized people may be spoken, thus no German.

*Reading and relaxation:* No German books may be read, except for the classics and works of a scholarly nature. Other books are optional.

*Calisthenics:* Daily.

*Singing:* Only softly, and after 6 p.m.

*Movies:* Prior arrangements required.

*Classes:* A weekly correspondence course in shorthand. Courses in English, French, math and history offered at any hour of the day or night. Payment in the form of tutoring, e.g., Dutch.

*Separate department* for the care of small household pets (with the exception of vermin, for which special permits are required).

*Mealtimes:*

> *Breakfast:* At 9 a.m. daily except holidays and Sundays; at approximately 11:30 a.m. on Sundays and holidays.
>
> *Lunch:* A light meal. From 1:15 p.m. to 1:45 p.m.
>
> *Dinner:* May or may not be a hot meal. Mealtime depends on news broadcasts.

*Obligations with respect to the Supply Corps:* Residents must be prepared to help with office work at all times.

*Baths:* The washtub is available to all residents after 9 a.m. on Sundays. Residents may bathe in the bathroom, kitchen, private office or front office, as they choose.

*Alcohol:* For medicinal purposes only.

The end.

Yours, Anne

*Dearest Kitty,*                                THURSDAY, NOVEMBER 19, 1942

Just as we thought, Mr. Dussel is a very nice man. Of course he didn't mind sharing a room with me; to be honest, I'm not exactly delighted at having a stranger use my things, but you have to make sacrifices for a good cause, and I'm glad I can make this small one. "If we can save even one of our friends, the rest doesn't matter," said Father, and he's absolutely right.

The first day Mr. Dussel was here, he asked me all sorts of questions – for example, what time the cleaning lady comes to the office, how we've arranged to use the washroom and when we're allowed to go to the toilet. You may laugh, but these things aren't so easy in a hiding place. During the daytime we can't make any noise that might be heard downstairs, and when someone else is there, like the cleaning lady, we have to be extra careful. I patiently explained all this to Mr. Dussel, but I was surprised to see how slow he is to catch on. He asks everything twice and still can't remember what you've told him.

Maybe he's just confused by the sudden change and he'll get over it. Otherwise, everything is going fine.

Mr. Dussel has told us much about the outside world we've missed for so long. He had sad news. Countless friends and acquaintances have been taken off to a dreadful fate. Night after night, green and gray military vehicles cruise the streets. They knock on every door, asking whether any Jews live there. If so, the whole family is immediately taken away. If not, they proceed to the next house. It's impossible to escape their clutches unless you go into hiding. They often go around with lists, knocking only on those doors where they know there's a big haul to be made. They frequently offer a bounty, so much per head. It's like the slave hunts of the olden days. I don't mean to make light of this; it's much too tragic for that. In the evenings when it's dark,

I often see long lines of good, innocent people, accompanied by crying children, walking on and on, ordered about by a handful of men who bully and beat them until they nearly drop. No one is spared. The sick, the elderly, children, babies and pregnant women – all are marched to their death.

We're so fortunate here, away from the turmoil. We wouldn't have to give a moment's thought to all this suffering if it weren't for the fact that we're so worried about those we hold dear, whom we can no longer help. I feel wicked sleeping in a warm bed, while somewhere out there my dearest friends are dropping from exhaustion or being knocked to the ground.

I get frightened myself when I think of close friends who are now at the mercy of the cruelest monsters ever to stalk the earth.

And all because they're Jews.

*Yours, Anne*

*Dearest Kitty,*

FRIDAY, NOVEMBER 20, 1942

We don't really know how to react. Up to now very little news about the Jews had reached us here, and we thought it best to stay as cheerful as possible. Every now and then Miep used to mention what had happened to a friend, and Mother or Mrs. van Daan would start to cry, so she decided it was better not to say any more. But we bombarded Mr. Dussel with questions, and the stories he had to tell were so gruesome and dreadful that we can't get them out of our heads. Once we've had time to digest the news, we'll probably go back to our usual joking and teasing. It won't do us or those outside any good if we continue to be as gloomy as we are now. And what would be the point of turning the Secret Annex into a Melancholy Annex?

No matter what I'm doing, I can't help thinking about those who are gone. I catch myself laughing and remember that it's a disgrace to be so cheerful. But am I supposed to spend the whole day crying? No, I can't do that. This gloom will pass.

Added to this misery there's another, but of a more personal nature, and it pales in comparison to the suffering I've just told you about. Still, I can't help telling you that lately I've begun to feel deserted. I'm surrounded by too great a void. I never used to give it much thought, since my mind was filled with my friends and having a good time. Now I think either about unhappy things or about myself. It's taken a while, but I've finally realized that Father, no matter how kind he may be, can't take the place of my former world. When it comes to my feelings, Mother and Margot ceased to count long ago.

But why do I bother you with this foolishness? I'm terribly ungrateful, Kitty, I know, but when I've been scolded for the umpteenth time and have all these other woes to think about as well, my head begins to reel!

*Yours, Anne*

*Dearest Kitty,*

SATURDAY, NOVEMBER 28, 1942

We've been using too much electricity and have now exceeded our ration. The result: excessive economy and the prospect of having the electricity cut off. No light for fourteen days; that's a pleasant thought, isn't it? But who knows, maybe it won't be so long! It's too dark to read after four or four-thirty, so we while away the time with all kinds of crazy activities: telling riddles, doing calisthenics in the dark, speaking English or French, reviewing books – after a while everything gets boring. Yesterday I discovered a new pastime: using a good pair of binoculars to peek into the lighted rooms of the neighbors. During the day our curtains can't be opened, not even an inch, but there's no harm when it's so dark.

I never knew that neighbors could be so interesting. Ours are, at any rate. I've come across a few at dinner, one family making home movies and the dentist across the way working on a frightened old lady.

Mr. Dussel, the man who was said to get along so well with children and to absolutely adore them, has turned out to be an old-fashioned disciplinarian and preacher of unbearably long sermons on manners. Since I have the singular pleasure (!) of sharing my far too narrow room with His Excellency, and since I'm generally considered to be the worst behaved of the three young people, it's all I can do to avoid having the same old scoldings and admonitions repeatedly flung at my head and to pretend not to hear. This wouldn't be so bad if Mr. Dussel weren't such a tattletale and hadn't singled out Mother to be the recipient of his reports. If Mr. Dussel's just read me the riot act, Mother lectures me all over again, this time throwing the whole book at me. And if I'm really lucky, Mrs. van D. calls me to account five minutes later and lays down the law as well!

Really, it's not easy being the badly brought-up center of attention of a family of nitpickers.

In bed at night, as I ponder my many sins and exaggerated shortcomings, I get so confused by the sheer amount of things I have to consider that I either laugh or cry, depending on my mood. Then I fall asleep with the strange feeling of wanting to be different than I am or being different than I want to be, or perhaps of behaving differently than I am or want to be.

Oh dear, now I'm confusing you too. Forgive me, but I don't like crossing things out, and in these times of scarcity, tossing away a piece of paper is clearly taboo. So I can only advise you not to reread the above passage and to make no attempt to get to the bottom of it, because you'll never find your way out again!

Yours, Anne

MONDAY, DECEMBER 7, 1942
Dearest Kitty,

Hanukkah and St. Nicholas Day nearly coincided this year; they were only one day apart. We didn't make much of a fuss with Hanukkah, merely exchanging a few small gifts and lighting the candles. Since candles are in short supply, we lit them for only ten minutes, but as long as we sing the song, that doesn't matter. Mr. van Daan made a menorah out of wood, so that was taken care of too.

St. Nicholas Day on Saturday was much more fun. During dinner Bep and Miep were so busy whispering to Father that our curiosity was aroused and we suspected they were up to something. Sure enough, at eight o'clock we all trooped downstairs through the hall in pitch darkness (it gave me the shivers, and I wished I was safely back upstairs!) to the alcove. We could switch on the light, since this room doesn't have any windows. When that was done, Father opened the big cabinet.

"Oh, how wonderful!" we all cried.

In the corner was a large basket decorated with colorful paper and a mask of Black Peter.

We quickly took the basket upstairs with us. Inside was a little gift for everyone, including an appropriate verse. Since you're familiar with the kinds of poems people write each other on St. Nicholas Day, I won't copy them down for you.

I received a Kewpie doll, Father got bookends, and so on. Well anyway, it was a nice idea, and since the eight of us had never celebrated St. Nicholas Day before, this was a good time to begin.

*Yours, Anne*

P S. We also had presents for everyone downstairs, a few things left over from the Good Old Days; plus Miep and Bep are always grateful for money.

Today we heard that Mr. van Daan's ashtray, Mr. Dussel's picture frame and Father's bookends were made by none other than Mr. Voskuijl. How anyone can be so clever with his hands is a mystery to me!

THURSDAY, DECEMBER 10, 1942

*Dearest Kitty,*

Mr. van Daan used to be in the meat, sausage and spice business. He was hired for his knowledge of spices, and yet, to our great delight, it's his sausage talents that have come in handy now.

We ordered a large amount of meat (under the counter, of course) that we were planning to preserve in case there were hard times ahead. Mr. van Daan decided to make bratwurst, sausages and mettwurst. I had fun watching him put the meat through the grinder: once, twice, three times. Then he added the remaining ingredients to the ground meat and used a long pipe to force the mixture into the casings. We ate the bratwurst with sauerkraut for lunch, but the sausages, which were going to be canned, had to dry first, so we hung them over a pole suspended from the ceiling. Everyone who came into the room burst into laughter when they saw the dangling sausages. It was such a comical sight.

The kitchen was a shambles. Mr. van Daan, clad in his wife's apron and looking fatter than ever, was working away at the meat. What with his bloody hands, red face and spotted apron, he looked like a real butcher. Mrs. van D. was trying to do everything at once: learning Dutch out of a book, stirring the soup, watching the meat, sighing and moaning about her broken rib.

That's what happens when old (!) ladies do such stupid exercises to get rid of their fat behinds! Dussel had an eye infection and was sitting next to the stove dabbing his eye with camomile tea. Pim, seated in the one ray of sunshine coming through the window, kept having to move his chair this way and that to stay out of the way. His rheumatism must have been bothering him because he was slightly hunched over and was keeping an eye on Mr. van Daan with an agonized expression on his face. He reminded me of those aged invalids you see in the poorhouse. Peter was romping around the room with Mouschi, the cat, while Mother, Margot and I were peeling boiled potatoes. When you get right down to it, none of us were doing our work properly, because we were all so busy watching Mr. van Daan

Dussel has opened his dental practice. Just for fun, I'll describe the session with his very first patient.

Mother was ironing, and Mrs. van D., the first victim, sat down on a chair in the middle of the room. Dussel, unpacking his case with an air of importance, asked for some eau de cologne, which could be used as a disinfectant, and vaseline, which would have to do for wax. He looked in Mrs. van D.'s mouth and found two teeth that made her wince with pain and utter incoherent cries every time he touched them. After a lengthy examination (lengthy as far as Mrs. van D. was concerned, since it actually took no longer than two minutes), Dussel began to scrape out a cavity. But Mrs. van D. had no intention of letting him. She flailed her arms and legs until Dussel finally let go of his probe and . . . it remained stuck in Mrs. van D.'s tooth. That really did it! Mrs. van D. lashed out wildly in all directions, cried (as much as you can with an instrument like that in your mouth), tried to remove it, but only managed to push it in even farther. Mr. Dussel calmly observed the scene, his hands on his hips, while the rest of the audience roared with laughter. Of course, that was very mean of us. If it'd been me, I'm sure I would have yelled even louder. After a great deal of squirming, kicking, screaming and shouting, Mrs. van D. finally managed to yank the thing out, and Mr. Dussel went on with his work as if nothing had happened. He was so quick that Mrs. van D. didn't have time to pull any more shenanigans. But then, he had more help than he's ever had before: no fewer than two assistants; Mr. van D. and I performed our job well. The whole scene resembled one of those engravings from the Middle Ages entitled "A Quack at Work." In the meantime, however, the patient was getting restless, since she had to keep an eye on "her" soup and "her" food. One thing is certain: it'll be a while before Mrs. van D. makes another dental appointment!

*Yours, Anne*

SUNDAY, DECEMBER 13, 1942

*Dearest Kitty,*

I'm sitting here nice and cozy in the front office, peering out through a chink in the heavy curtains. It's dusky, but there's just enough light to write by.

It's really strange watching people walk past. They all seem to be in such a hurry that they nearly trip over their own feet. Those on bicycles whiz by so fast I can't even tell who's on the bike. The people in this neighborhood aren't particularly attractive to look at. The children especially are so dirty you wouldn't want to touch them with a ten-foot pole. Real slum kids with runny noses. I can hardly understand a word they say.

Yesterday afternoon, when Margot and I were taking a bath, I said, "What if we took a fishing rod and reeled in each of those kids one by one as they walked by, stuck them in the tub, washed and mended their clothes and then . . ."

"And then tomorrow they'd be just as dirty and tattered as they were before," Margot replied.

But I'm babbling. There are also other things to look at: cars, boats and the rain. I can hear the streetcar and the children and I'm enjoying myself.

Our thoughts are subject to as little change as we are. They're like a merry-go-round, turning from the Jews to food, from food to politics. By the way, speaking of Jews, I saw two yesterday when I was peeking through the curtains. I felt as though I were gazing at one of the Seven Wonders of the World. It gave me such a funny feeling, as if I'd denounced them to the authorities and was now spying on their misfortune.

Across from us is a houseboat. The captain lives there with his wife and children. He has a small yapping dog. We know the little dog only by its bark and by its tail, which we can see whenever it runs around the deck. Oh, what a shame, it's just started raining and most of the people are hidden under their umbrellas. All I can see are raincoats, and now and again the back of a stocking-capped head. Actually, I don't even need to look. By now I can recognize the women at a glance: gone to fat from eating potatoes, dressed in a red or green coat and worn-out shoes, a shopping bag dangling from their arms, with faces that are either grim or good humored, depending on the mood of their husbands.

Yours, Anne

Dearest Kitty,                          TUESDAY, DECEMBER 22, 1942

The Annex was delighted to hear that we'll all be receiving an extra quarter pound of butter for Christmas. According to the newspaper, everyone is entitled to half a pound, but they mean those lucky souls who get their ration books from the government, not Jews in hiding like us who can only afford to buy four rather than eight ration books on the black market. Each of us is going to bake something with the butter. This morning I made two cakes and a batch of cookies. It's very busy upstairs, and Mother has informed me that I'm not to do any studying or reading until all the household chores have been finished.

Mrs. van Daan is lying in bed nursing her bruised rib. She complains all day long, constantly demands that the bandages be changed and is generally dissatisfied with everything. I'll be glad when she gets back on her feet and can clean up after herself because, I must admit, she's extraordinarily hardworking and neat, and as long as she's in good physical and mental condition, she's quite cheerful.

As if I don't hear "shh, shh" enough during the day because I'm always making "too much" noise, my dear roommate has come up with the idea of saying "shh, shh" to me all night too. According to him, I shouldn't even turn over. I refuse to take any notice of him, and the next time he shushes me, I'm going to shush him right back.

He gets more exasperating and egotistical as the days go by.

Except for the first week, I haven't seen even one of the cookies he so generously promised me. He's particularly infuriating on Sundays, when he switches on the light at the crack of dawn to exercise for ten minutes.

To me, the torment seems to last for hours, since the chairs I use to make my bed longer are constantly being jiggled under my sleepy head. After rounding off his limbering-up exercises with a few vigorous arm swings, His Lordship begins dressing. His underwear is hanging on a hook, so first he lumbers over to get it and then lumbers back, past my bed. But his tie is on the table, so once again he pushes and bumps his way past the chairs.

But I mustn't waste any more of your time griping about disgusting old men. It won't help matters anyway. My plans for revenge, such as unscrewing the lightbulb, locking the door and hiding his clothes, have unfortunately had to be abandoned in the interests of peace.

Oh, I'm becoming so sensible! We've got to be reasonable about everything we do here: studying, listening, holding our tongues, helping others, being kind, making compromises and I don't know what else! I'm afraid my common sense, which was in short supply to begin with, will be used up too quickly and I won't have any left by the time the war is over. *Yours, Anne*

*Dearest Kitty,*                    WEDNESDAY, JANUARY 13, 1943

This morning I was constantly interrupted, and as a result I haven't been able to finish a single thing I've begun.

We have a new pastime, namely, filling packages with powdered gravy. The gravy is one of Gies & Co.'s products. Mr. Kugler hasn't been able to find anyone else to fill the packages, and besides, it's cheaper if we do the job. It's the kind of work they do in prisons. It's incredibly boring and makes us dizzy and giggly.

Terrible things are happening outside. At any time of night and day, poor helpless people are being dragged out of their homes. They're allowed to take only a knapsack and a little cash with them, and even then, they're robbed of these possessions on the way. Families are torn apart; men, women and children are separated. Children come home from school to find that their parents have disappeared. Women return from shopping to find their houses sealed, their families gone. The Christians in Holland are also living in fear because their sons are being sent to Germany. Everyone is scared. Every night hundreds of planes pass over Holland on their way to German cities, to sow their bombs on German soil. Every hour hundreds, or maybe even thousands, of people are being killed in Russia and Africa. No one can keep out of the conflict, the entire world is at war, and even though the Allies are doing better, the end is nowhere in sight.

As for us, we're quite fortunate. Luckier than millions of people. It's quiet and safe here, and we're using our money to buy food. We're so selfish that we talk about "after the war" and look forward to new clothes and shoes, when actually we should be saving every penny to help others when the war is over, to salvage whatever we can.

The children in this neighborhood run around in thin shirts and wooden shoes. They have no coats, no socks, no caps and no one to help them. Gnawing on a carrot to still their hunger pangs, they walk from their cold houses through cold streets to an even colder classroom. Things have gotten so bad in Holland that hordes of children stop passersby in the streets to beg for a piece of bread.

I could spend hours telling you about the suffering the war has brought, but I'd only make myself more miserable. All we can do is wait, as calmly as possible, for it to end. Jews and Christians alike are waiting, the whole world is waiting, and many are waiting for death.

*Yours, Anne*

SATURDAY, JANUARY 30, 1943

*Dearest Kitty,*

I'm seething with rage, yet I can't show it. I'd like to scream, stamp my foot, give Mother a good shaking, cry and I don't know what else because of the nasty words, mocking looks and accusations that she hurls at me day after day, piercing me like arrows from a tightly strung bow, which are nearly impossible to pull from my body. I'd like to scream at Mother, Margot, the van Daans, Dussel and Father too: "Leave me alone, let me have at

least one night when I don't cry myself to sleep with my eyes
burning and my head pounding. Let me get away, away from
everything, away from this world!" But I can't do that. I can't
let them see my doubts, or the wounds they've inflicted on me.
I couldn't bear their sympathy or their good-humored derision.
It would only make me want to scream even more.

Everyone thinks I'm showing off when I talk, ridiculous when
I'm silent, insolent when I answer, cunning when I have a good
idea, lazy when I'm tired, selfish when I eat one bite more than
I should, stupid, cowardly, calculating, etc., etc. All day long I
hear nothing but what an exasperating child I am, and although
I laugh it off and pretend not to mind, I do mind. I wish I could
ask God to give me another personality, one that doesn't antago-
nize everyone.

But that's impossible. I'm stuck with the character I was born
with, and yet I'm sure I'm not a bad person. I do my best to please
everyone, more than they'd ever suspect in a million years. When
I'm upstairs, I try to laugh it off because I don't want them to see
my troubles.

More than once, after a series of absurd reproaches, I've
snapped at Mother: "I don't care what you say. Why don't you
just wash your hands of me – I'm a hopeless case." Of course,
she'd tell me not to talk back and virtually ignore me for two
days. Then suddenly all would be forgotten and she'd treat me
like everyone else.

It's impossible for me to be all smiles one day and venomous
the next. I'd rather choose the golden mean, which isn't so
golden, and keep my thoughts to myself. Perhaps sometime I'll
treat the others with the same contempt as they treat me. Oh, if
only I could.

*Yours, Anne*

*Dearest Kitty,*                                    FRIDAY, FEBRUARY 5, 1943

Though it's been ages since I've written to you about the
squabbles, there's still no change. In the beginning Mr. Dussel
took our soon-forgotten clashes very seriously, but now he's
grown used to them and no longer tries to mediate.

Margot and Peter aren't exactly what you'd call "young";

they're both so quiet and boring. Next to them, I stick out like a sore thumb, and I'm always being told, "Margot and Peter don't act that way. Why don't you follow your sister's example!" I hate that.

I confess that I have absolutely no desire to be like Margot. She's too weak-willed and passive to suit me; she lets herself be swayed by others and always backs down under pressure. I want to have more spunk! But I keep ideas like these to myself. They'd only laugh at me if I offered this in my defense.

During meals the air is filled with tension. Fortunately, the outbursts are sometimes held in check by the "soup eaters," the people from the office who come up to have a cup of soup for lunch.

This afternoon Mr. van Daan again brought up the fact that Margot eats so little. "I suppose you do it to keep your figure," he added in a mocking tone.

Mother, who always comes to Margot's defense, said in a loud voice, "I can't stand that stupid chatter of yours a minute longer."

Mrs. van D. turned red as a beet. Mr. van D. stared straight ahead and said nothing.

Still, we often have a good laugh. Not long ago Mrs. van D. was entertaining us with some bit of nonsense or another. She was talking about the past, about how well she got along with her father and what a flirt she was. "And you know," she continued, "my father told me that if a gentleman ever got fresh, I was to say, 'Remember, sir, that I'm a lady,' and he'd know what I meant." We split our sides laughing, as if she'd told us a good joke.

Even Peter, though he's usually quiet, occasionally gives rise to hilarity. He has the misfortune of adoring foreign words without knowing what they mean. One afternoon we couldn't use the toilet because there were visitors in the office. Unable to wait, he went to the bathroom but didn't flush the toilet. To warn us of the unpleasant odor, he tacked a sign to the bathroom door: "RSVP – gas!" Of course, he meant "Danger – gas!" but he thought "RSVP" looked more elegant. He didn't have the faintest idea that it meant "please reply."

*Yours, Anne*

*Dearest Kitty,*

Pim is expecting the invasion any day now. Churchill has had pneumonia, but is gradually getting better. Gandhi, the champion of Indian freedom, is on one of his umpteenth hunger strikes.

Mrs. van D. claims she's fatalistic. But who's the most afraid when the guns go off? None other than Petronella van Daan.

Jan brought along the episcopal letter that the bishops addressed to their parishioners. It was beautiful and inspiring. "People of the Netherlands, stand up and take action. Each of us must choose our own weapons to fight for the freedom of our country, our people and our religion! Give your help and support. Act now!" This is what they're preaching from the pulpit. Will it do any good? It's definitely too late to help our fellow Jews.

Guess what's happened to us now? The owner of the building sold it without informing Mr. Kugler and Mr. Kleiman. One morning the new landlord arrived with an architect to look the place over. Thank goodness Mr. Kleiman was in the office. He showed the gentlemen all there was to see, with the exception of the Secret Annex. He claimed he'd left the key at home and the new owner asked no further questions. If only he doesn't come back demanding to see the Annex. In that case, we'll be in big trouble!

Father emptied a card file for Margot and me and filled it with index cards that are blank on one side. This is to become our reading file, in which Margot and I are supposed to note down the books we've read, the author and the date. I've learned two new words: "brothel" and "coquette." I've bought a separate notebook for new words.

There's a new division of butter and margarine. Each person is to get their portion on their own plate. The distribution is very unfair. The van Daans, who always make breakfast for everyone, give themselves one and a half times more than they do us. My parents are much too afraid of an argument to say anything, which is a shame, because I think people like that should always be given a taste of their own medicine.

*Yours, Anne*

*Dearest Kitty,*                    THURSDAY, MARCH 4, 1943

Mrs. van D. has a new nickname – we've started calling her Mrs. Beaverbrook. Of course, that doesn't mean anything to you, so let me explain. A certain Mr. Beaverbrook often talks on the English radio about what he considers to be the far too lenient bombardment of Germany. Mrs. van Daan, who always contradicts everyone, including Churchill and the news reports, is in complete agreement with Mr. Beaverbrook. So we thought it would be a good idea for her to be married to him, and since she was flattered by the notion, we've decided to call her Mrs. Beaverbrook from now on.

We're getting a new warehouse employee, since the old one is being sent to Germany. That's bad for him but good for us because the new one won't be familiar with the building. We're still afraid of the men who work in the warehouse.

Gandhi is eating again.

The black market is doing a booming business. If we had enough money to pay the ridiculous prices, we could stuff ourselves silly. Our greengrocer buys potatoes from the "Wehrmacht" and brings them in sacks to the private office. Since he suspects we're hiding here, he makes a point of coming during lunchtime, when the warehouse employees are out.

So much pepper is being ground at the moment that we sneeze and cough with every breath we take. Everyone who comes upstairs greets us with an "ah-CHOO." Mrs. van D. swears she won't go downstairs; one more whiff of pepper and she's going to get sick.

I don't think Father has a very nice business. Nothing but pectin and pepper. As long as you're in the food business, why not make candy?

A veritable thunderstorm of words came crashing down on me again this morning. The air flashed with so many coarse expressions that my ears were ringing with "Anne's bad this" and "van Daans' good that." Fire and brimstone!

*Yours, Anne*

*Dearest Kitty,*

We had a short circuit last night, and besides that, the guns were booming away until dawn. I still haven't gotten over my fear of planes and shooting, and I crawl into Father's bed nearly every night for comfort. I know it sounds childish, but wait till it happens to you! The ack-ack guns make so much noise you can't hear your own voice. Mrs. Beaverbrook, the fatalist, practically burst into tears and said in a timid little voice, "Oh, it's so awful. Oh, the guns are so loud!" – which is another way of saying "I'm so scared."

It didn't seem nearly as bad by candlelight as it did in the dark. I was shivering, as if I had a fever, and begged Father to relight the candle. He was adamant: there was to be no light. Suddenly we heard a burst of machine-gun fire, and that's ten times worse than anti-aircraft guns. Mother jumped out of bed and, to Pim's great annoyance, lit the candle. Her resolute answer to his grumbling was, "After all, Anne is not an ex-soldier!" And that was the end of that!

Have I told you any of Mrs. van D.'s other fears? I don't think so. To keep you up to date on the latest adventures in the Secret Annex, I should tell you this as well. One night Mrs. van D. thought she heard loud footsteps in the attic, and she was so afraid of burglars, she woke her husband. At that very same moment, the thieves disappeared, and the only sound Mr. van D. could hear was the frightened pounding of his fatalistic wife's heart. "Oh, Putti!" she cried. (Putti is Mrs. van D.'s pet name for her husband.) "They must have taken all our sausages and dried beans. And what about Peter? Oh, do you think Peter's still safe and sound in his bed?"

"I'm sure they haven't stolen Peter. Stop being such a ninny, and let me get back to sleep!"

Impossible. Mrs. van D. was too scared to sleep.

A few nights later the entire van Daan family was awakened by ghostly noises. Peter went to the attic with a flashlight and – scurry, scurry – what do you think he saw running away? A whole slew of enormous rats!

Once we knew who the thieves were, we let Mouschi sleep in

the attic and never saw our uninvited guests again . . . at least not at night.

A few evenings ago (it was seven-thirty and still light), Peter went up to the loft to get some old newspapers. He had to hold on tightly to the trapdoor to climb down the ladder. He put down his hand without looking, and nearly fell off the ladder from shock and pain. Without realizing it, he'd put his hand on a large rat, which had bitten him in the arm. By the time he reached us, white as a sheet and with his knees knocking, the blood had soaked through his pajamas. No wonder he was so shaken — petting a rat isn't much fun, especially when it takes a chunk out of your arm.

*Yours, Anne*

FRIDAY, MARCH 12, 1943

*Dearest Kitty,*

May I introduce: Mama Frank, the children's advocate! Extra butter for the youngsters, the problems facing today's youth — you name it, and Mother defends the younger generation. After a skirmish or two, she always gets her way.

One of the jars of pickled tongue is spoiled. A feast for Mouschi and Boche.

You haven't met Boche yet, despite the fact that she was here before we went into hiding. She's the warehouse and office cat, who keeps the rats at bay in the storeroom. Her odd, political name can easily be explained. For a while the firm Gies & Co. had two cats: one for the warehouse and one for the attic. Their paths crossed from time to time, which invariably resulted in a fight. The warehouse cat was always the aggressor, while the attic cat was ultimately the victor, just as in politics. So the warehouse cat was named the German, or "Boche," and the attic cat the Englishman, or "Tommy." Sometime after that they got rid of Tommy, but Boche is always there to amuse us when we go downstairs.

We've eaten so many brown beans and navy beans that I can't stand to look at them. Just thinking about them makes me sick.

Our evening serving of bread has been canceled.

Daddy just said that he's not in a very cheerful mood. His eyes look so sad again, the poor man!

I can't tear myself away from the book *A Knock at the Door* by Ina Bakker Boudier. This family saga is extremely well written, but the parts dealing with war, writers and the emancipation of women aren't very good. To be honest, these subjects don't interest me much.

Terrible bombing raids on Germany. Mr. van Daan is grouchy. The reason: the cigarette shortage.

The debate about whether or not to start eating the canned food ended in our favor.

I can't wear any of my shoes, except my ski boots, which are not very practical around the house. A pair of straw thongs that were purchased for 6.50 guilders were worn down to the soles within a week. Maybe Miep will be able to scrounge up something on the black market.

It's time to cut Father's hair. Pim swears that I do such a good job he'll never go to another barber after the war. If only I didn't nick his ear so often!

*Yours, Anne*

*My dearest Kitty,* THURSDAY, MARCH 18, 1943

Turkey's entered the war. Great excitement. Anxiously awaiting radio reports.

*Dearest Kitty,* FRIDAY, MARCH 19, 1943

In less than an hour, joy was followed by disappointment. Turkey hasn't entered the war yet. It was only a cabinet minister talking about Turkey giving up its neutrality sometime soon. The newspaper vendor in Dam Square was shouting "Turkey on England's side!" and the papers were being snatched out of his hands. This was how we'd heard the encouraging rumor.

Thousand-guilder notes are being declared invalid. That'll be a blow to the black marketeers and others like them, but even more to people in hiding and anyone else with money that can't be accounted for. To turn in a thousand-guilder bill, you have to be able to state how you came by it and provide proof. They can still be used to pay taxes, but only until next week. The five-hundred notes will lapse at the same time. Gies & Co. still had some unaccounted-for thousand-guilder bills, which they used to pay their estimated taxes for the coming years, so every-thing seems to be aboveboard.

Dussel has received an old-fashioned, foot-operated dentist's drill. That means I'll probably be getting a thorough checkup soon.

Dussel is terribly lax when it comes to obeying the rules of the house. Not only does he write letters to his Charlotte, he's also carrying on a chatty correspondence with various other people. Margot, the Annex's Dutch teacher, has been correcting these letters for him. Father has forbidden him to keep up the practice and Margot has stopped correcting the letters, but I think it won't be long before he starts up again.

The Führer has been talking to wounded soldiers. We listened on the radio, and it was pathetic. The questions and answers went something like this:

"My name is Heinrich Scheppel."

"Where were you wounded?"

"Near Stalingrad."

"What kind of wound is it?"

"Two frostbitten feet and a fracture of the left arm."

This is an exact report of the hideous puppet show aired on the radio. The wounded seemed proud of their wounds — the more the better. One was so beside himself at the thought of shaking hands (I presume he still had one) with the Führer that he could barely say a word.

I happened to drop Dussel's soap on the floor and step on it. Now there's a whole piece missing. I've already asked Father to compensate him for the damages, especially since Dussel only gets one bar of inferior war-time soap a month.

*Yours, Anne*

*Dearest Kitty,*

THURSDAY, MARCH 25, 1943

Mother, Father, Margot and I were sitting quite pleasantly together last night when Peter suddenly came in and whispered in Father's ear. I caught the words "a barrel falling over in the warehouse" and "someone fiddling with the door."

Margot heard it too, but was trying to calm me down, since I'd turned white as chalk and was extremely nervous. The three of us waited while Father and Peter went downstairs. A minute or two later Mrs. van Daan came up from where she'd been listening to the radio and told us that Pim had asked her to turn it off and tiptoe upstairs. But you know what happens when you're trying to be quiet – the old stairs creaked twice as loud. Five minutes later Peter and Pim, the color drained from their faces, appeared again to relate their experiences.

They had positioned themselves under the staircase and waited. Nothing happened. Then all of a sudden they heard a couple of bangs, as if two doors had been slammed shut inside the house. Pim bounded up the stairs, while Peter went to warn Dussel, who finally presented himself upstairs, though not without kicking up a fuss and making a lot of noise. Then we all tiptoed in our stockinged feet to the van Daans on the next floor. Mr. van D. had a bad cold and had already gone to bed, so we gathered around his bedside and discussed our suspicions in a whisper. Every time Mr. van D. coughed loudly, Mrs. van D. and I nearly had a nervous fit. He kept coughing until someone came up with the bright idea of giving him codeine. His cough subsided immediately.

Once again we waited and waited, but heard nothing. Finally we came to the conclusion that the burglars had taken to their heels when they heard footsteps in an otherwise quiet building. The problem now was that the chairs in the private office were neatly grouped around the radio, which was tuned to England. If the burglars had forced the door and the air-raid wardens were to notice it and call the police, there could be very serious repercussions. So Mr. van Daan got up, pulled on his coat and pants, put on his hat and cautiously followed Father down the stairs, with Peter (armed with a heavy hammer, to be on the safe side) right behind him. The ladies (including Margot and me) waited in suspense until the men returned five minutes later and reported that there was no sign of any activity in the building. We agreed not to run any water or flush the toilet; but since everyone's stomach was churning from all the tension, you can imagine the stench after we'd each had a turn in the bathroom.

Incidents like these are always accompanied by other disasters, and this was no exception. Number one: the Westertoren bells stopped chiming, and I'd always found them so comforting. Number two: Mr. Voskuijl left early last night, and we weren't sure if he'd given Bep the key and she'd forgotten to lock the door.

But that was of little importance now. The night had just begun, and we still weren't sure what to expect. We were somewhat reassured by the fact that between eight-fifteen – when the burglar had first entered the building and put our lives in jeopardy – and ten-thirty, we hadn't heard a sound. The more we thought about it, the less likely it seemed that a burglar would have forced a door so early in the evening, when there were still people out on the streets. Besides that, it occurred to us that the warehouse manager at the Keg Company next door might still have been at work. What with the excitement and the thin walls, it's easy to mistake the sounds. Besides, your imagination often plays tricks on you in moments of danger.

So we went to bed, though not to sleep. Father and Mother and Mr. Dussel were awake most of the night, and I'm not exaggerating when I say that I hardly got a wink of sleep. This morning the men went downstairs to see if the outside door was still locked, but all was well!

Of course, we gave the entire office staff a blow-by-blow account of the incident, which had been far from pleasant. It's much easier to laugh at these kinds of things after they've happened, and Bep was the only one who took us seriously.

Yours, Anne

PS. This morning the toilet was clogged, and Father had to stick in a long wooden pole and fish out several pounds of excrement and strawberry recipes (which is what we use for toilet paper these days). Afterward we burned the pole.

Dearest Kitty,                     SATURDAY, MARCH 27, 1943

We've finished our shorthand course and are now working on improving our speed. Aren't we smart! Let me tell you more about my "time killers" (this is what I call my courses, because all we ever do is try to make the days go by as quickly as possible so we're that much closer to the end of our time here). I adore mythology, especially the Greek and Roman gods. Everyone here thinks my interest is just a passing fancy, since they've never heard of a teenager with an appreciation of mythology. Well then, I guess I'm the first!

Mr. van Daan has a cold. Or rather, he has a scratchy throat, but he's making an enormous to-do over it. He gargles with camomile tea, coats the roof of his mouth with a tincture of myrrh and rubs Mentholatum over his chest, nose, gums and tongue. And to top it off, he's in a foul mood!

Rauter, some German bigwig, recently gave a speech. "All Jews must be out of the German-occupied territories before July 1. The province of Utrecht will be cleansed of Jews [as if they were cockroaches] between April 1 and May 1, and the provinces of North and South Holland between May 1 and June 1." These poor people are being shipped off to filthy slaughterhouses like a herd of sick and neglected cattle. But I'll say no more on the subject. My own thoughts give me nightmares!

One good piece of news is that the Labor Exchange was set on fire in an act of sabotage. A few days later the County Clerk's Office also went up in flames. Men posing as German police bound and gagged the guards and managed to destroy some important documents.

*Yours, Anne*

THURSDAY, APRIL 1, 1943
*Dearest Kitty,*

I'm not really in the mood for pranks (see the date). On the contrary, today I can safely quote the saying "Misfortunes never come singly."

First, Mr. Kleiman, our merry sunshine, had another bout of gastrointestinal hemorrhaging yesterday and will have to stay in bed for at least three weeks. I should tell you that his stomach has been bothering him quite a bit, and there's no cure. Second, Bep has the flu. Third, Mr. Voskuijl has to go to the hospital next week. He probably has an ulcer and will have to undergo surgery. Fourth, the managers of Pomosin Industries came from Frankfurt to discuss the new Opekta deliveries. Father had gone over the important points with Mr. Kleiman, and there wasn't enough time to give Mr. Kugler a thorough briefing.

The gentlemen arrived from Frankfurt, and Father was already shaking at the thought of how the talks would go. "If only I could be there, if only I were downstairs," he exclaimed.

"Go lie down with your ear to the floor. They'll be brought to the private office, and you'll be able to hear everything."

Father's face cleared, and yesterday morning at ten-thirty Margot and Pim (two ears are better than one) took up their posts on the floor. By noon the talks weren't finished, but Father was in no shape to continue his listening campaign. He was in agony from having to lie for hours in such an unusual and uncomfortable position. At two-thirty we heard voices in the hall, and I took his place; Margot kept me company. The conversation was so long-winded and boring that I suddenly fell asleep on the cold, hard linoleum. Margot didn't dare touch me for fear they'd hear us, and of course she couldn't shout. I slept for a good half hour and then awoke with a start, having forgotten every word of the important discussion. Luckily, Margot had paid more attention.

Yours, Anne

FRIDAY, APRIL 2, 1943

*Dearest Kitty,*

Oh my, another item has been added to my list of sins. Last night I was lying in bed, waiting for Father to tuck me in and say my prayers with me, when Mother came into the room, sat on my bed and asked very gently, "Anne, Daddy isn't ready. How about if I listen to your prayers tonight?"

"No, Momsy," I replied.

Mother got up, stood beside my bed for a moment and then slowly walked toward the door. Suddenly she turned, her face contorted with pain, and said, "I don't want to be angry with you. I can't make you love me!" A few tears slid down her cheeks as she went out the door.

I lay still, thinking how mean it was of me to reject her so cruelly, but I also knew that I was incapable of answering her any other way. I can't be a hypocrite and pray with her when I don't feel like it. It just doesn't work that way. I felt sorry for Mother — very, very sorry — because for the first time in my life I noticed she wasn't indifferent to my coldness. I saw the sorrow in her face when she talked about not being able to make me love her.

It's hard to tell the truth, and yet the truth is that she's the one who's rejected me. She's the one whose tactless comments and cruel jokes about matters I don't think are funny have made me insensitive to any sign of love on her part. Just as my heart sinks every time I hear her harsh words, that's how her heart sank when she realized there was no more love between us.

She cried half the night and didn't get any sleep. Father has avoided looking at me, and if his eyes do happen to cross mine, I can read his unspoken words: "How can you be so unkind? How dare you make your mother so sad!"

Everyone expects me to apologize, but this is not something I can apologize for, because I told the truth, and sooner or later Mother was bound to find out anyway. I seem to be indifferent to Mother's tears and Father's glances, and I am, because both of them are now feeling what I've always felt. I can only feel sorry for Mother, who will have to figure out what her attitude should be all by herself. For my part, I will continue to remain silent and aloof, and I don't intend to shrink from the truth, because the longer it's postponed, the harder it will be for them to accept it when they do hear it!

*Yours, Anne*

*Dearest Kitty,*
                                    TUESDAY, APRIL 27, 1943

The house is still trembling from the aftereffects of the quarrels. Everyone is mad at everyone else: Mother and I, Mr. van Daan and Father, Mother and Mrs. van D. Terrific atmosphere, don't you think? Once again Anne's usual list of shortcomings has been extensively aired.

Our German visitors were back last Saturday. They stayed until six. We all sat upstairs, not daring to move an inch. If there's no one else working in the building or in the neighborhood, you can hear every single step in the private office. I've got ants in my pants again from having to sit still so long.

Mr. Voskuijl has been hospitalized, but Mr. Kleiman's back at the office. His stomach stopped bleeding sooner than it normally does. He told us that the County Clerk's Office took an extra beating because the firemen flooded the entire building instead of just putting out the fire. That does my heart good!

The Carlton Hotel has been destroyed. Two British planes loaded with firebombs landed right on top of the German Officers' Club. The entire corner of Vijzelstraat and Singel has gone up in flames. The number of air strikes on German cities is increasing daily. We haven't had a good night's rest in ages, and I have bags under my eyes from lack of sleep.

Our food is terrible. Breakfast consists of plain, unbuttered bread and ersatz coffee. For the last two weeks lunch has been either spinach or cooked lettuce with huge potatoes that have a rotten, sweetish taste. If you're trying to diet, the Annex is the place to be! Upstairs they complain bitterly, but we don't think it's such a tragedy.

All the Dutch men who either fought or were mobilized in 1940 have been called up to work in prisoner-of-war camps. I bet they're taking this precaution because of the invasion!

Yours, Anne

SATURDAY, MAY 1, 1943

*Dearest Kitty,*

Yesterday was Dussel's birthday. At first he acted as if he didn't want to celebrate it, but when Miep arrived with a large shopping bag overflowing with gifts, he was as excited as a little kid. His darling "Lotje" has sent him eggs, butter, cookies, lemonade, bread, cognac, spice cake, flowers, oranges, chocolate, books and writing paper. He piled his presents on a table and displayed them for no fewer than three days, the silly old goat!

You mustn't get the idea that he's starving. We found bread, cheese, jam and eggs in his cupboard. It's absolutely disgraceful that Dussel, whom we've treated with such kindness and whom we took in to save from destruction, should stuff himself behind our backs and not give us anything. After all, we've shared all we had with him! But what's worse, in our opinion, is that he's so stingy with respect to Mr. Kleiman, Mr. Voskuijl and Bep. He doesn't give them a thing. In Dussel's view the oranges that Kleiman so badly needs for his sick stomach will benefit his own stomach even more.

Tonight the guns have been banging away so much that I've already had to gather up my belongings four times. Today I packed a suitcase with the stuff I'd need in case we had to flee, but as Mother correctly noted, "Where would you go?"

All of Holland is being punished for the workers' strikes. Martial law has been declared, and everyone is going to get one less butter coupon. What naughty children.

I washed Mother's hair this evening, which is no easy task these days. We have to use a very sticky liquid cleanser because there's no more shampoo. Besides that, Moms had a hard time combing her hair because the family comb has only ten teeth left.

*Yours, Anne*

SUNDAY, MAY 2, 1943

When I think about our lives here, I usually come to the conclusion that we live in a paradise compared to the Jews who aren't in hiding. All the same, later on, when everything has returned to normal, I'll probably wonder how we, who always lived in such comfortable circumstances, could have "sunk" so low. With respect to manners, I mean. For example, the same oilcloth has covered the dining table ever since we've been here. After so much use, it's hardly what you'd call spotless. I do my best to clean it, but since the dishcloth was also purchased before we went into hiding and consists of more holes than cloth, it's a thankless task. The van Daans have been sleeping all winter long on the same flannel sheet, which can't be washed because detergent is rationed and in short supply. Besides, it's of such poor quality that it's practically useless. Father is walking around in frayed trousers, and his tie is also showing signs of wear and tear. Mama's corset snapped today and is beyond repair, while Margot is wearing a bra that's two sizes too small. Mother and Margot have shared the same three undershirts the entire winter, and mine are so small they don't even cover my stomach. These are all things that can be overcome, but I sometimes wonder: how can we, whose every possession, from my underpants to Father's shaving brush, is so old and worn, ever hope to regain the position we had before the war?

SUNDAY, MAY 2, 1943

*The Attitude of the Annex Residents Toward the War*

*Mr. van Daan.* In the opinion of us all, this revered gentleman has great insight into politics. Nevertheless, he predicts we'll have to stay here until the end of '43. That's a very long time, and yet it's possible to hold out until then. But who can assure us that this war, which has caused nothing but pain and sorrow, will then be over? And that nothing will have happened to us and our helpers long before that time? No one! That's why each and every day is filled with tension. Expectation and hope generate tension, as does fear — for example, when we hear a noise inside or outside the house, when the guns go off or when we read new "proclamations" in the paper, since we're afraid our helpers might be forced to go into hiding themselves sometime. These days everyone is talking about having to hide. We don't know how many people are actually in hiding; of course, the number is relatively small compared to the general population, but later on we'll no doubt be astonished at how many good people in Holland were willing to take Jews and Christians, with or without money, into their homes. There're also an unbelievable number of people with false identity papers.

*Mrs. van Daan.* When this beautiful damsel (by her own account) heard that it was getting easier these days to obtain false IDs, she immediately proposed that we each have one made. As if there were nothing to it, as if Father and Mr. van Daan were made of money.

Mrs. van Daan is always saying the most ridiculous things, and her Putti is often exasperated. But that's not surprising, because one day Kerli announces, "When this is all over, I'm going to have myself baptized"; and the next, "As long as I can remember, I've wanted to go to Jerusalem. I only feel at home with other Jews!"

*Pim* is a big optimist, but he always has his reasons.

*Mr. Dussel* makes up everything as he goes along, and anyone wishing to contradict His Majesty had better think twice. In Albert Dussel's home his word is law, but that doesn't suit Anne Frank in the least.

What the other members of the Annex family think about the war doesn't matter. When it comes to politics, these four are the only ones who count. Actually, only two of them do, but Madame van Daan and Dussel include themselves as well.

*Dearest Kit,*                                        TUESDAY, MAY 18, 1943

I recently witnessed a fierce dogfight between German and English pilots. Unfortunately, a couple of Allied airmen had to jump out of their burning plane. Our milkman, who lives in Halfweg, saw four Canadians sitting along the side of the road, and one of them spoke fluent Dutch. He asked the milkman if he had a light for his cigarette, and then told him the crew had consisted of six men. The pilot had been burned to death, and the fifth crew member had hidden himself somewhere. The German Security Police came to pick up the four remaining men, none of whom were injured. After parachuting out of a flaming plane, how can anyone have such presence of mind?

Although it's undeniably hot, we have to light a fire every other day to burn our vegetable peelings and garbage. We can't throw anything into the trash cans, because the warehouse employees might see it. One small act of carelessness and we're done for!

All college students are being asked to sign an official statement to the effect that they "sympathize with the Germans and approve of the New Order." Eighty percent have decided to obey the dictates of their conscience, but the penalty will be severe. Any student refusing to sign will be sent to a German labor camp. What's to become of the youth of our country if they've all got to do hard labor in Germany?

Last night the guns were making so much noise that Mother shut the window; I was in Pim's bed. Suddenly, right above our heads, we heard Mrs. van D. leap up, as if she'd been bitten by Mouschi. This was followed by a loud boom, which sounded as if a firebomb had landed beside my bed. "Lights! Lights!" I screamed.

Pim switched on the lamp. I expected the room to burst into flames any minute. Nothing happened. We all rushed upstairs to see what was going on. Mr. and Mrs. van D. had seen a red glow through the open window, and he thought there was a fire nearby, while she was certain our house was ablaze. Mrs. van D. was already standing beside her bed with her knees knocking when the boom came. Dussel stayed upstairs to smoke a cigarette, and we crawled back into bed. Less than fifteen minutes later the shooting started again. Mrs. van D. sprang out of bed and went downstairs to Dussel's room to seek the comfort she was unable to find with her spouse. Dussel welcomed her with the words "Come into my bed, my child!"

We burst into peals of laughter, and the roar of the guns bothered us no more; our fears had all been swept away.

*Yours, Anne*

*Dearest Kitty,* SUNDAY, JUNE 13, 1943

The poem Father composed for my birthday is too nice to keep to myself.

Since Pim writes his verses only in German, Margot volunteered to translate it into Dutch. See for yourself whether Margot hasn't done herself proud. It begins with the usual summary of the year's events and then continues:

*As youngest among us, but small no more,*
*Your life can be trying, for we have the chore*
*Of becoming your teachers, a terrible bore.*
*"We've got experience! Take it from me!"*
*"We've done this all before, you see.*
*We know the ropes, we know the game."*
*Since time immemorial, always the same.*
*One's own shortcomings are nothing but fluff*
*But everyone else's are heavier stuff.*
*Faultfinding comes easy when this is our plight,*
*But it's hard for your parents, try as they might,*
*To treat you with fairness, and kindness as well;*
*Nitpicking's a habit that's hard to dispel.*
*When you're living with old folks, all you can do*
*Is put up with their nagging — it's hard but it's true.*
*The pill may be bitter, but down it must go,*
*For it's meant to keep the peace, you know.*

*The many months here have not been in vain,*
*Since wasting time goes against your grain.*
*You read and study nearly all the day,*
*Determined to chase the boredom away.*
*The more difficult question, much harder to bear,*
*Is "What on earth do I have to wear?*
*I've got no more panties, my clothes are too tight,*
*My shirt is a loincloth, I'm really a sight!*
*To put on my shoes I must cut off my toes,*
*Oh dear, I'm plagued with so many woes!"*

Margot had trouble getting the part about food to rhyme, so I'm leaving it out. But aside from that, don't you think it's a good poem?

For the rest, I've been thoroughly spoiled and have received a number of lovely presents, including a big book on my favorite subject, Greek and Roman mythology. Nor can I complain about the lack of candy; everyone had dipped into their last reserves. As the Benjamin of the Annex, I got more than I deserve.

                                                              *Yours, Anne*

*Dearest Kitty,*                          TUESDAY, JUNE 15, 1943

Heaps of things have happened, but I often think I'm boring you with my dreary chitchat and that you'd just as soon have fewer letters. So I'll keep the news brief.

Mr. Voskuijl wasn't operated on for his ulcer after all. Once the doctors had him on the operating table and opened him up, they saw that he had cancer. It was in such an advanced stage that an operation was pointless. So they stitched him up again, kept him in the hospital for three weeks, fed him well and sent him back home. But they made an unforgivable error: they told the poor man exactly what was in store for him. He can't work anymore, and he's just sitting at home, surrounded by his eight children, brooding about his approaching death. I feel very sorry for him and hate not being able to go out; otherwise, I'd visit him as often as I could and help take his mind off matters. Now the good man can no longer let us know what's being said and done in the warehouse, which is a disaster for us. Mr. Voskuijl was our greatest source of help and support when it came to safety measures. We miss him very much.

Next month it's our turn to hand over our radio to the authorities. Mr. Kleiman has a small set hidden in his home that he's giving us to replace our beautiful cabinet radio. It's a pity we have to turn in our big Philips, but when you're in hiding, you can't afford to bring the authorities down on your heads. Of course, we'll put the "baby" radio upstairs. What's a clandestine radio when there are already clandestine Jews and clandestine money?

All over the country people are trying to get hold of an old radio that they can hand over instead of their "morale booster." It's true. as the reports from outside grow worse and worse, the radio, with its wondrous voice, helps us not to lose heart and to keep telling ourselves, "Cheer up, keep your spirits high, things are bound to get better!"

Yours, Anne

*Dear Kitty,*

To get back to the subject of child-rearing (for the umpteenth time), let me tell you that I'm doing my best to be helpful, friendly and kind and to do all I can to keep the rain of rebukes down to a light drizzle. It's not easy trying to behave like a model child with people you can't stand, especially when you don't mean a word of it. But I can see that a little hypocrisy gets me a lot further than my old method of saying exactly what I think (even though no one ever asks my opinion or cares one way or another). Of course, I often forget my role and find it impossible to curb my anger when they're unfair, so that they spend the next month saying I'm the most impertinent girl in the world. Don't you think I'm to be pitied sometimes? It's a good thing I'm not the grouchy type, because then I might become sour and bad-tempered. I can usually see the humorous side of their scoldings, but it's easier when somebody else is being raked over the coals.

Further, I've decided (after a great deal of thought) to drop the shorthand. First, so that I have more time for my other subjects, and second, because of my eyes. That's a sad story. I've become very nearsighted and should have had glasses ages ago. (Ugh, won't I look like a dope!). But as you know, people in hiding can't . . .

Yesterday all anyone here could talk about was Anne's eyes, because Mother had suggested I go to the ophthalmologist with Mrs. Kleiman. Just hearing this made my knees weak, since it's no small matter. Going outside! Just think of it, walking down the *street!* I can't imagine it. I was petrified at first, and then glad. But it's not as simple as all that; the various authorities who had to approve such a step were unable to reach a quick decision. They first had to carefully weigh all the difficulties and risks, though Miep was ready to set off immediately with me in tow. In the meantime, I'd taken my gray coat from the closet, but it was so small it looked as if it might have belonged to my little sister. We lowered the hem, but I still couldn't button it. I'm really curious to see what they decide, only I don't think they'll ever work out a plan, because the British have landed in Sicily and Father's all set for a "quick finish."

Bep's been giving Margot and me a lot of office work to do. It makes us both feel important, and it's a big help to her. Anyone can file letters and make entries in a sales book, but we do it with remarkable accuracy.

Miep has so much to carry she looks like a pack mule. She goes forth nearly every day to scrounge up vegetables, and then bicycles back with her purchases in large shopping bags. She's also the one who brings five library books with her every Saturday. We long for Saturdays because that means books. We're like a bunch of little kids with a present. Ordinary people don't know how much books can mean to someone who's cooped up. Our only diversions are reading, studying and listening to the radio.

*Yours, Anne*

TUESDAY, JULY 13, 1943

*The Best Little Table*

Yesterday afternoon Father gave me permission to ask Mr. Dussel whether he would please be so good as to allow me (see how polite I am?) to use the table in our room two afternoons a week, from four to five-thirty. I already sit there every day from two-thirty to four while Dussel takes a nap, but the rest of the time the room and the table are off-limits to me. It's impossible to study next door in the afternoon, because there's too much going on. Besides, Father sometimes likes to sit at the desk during the afternoon.

So it seemed like a reasonable request, and I asked Dussel very politely. What do you think the learned gentleman's reply was? "No." Just plain "No!"

I was incensed and wasn't about to let myself be put off like that. I asked him the reason for his "No," but this didn't get me anywhere. The gist of his reply was: "I have to study too, you know, and if I can't do that in the afternoons, I won't be able to fit it in at all. I have to finish the task I've set for myself, otherwise, there's no point in starting. Besides, you aren't serious about your studies. Mythology — what kind of work is that? Reading and knitting don't count either. I use that table and I'm not going to give it up!"

I replied, "Mr. Dussel, I do take my work seriously. I can't study next door in the afternoons, and I would appreciate it if you would reconsider my request!"

Having said these words, the insulted Anne turned around and pretended the learned doctor wasn't there. I was seething with rage and felt that Dussel had been incredibly rude (which he certainly had been) and that I'd been very polite.

That evening, when I managed to get hold of Pim, I told him what had happened and we discussed what my next step should be, because I had no intention of giving up and preferred to deal with the matter myself. Pim gave me a rough idea of how to approach Dussel, but cautioned me to wait until the next day, since I was in such a flap. I ignored this last piece of advice and waited for Dussel after the dishes had been done. Pim was sitting next door and that had a calming effect.

I began, "Mr. Dussel, you seem to believe further discussion of the matter is pointless, but I beg you to reconsider."

Dussel gave me his most charming smile and said, "I'm always prepared to discuss the matter, even though it's already been settled."

I went on talking, despite Dussel's repeated interruptions.

"When you first came here," I said, "we agreed that the room was to be shared by the two of us. If we were to divide it fairly, you'd have the entire morning and I'd have the entire afternoon! I'm not asking for that much, but two afternoons a week does seem reasonable to me."

Dussel leapt out of his chair as if he'd sat on a pin. "You have no business talking about your rights to the room. Where am I supposed to go? Maybe I should ask Mr. van Daan to build me a cubbyhole in the attic. You're not the only one who can't find a quiet place to work. You're always looking for a fight. If your sister Margot, who has more right to work space than you do, had come to me with the same request, I'd never even have thought of refusing, but you . . ."

And once again he brought up the business about the mythology and the knitting, and once again Anne was insulted. However, I showed no sign of it and let Dussel finish: "But no, it's impossible to talk to you. You're shamefully self-centered. No one else matters, as long as you get your way. I've never seen such a child. But after all is said and done, I'll be obliged to let you have your way, since I don't want people saying later on that Anne Frank failed her exams because Mr. Dussel refused to relinquish his table!"

He went on and on until there was such a deluge of words I could hardly keep up. For one fleeting moment I thought, "Him and his lies. I'll smack his ugly mug so hard he'll go bouncing off the wall!" But the next moment I thought, "Calm down, he's not worth getting so upset about!"

At long last Mr. Dussel's fury was spent, and he left the room with an expression of triumph mixed with wrath, his coat pockets bulging with food.

I went running over to Father and recounted the entire story, or at least those parts he hadn't been able to follow himself. Pim decided to talk to Dussel that very same evening, and they spoke for more than half an hour. They first discussed whether Anne should be allowed to use the table, yes or no. Father said that he and Dussel had dealt with the subject once before, at which time he'd professed to agree with Dussel because he didn't want to contradict the elder in front of the younger, but that, even then, he hadn't thought it was fair. Dussel felt I had no right to talk as if he were an intruder laying claim to everything in sight. But Father protested strongly, since he himself had heard me say nothing of the kind. And so the conversation went back and forth, with Father defending my "selfishness" and my "busy-work" and Dussel grumbling the whole time.

Dussel finally had to give in, and I was granted the opportunity to work without interruption two afternoons a week. Dussel looked very sullen, didn't speak to me for two days and made sure he occupied the table from five to five-thirty – all very child-ish, of course.

Anyone who's so petty and pedantic at the age of fifty-four was born that way and is never going to change.

FRIDAY, JULY 16, 1943

*Dearest Kitty,*

There's been another break-in, but this time a real one! Peter went down to the warehouse this morning at seven, as usual, and noticed at once that both the warehouse door and the street door were open. He immediately reported this to Pim, who went to the private office, tuned the radio to a German station and locked the door. Then they both went back upstairs. In such cases our orders are "not to wash ourselves or run any water, to be quiet, to be dressed by eight and not to go to the bathroom," and as usual we followed these to the letter. We were all glad we'd slept so well and hadn't heard anything. For a while we were indignant because no one from the office came upstairs the entire morning; Mr. Kleiman left us on tenterhooks until eleven-thirty. He told us that the burglars had forced the outside door and the ware-house door with a crowbar, but when they didn't find anything worth stealing, they tried their luck on the next floor. They stole two cashboxes containing 40 guilders, blank checkbooks and, worst of all, coupons for 330 pounds of sugar, our entire allot-ment. It won't be easy to wangle new ones.

Mr. Kugler thinks this burglar belongs to the same gang as the one who made an unsuccessful attempt six weeks ago to open all three doors (the warehouse door and the two outside doors).

The burglary caused another stir, but the Annex seems to thrive on excitement. Naturally, we were glad the cash register and the typewriters had been safely tucked away in our clothes closet.

*Yours, Anne*

PS. Landing in Sicily. Another step closer to the . . . !

*Dearest Kitty,*                               MONDAY, JULY 19, 1943

North Amsterdam was very heavily bombed on Sunday. There was apparently a great deal of destruction. Entire streets are in ruins, and it will take a while for them to dig out all the bodies. So far there have been two hundred dead and countless wounded; the hospitals are bursting at the seams. We've been told of children searching forlornly in the smoldering ruins for their dead parents. It still makes me shiver to think of the dull, distant drone that signified the approaching destruction.

FRIDAY, JULY 23, 1943

Bep is currently able to get hold of notebooks, especially journals and ledgers, useful for my bookkeeping sister! Other kinds are for sale as well, but don't ask what they're like or how long they'll last. At the moment they're all labeled "No Coupons Needed!" Like everything else you can purchase without ration stamps, they're totally worthless. They consist of twelve sheets of gray paper with narrow lines that slant across the page. Margot is thinking about taking a course in calligraphy; I've advised her to go ahead and do it. Mother won't let me because of my eyes, but I think that's silly. Whether I do that or something else, it all comes down to the same thing.

Since you've never been through a war, Kitty, and since you know very little about life in hiding, in spite of my letters, let me tell you, just for fun, what we each want to do first when we're able to go outside again.

Margot and Mr. van Daan wish, above all else, to have a hot bath, filled to the brim, which they can lie in for more than half an hour. Mrs. van Daan would like a cake, Dussel can think of nothing but seeing his Charlotte, and Mother is dying for a cup of real coffee. Father would like to visit Mr. Voskuijl, Peter would go downtown, and as for me, I'd be so overjoyed I wouldn't know where to begin.

Most of all I long to have a home of our own, to be able to move around freely and have someone help me with my homework again, at last. In other words, to go back to school!

Bep has offered to get us some fruit, at so-called bargain prices: grapes 2.50 guilders a pound, gooseberries 70 cents a pound, one peach 50 cents, melons 75 cents a pound. No wonder the papers write every evening in big, fat letters: "Keep Prices Down!"

*Dear Kitty,*                                    MONDAY, JULY 26, 1943

Yesterday was a very tumultuous day, and we're still all wound up. Actually, you may wonder if there's ever a day that passes without some kind of excitement.

The first warning siren went off in the morning while we were at breakfast, but we paid no attention, because it only meant that the planes were crossing the coast. I had a terrible headache, so I lay down for an hour after breakfast and then went to the office at around two. At two-thirty Margot had finished her office work and was just gathering her things together when the sirens began wailing again. So she and I trooped back upstairs. None too soon, it seems, for less than five minutes later the guns were booming so loudly that we went and stood in the hall. The house shook and the bombs kept falling. I was clutching my "escape bag," more because I wanted to have something to hold on to than because I wanted to run away. I know we can't leave here, but if we had to, being seen on the streets would be just as dangerous as getting caught in an air raid. After half an hour the drone of engines faded and the house began to hum with activity again. Peter emerged from his lookout post in the front attic, Dussel remained in the front office, Mrs. van D. felt safest in the private office, Mr. van Daan had been watching from the loft, and those of us on the landing spread out to watch the columns of smoke rising from the harbor. Before long the smell of fire was everywhere, and outside it looked as if the city were enveloped in a thick fog.

A big fire like that is not a pleasant sight, but fortunately for us it was all over, and we went back to our various chores. Just as we were starting dinner: another air-raid alarm. The food was good, but I lost my appetite the moment I heard the siren.

Nothing happened, however, and forty-five minutes later the all clear was sounded. After the dishes had been washed: another air-raid warning, gunfire and swarms of planes. "Oh, gosh, twice in one day," we thought, "that's twice too many." Little good that did us, because once again the bombs rained down, this time on the other side of the city. According to British reports, Schiphol Airport was bombed. The planes dived and climbed, the air was abuzz with the drone of engines. It was very scary, and the whole time I kept thinking, "Here it comes, this is it."

I can assure you that when I went to bed at nine, my legs were still shaking. At the stroke of midnight I woke up again: more planes! Dussel was undressing, but I took no notice and leapt up, wide awake, at the sound of the first shot. I stayed in Father's bed until one, in my own bed until one-thirty, and was back in Father's bed at two. But the planes kept on coming. At last they stopped firing and I was able to go back "home" again. I finally fell asleep at half past two.

Seven o'clock. I awoke with a start and sat up in bed. Mr. van Daan was with Father. My first thought was: burglars. "Everything," I heard Mr. van Daan say, and I thought everything had been stolen. But no, this time it was wonderful news, the best we've had in months, maybe even since the war began. Mussolini has resigned and the King of Italy has taken over the government.

We jumped for joy. After the awful events of yesterday, finally something good happens and brings us ... hope! Hope for an end to the war, hope for peace.

Mr. Kugler dropped by and told us that the Fokker aircraft factory had been hit hard. Meanwhile, there was another air-raid alarm this morning, with planes flying over, and another warning siren. I've had it up to here with alarms. I've hardly slept, and the last thing I want to do is work. But now the suspense about Italy and the hope that the war will be over by the end of the year are keeping us awake ...

Yours, Anne

THURSDAY, JULY 29, 1943

Dearest Kitty,

Mrs. van Daan, Dussel and I were doing the dishes, and I was extremely quiet. This is very unusual for me and they were sure to notice, so in order to avoid any questions, I quickly racked my brains for a neutral topic. I thought the book *Henry from Across the Street* might fit the bill, but I couldn't have been more wrong; if Mrs. van Daan doesn't jump down my throat, Mr. Dussel does. It all boiled down to this: Mr. Dussel had recommended the book to Margot and me as an example of excellent writing. We thought it was anything but that. The little boy had been portrayed well, but as for the rest . . . the less said the better. I mentioned something to that effect while we were doing the dishes, and Dussel launched into a veritable tirade.

"How can you possibly understand the psychology of a man? That of a child isn't so difficult [!]. But you're far too young to read a book like that. Even a twenty-year-old man would be unable to comprehend it." (So why did he go out of his way to recommend it to Margot and me?)

Mrs. van D. and Dussel continued their harangue: "You know way too much about things you're not supposed to. You've been brought up all wrong. Later on, when you're older, you won't be able to enjoy anything anymore. You'll say, 'Oh, I read that twenty years ago in some book.' You'd better hurry if you want to catch a husband or fall in love, since everything is bound to be a disappointment to you. You already know all there is to know in theory. But in practice? That's another story!"

Can you imagine how I felt? I astonished myself by calmly replying, "You may think I haven't been raised properly, but many people would disagree!"

They apparently believe that good child-rearing includes trying to pit me against my parents, since that's all they ever do. And not telling a girl my age about grown-up subjects is fine. We can all see what happens when people are raised that way.

At that moment I could have slapped them both for poking fun at me. I was beside myself with rage, and if I only knew how much longer we had to put up with each other's company, I'd start counting the days.

Mrs. van Daan's a fine one to talk! She sets an example all right – a bad one! She's known to be exceedingly pushy, egotistical, cunning, calculating and perpetually dissatisfied. Add to that, vanity and coquettishness and there's no question about it: she's a thoroughly despicable person. I could write an entire book about Madame van Daan, and who knows, maybe someday I will. Anyone can put on a charming exterior when they want to. Mrs. van D. is friendly to strangers, especially men, so it's easy to make a mistake when you first get to know her.

Mother thinks that Mrs. van D. is too stupid for words, Margot that she's too unimportant, Pim that she's too ugly (literally and figuratively!), and after long observation (I'm never prejudiced at the beginning), I've come to the conclusion that she's all three of the above, and lots more besides. She has so many bad traits, why should I single out just one of them?

*Yours, Anne*

PS. Will the reader please take into consideration that this story was written before the writer's fury had cooled?

TUESDAY, AUGUST 3, 1943

*Dearest Kitty,*

Things are going well on the political front. Italy has banned the Fascist Party. The people are fighting the Fascists in many places – even the army has joined the fight. How can a country like that continue to wage war against England?

Our beautiful radio was taken away last week. Dussel was very angry at Mr. Kugler for turning it in on the appointed day. Dussel is slipping lower and lower in my estimation, and he's already below zero. Whatever he says about politics, history, geography or anything else is so ridiculous that I hardly dare repeat it: Hitler will fade from history; the harbor in Rotterdam is bigger than the one in Hamburg; the English are idiots for not taking the opportunity to bomb Italy to smithereens; etc., etc.

We just had a third air raid. I decided to grit my teeth and practice being courageous.

Mrs. van Daan, the one who always said "Let them fall" and "Better to end with a bang than not to end at all," is the most cowardly one among us. She was shaking like a leaf this morning and even burst into tears. She was comforted by her husband, with whom she recently declared a truce after a week of squabbling; I nearly got sentimental at the sight.

Mouschi has now proved, beyond a shadow of a doubt, that having a cat has disadvantages as well as advantages. The whole house is crawling with fleas, and it's getting worse each day. Mr. Kleiman sprinkled yellow powder in every nook and cranny, but the fleas haven't taken the slightest notice. It's making us all very jittery; we're forever imagining a bite on our arms and legs or other parts of our bodies, so we leap up and do a few exercises, since it gives us an excuse to take a better look at our arms or necks. But now we're paying the price for having had so little physical exercise; we're so stiff we can hardly turn our heads. The real calisthenics fell by the wayside long ago.

*Yours, Anne*

WEDNESDAY, AUGUST 4, 1943

*Dearest Kitty,*

Now that we've been in hiding for a little over a year, you know a great deal about our lives. Still, I can't possibly tell you everything, since it's all so different compared to ordinary times and ordinary people. Nevertheless, to give you a closer look into our lives, from time to time I'll describe part of an ordinary day. I'll start with the evening and night.

*Nine in the evening.* Bedtime always begins in the Annex with an enormous hustle and bustle. Chairs are shifted, beds pulled out, blankets unfolded – nothing stays where it is during the daytime. I sleep on a small divan, which is only five feet long, so we have to add a few chairs to make it longer. Comforter, sheets, pillows, blankets: everything has to be removed from Dussel's bed, where it's kept during the day.

In the next room there's a terrible creaking: that's Margot's folding bed being set up. More blankets and pillows, anything to make the wooden slats a bit more comfortable. Upstairs it sounds like thunder, but it's only Mrs. van D.'s bed being shoved against the window so that Her Majesty, arrayed in her pink bed jacket, can sniff the night air through her delicate little nostrils.

*Nine o'clock.* After Peter's finished, it's my turn for the bathroom. I wash myself from head to toe, and more often than not I find a tiny flea floating in the sink (only during the hot months, weeks or days). I brush my teeth, curl my hair, manicure my nails and dab peroxide on my upper lip to bleach the black hairs – all this in less than half an hour.

*Nine-thirty.* I throw on my bathrobe. With soap in one hand,

and potty, hairpins, panties, curlers and a wad of cotton in the other, I hurry out of the bathroom. The next in line invariably calls me back to remove the gracefully curved but unsightly hairs that I've left in the sink.

*Ten o'clock.* Time to put up the blackout screen and say good-night. For the next fifteen minutes, at least, the house is filled with the creaking of beds and the sigh of broken springs, and then, provided our upstairs neighbors aren't having a marital spat in bed, all is quiet.

*Eleven-thirty.* The bathroom door creaks. A narrow strip of light falls into the room. Squeaking shoes, a large coat, even larger than the man inside it . . . Dussel is returning from his nightly work in Mr. Kugler's office. I hear him shuffling back and forth for ten whole minutes, the rustle of paper (from the food he's tucking away in his cupboard) and the bed being made up. Then the figure disappears again, and the only sound is the occasional suspicious noise from the bathroom.

*Approximately three o'clock.* I have to get up to use the tin can under my bed, which, to be on the safe side, has a rubber mat underneath in case of leaks. I always hold my breath while I go, since it clatters into the can like a brook down a mountainside. The potty is returned to its place, and the figure in the white nightgown (the one that causes Margot to exclaim every evening, "Oh, that indecent nighty!') climbs back into bed. A certain somebody lies awake for about fifteen minutes, listening to the sounds of the night. In the first place, to hear whether there are any burglars downstairs, and then to the various beds – upstairs, next door and in my room – to tell whether the others are asleep or half awake. This is no fun, especially when it concerns a member of the family named Dr. Dussel. First, there's the sound of a fish gasping for air, and this is repeated nine or ten times. Then, the lips are moistened profusely. This is alternated with little smacking sounds, followed by a long period of toss-ing and turning and rearranging the pillows. After five minutes of perfect quiet, the same sequence repeats itself three more times, after which he's presumably lulled himself back to sleep for a while.

Sometimes the guns go off during the night, between one and

four. I'm never aware of it before it happens, but all of a sudden I find myself standing beside my bed, out of sheer habit. Occasionally I'm dreaming so deeply (of irregular French verbs or a quarrel upstairs) that I realize only when my dream is over that the shooting has stopped and that I've remained quietly in my room. But usually I wake up. Then I grab a pillow and a handkerchief, throw on my robe and slippers and dash next door to Father, just the way Margot described in this birthday poem:

> When shots ring out in the dark of night,
> The door creaks open and into sight
> Come a hanky, a pillow, a figure in white . . .

Once I've reached the big bed, the worst is over, except when the shooting is extra loud.

*Six forty-five.* Brrring . . . the alarm clock, which raises its shrill voice at any hour of the day or night, whether you want it to or not. Creak . . . wham . . . Mrs. van D. turns it off. Screak . . . Mr. van D. gets up, puts on the water and races to the bathroom.

*Seven-fifteen.* The door creaks again. Dussel can go to the bathroom. Alone at last, I remove the blackout screen . . . and a new day begins in the Annex.

*Yours, Anne*

THURSDAY, AUGUST 5, 1943

*Dearest Kitty,*

Today let's talk about the lunch break.

*It's twelve-thirty.* The whole gang breathes a sigh of relief: Mr. van Maaren, the man with the shady past, and Mr. de Kok have gone home for lunch.

Upstairs you can hear the thud of the vacuum cleaner on Mrs. van D.'s beautiful and only rug. Margot tucks a few books under her arm and heads for the class for "slow learners," which is what Dussel seems to be. Pim goes and sits in a corner with his constant companion, Dickens, in hopes of finding a bit of peace and quiet. Mother hastens upstairs to help the busy little housewife, and I tidy up both the bathroom and myself at the same time.

*Twelve forty-five.* One by one they trickle in: first Mr. Gies and then either Mr. Kleiman or Mr. Kugler, followed by Bep and sometimes even Miep.

*One.* Clustered around the radio, they all listen raptly to the BBC. This is the only time the members of the Annex family don't interrupt each other, since even Mr. van Daan can't argue with the speaker.

*One-fifteen.* Food distribution. Everyone from downstairs gets a cup of soup, plus dessert, if there happens to be any. A contented Mr. Gies sits on the divan or leans against the desk with his newspaper, cup and usually the cat at his side. If one of the three is missing, he doesn't hesitate to let his protest be heard. Mr. Kleiman relates the latest news from town, and he's an excellent source. Mr. Kugler hurries up the stairs, gives a short but solid knock on the door and comes in either wringing his hands or rubbing them in glee, depending on whether he's quiet and in a bad mood or talkative and in a good mood.

*One forty-five.* Everyone rises from the table and goes about their business. Margot and Mother do the dishes, Mr. and Mrs. van D. head for the divan, Peter for the attic, Father for his divan, Dussel too, and Anne does her homework.

What comes next is the quietest hour of the day; when they're all asleep, there are no disturbances. To judge by his face, Dussel is dreaming of food. But I don't look at him long, because the time whizzes by and before you know it, it'll be 4 p.m. and the pedantic Dr. Dussel will be standing with the clock in his hand because I'm one minute late clearing off the table.

*Yours, Anne*

*Dearest Kitty,*                       SATURDAY, AUGUST 7, 1943

A few weeks ago I started writing a story, something I made up from beginning to end, and I've enjoyed it so much that the products of my pen are piling up.

*Yours, Anne*

*Dearest Kitty,*                       MONDAY, AUGUST 9, 1943

We now continue with a typical day in the Annex. Since we've already had lunch, it's time to describe dinner.

*Mr. van Daan.* Is served first, and takes a generous portion of whatever he likes. Usually joins in the conversation, never fails to give his opinion. Once he's spoken, his word is final. If anyone dares to suggest otherwise, Mr. van D. can put up a good fight. Oh, he can hiss like a cat . . . but I'd rather he didn't. Once you've seen it, you never want to see it again. His opinion is the best, he knows the most about everything. Granted, the man has a good head on his shoulders, but it's swelled to no small degree.

*Madame.* Actually, the best thing would be to say nothing. Some days, especially when a foul mood is on the way, her face is hard to read. If you analyze the discussions, you realize she's not the subject, but the guilty party! A fact everyone prefers to ignore. Even so, you could call her the instigator. Stirring up trouble, now *that's* what Mrs. van Daan calls fun. Stirring up trouble between Mrs. Frank and Anne. Margot and Mr. Frank aren't quite as easy.

But let's return to the table. Mrs. van D. may think she doesn't always get enough, but that's not the case. The choicest potatoes, the tastiest morsel, the tenderest bit of whatever there is, that's Madame's motto. The others can all have their turn, as long as I get the best. (Exactly what she accuses Anne Frank of doing.) Her second watchword is: keep talking. As long as somebody's listening, it doesn't seem to occur to her to wonder whether they're interested. She must think that whatever Mrs. van Daan says will interest everyone.

Smile coquettishly, pretend you know everything, offer everyone a piece of advice and mother them – that's sure to make a good impression. But if you take a better look, the good impression fades. One, she's hardworking; two, cheerful; three, coquettish and sometimes a cute face. That's Petronella van Daan.

*The third diner.* Says very little. Young Mr. van Daan is usually quiet and hardly makes his presence known. As far as his appetite is concerned, he's a Danaïdean vessel that never gets full. Even after the most substantial meal, he can look you calmly in the eye and claim he could have eaten twice as much.

*Number four – Margot.* Eats like a bird and doesn't talk at all. She eats only vegetables and fruit. "Spoiled," in the opinion of the van Daans. "Too little exercise and fresh air," in ours.

*Beside her – Mama.* Has a hearty appetite, does her share of the talking. No one has the impression, as they do with Mrs. van Daan, that this is a housewife. What's the difference between the two? Well, Mrs. van D. does the cooking and Mother does the dishes and polishes the furniture.

*Numbers six and seven.* I won't say much about Father and me. The former is the most modest person at the table. He always looks to see whether the others have been served first. He needs nothing for himself; the best things are for the children. He's goodness personified. Seated next to him is the Annex's little bundle of nerves.

*Dussel.* Help yourself, keep your eyes on the food, eat and don't talk. And if you have to say something, then for goodness' sake talk about food. That doesn't lead to quarrels, just to bragging. He consumes enormous portions, and "no" is not part of his vocabulary, whether the food is good or bad.

Pants that come up to his chest, a red jacket, black patent-leather slippers and horn-rimmed glasses – that's how he looks when he's at work at the little table, always studying and never progressing. This is interrupted only by his afternoon nap, food and – his favorite spot – the bathroom. Three, four or five times a day there's bound to be someone waiting outside the bathroom door, hopping impatiently from one foot to another, trying to hold it in and barely managing. Does Dussel care? Not a whit. From seven-fifteen to seven-thirty, from twelve-thirty to one, from two to two-fifteen, from four to four-fifteen, from six to six-fifteen, from eleven-thirty to twelve. You can set your watch by them; these are the times for his "regular sessions." He never deviates or lets himself be swayed by the voices outside the door, begging him to open up before a disaster occurs.

*Number nine* is not part of our Annex family, although she does share our house and table. Bep has a healthy appetite. She cleans her plate and isn't choosy. Bep's easy to please and that pleases us. She can be characterized as follows: cheerful, good-humored, kind and willing.

*Dearest Kitty,*                    TUESDAY, AUGUST 10, 1943

A new idea: during meals I talk more to myself than to the others, which has two advantages. First, they're glad they don't have to listen to my continuous chatter, and second, I don't have to get annoyed by their opinions. I don't think my opinions are stupid but other people do, so it's better to keep them to myself. I apply the same tactic when I have to eat something I loathe. I put the dish in front of me, pretend it's delicious, avoid looking at it as much as possible, and it's gone before I've had time to realize what it is. When I get up in the morning, another very disagreeable moment, I leap out of bed, think to myself, "You'll be slipping back under the covers soon," walk to the window, take down the blackout screen, sniff at the crack until I feel a bit of fresh air, and I'm awake. I strip the bed as fast as I can so I won't be tempted to get back in. Do you know what Mother calls this sort of thing? The art of living. Isn't that a funny expression?

We've all been a little confused this past week because our dearly beloved Westertoren bells have been carted off to be melted down for the war, so we have no idea of the exact time, either night or day. I still have hopes that they'll come up with a substitute, made of tin or copper or some such thing, to remind the neighborhood of the clock.

Everywhere I go, upstairs or down, they all cast admiring glances at my feet, which are adorned by a pair of exceptionally beautiful (for times like these!) shoes. Miep managed to snap them up for 27.50 guilders. Burgundy-colored suede and leather with medium-sized high heels. I feel as if I'm on stilts, and look even taller than I already am.

Yesterday was my unlucky day. I pricked my right thumb with the blunt end of a big needle. As a result, Margot had to peel potatoes for me (take the good with the bad), and writing was awkward. Then I bumped into the cupboard door so hard it nearly knocked me over, and was scolded for making such a racket. They wouldn't let me run water to bathe my forehead, so now I'm walking around with a giant lump over my right eye. To make matters worse, the little toe on my right foot got stuck in the vacuum cleaner. It bled and hurt, but my other ailments were already causing me so much trouble that I let this one slide, which was stupid of me, because now I'm walking around with an infected toe. What with the salve, the gauze and the tape, I can't get my heavenly new shoe on my foot.

Dussel has put us in danger for the umpteenth time. He

actually had Miep bring him a book, an anti-Mussolini tirade, which has been banned. On the way here she was knocked down by an SS motorcycle. She lost her head and shouted "You brutes!" and went on her way. I don't dare think what would have happened if she'd been taken down to headquarters.

*Yours, Anne*

### *A Daily Chore in Our Little Community: Peeling Potatoes!*

One person goes to get some newspapers; another, the knives (keeping the best for himself, of course); the third, the potatoes; and the fourth, the water.

Mr. Dussel begins. He may not always peel them very well, but he does peel nonstop, glancing left and right to see if everyone is doing it the way he does. No, they're not!

"Look, Anne, I am taking peeler in my hand like so and going from the top to bottom! *Nein*, not so . . . but so!"

"I think my way is easier, Mr. Dussel," I say tentatively.

"But this is best way, Anne. This you can take from me. Of course, it is no matter, you do the way you want."

We go on peeling. I glance at Dussel out of the corner of my eye. Lost in thought, he shakes his head (over me, no doubt), but says no more.

I keep on peeling. Then I look at Father, on the other side of me. To Father, peeling potatoes is not a chore, but precision work. When he reads, he has a deep wrinkle in the back of his head. But when he's preparing potatoes, beans or vegetables, he seems to be totally absorbed in his task. He puts on his potato-peeling face, and when it's set in that particular way, it would be impossible for him to turn out anything less than a perfectly peeled potato.

I keep on working. I glance up for a second, but that's all the time I need. Mrs. van D. is trying to attract Dussel's attention. She starts by looking in his direction, but Dussel pretends not to notice. She winks, but Dussel goes on peeling. She laughs, but Dussel still doesn't look up. Then Mother laughs too, but Dussel pays them no mind. Having failed to achieve her goal, Mrs. van D. is obliged to change tactics. There's a brief silence. Then she says, "Putti, why don't you put on an apron? Otherwise, I'll have to spend all day tomorrow trying to get the spots out of your suit!"

"I'm not getting it dirty."

Another brief silence. "Putti, why don't you sit down?"

"I'm fine this way. I like standing up!"

Silence.

"Putti, look out, *du spritzt schon!*"*

"I know, Mommy, but I'm being careful."

Mrs. van D. casts about for another topic. "Tell me, Putti, why aren't the British carrying out any bombing raids today?"

"Because the weather's bad, Kerli!"

"But yesterday it was such nice weather and they weren't flying then either."

"Let's drop the subject."

"Why? Can't a person talk about that or offer an opinion?"

"No!"

"Well, why in the world not?"

"Oh, be quiet, *Mammichen!*"†

"Mr. Frank always answers his wife."

Mr. van D. is trying to control himself. This remark always rubs him the wrong way, but Mrs. van D.'s not one to quit: "Oh, there's never going to be an invasion!"

Mr. van D. turns white, and when she notices it, Mrs. van D. turns red, but she's not about to be deterred: "The British aren't doing a thing!"

The bomb bursts. "And now shut up, *Donnerwetter noch mal!*"‡

Mother can barely stifle a laugh, and I stare straight ahead.

Scenes like these are repeated almost daily, unless they've just had a terrible fight. In that case, neither Mr. nor Mrs. van D. says a word.

It's time for me to get some more potatoes. I go up to the attic, where Peter is busy picking fleas from the cat. He looks up, the cat notices it, and whoosh ... he's gone. Out the window and into the rain gutter.

Peter swears; I laugh and slip out of the room.

*Now you're splashing!
†Mommy.
‡For crying out loud!

### Freedom in the Annex

*Five-thirty.* Bep's arrival signals the beginning of our nightly freedom. Things get going right away. I go upstairs with Bep, who usually has her dessert before the rest of us. The moment she sits down, Mrs. van D. begins stating her wishes. Her list usually starts with "Oh, by the way, Bep, something else I'd like . . ." Bep winks at me. Mrs. van D. doesn't miss a chance to make her wishes known to whoever comes upstairs. It must be one of the reasons none of them like to go up there.

*Five forty-five.* Bep leaves. I go down two floors to have a look around: first to the kitchen, then to the private office and then to the coal bin to open the cat door for Mouschi.

After a long tour of inspection, I wind up in Mr. Kugler's office. Mr. van Daan is combing all the drawers and files for today's mail. Peter picks up Boche and the warehouse key; Pim lugs the typewriters upstairs; Margot looks around for a quiet place to do her office work; Mrs. van D. puts a kettle of water on the stove; Mother comes down the stairs with a pan of potatoes; we all know our jobs.

Soon Peter comes back from the warehouse. The first question they ask him is whether he's remembered the bread. No, he hasn't. He crouches before the door to the front office to make himself as small as possible and crawls on his hands and knees to the steel cabinet, takes out the bread and starts to leave. At any rate, that's what he intends to do, but before he knows what's happened, Mouschi has jumped over him and gone to sit under the desk.

Peter looks all around him. Aha, there's the cat! He crawls back into the office and grabs the cat by the tail. Mouschi hisses, Peter sighs. What has he accomplished? Mouschi's now sitting by the window licking herself, very pleased at having escaped Peter's clutches. Peter has no choice but to lure her with a piece of bread. Mouschi takes the bait, follows him out, and the door closes.

I watch the entire scene through a crack in the door.

Mr. van Daan is angry and slams the door. Margot and I exchange looks and think the same thing: he must have worked himself into a rage again because of some blunder on Mr. Kugler's part, and he's forgotten all about the Keg Company next door.

Another step is heard in the hallway. Dussel comes in, goes toward the window with an air of propriety, sniffs ... coughs, sneezes and clears his throat. He's out of luck – it was pepper. He continues on to the front office. The curtains are open, which means he can't get at his writing paper. He disappears with a scowl.

Margot and I exchange another glance. "One less page for his sweetheart tomorrow," I hear her say. I nod in agreement.

An elephant's tread is heard on the stairway. It's Dussel, seeking comfort in his favorite spot.

We continue working. Knock, knock, knock ... Three taps means dinnertime!

MONDAY, AUGUST 23, 1943

*Wenn Die Uhr Halb Neune Schlägt ...* *

Margot and Mother are nervous. "Shh ... Father. Be quiet, Otto. Shh ... Pim! It's eight-thirty. Come here, you can't run the water anymore. Walk softly!" A sample of what's said to Father in the bathroom. At the stroke of half past eight, he has to be in the living room. No running water, no flushing toilet, no walking around, no noise whatsoever. As long as the office staff hasn't arrived, sounds travel more easily to the warehouse.

The door opens upstairs at eight twenty, and this is followed by three gentle taps on the floor ... Anne's hot cereal. I clamber up the stairs to get my doggie dish.

Back downstairs, everything has to be done quickly, quickly: I comb my hair, put away the potty, shove the bed back in place. Quiet! The clock is striking eight-thirty! Mrs. van D. changes shoes and shuffles through the room in her slippers; Mr. van D. too – a veritable Charlie Chaplin. All is quiet.

The ideal family scene has now reached its high point. I want to read or study and Margot does too. Father and Mother ditto. Father is sitting (with Dickens and the dictionary, of course) on the edge of the sagging, squeaky bed, which doesn't even have

* When the clock strikes half past eight.

a decent mattress. Two bolsters can be piled on top of each other. "I don't need these," he thinks. "I can manage without them!"

Once he starts reading, he doesn't look up. He laughs now and then and tries to get Mother to read a passage.

"I don't have the time right now!"

He looks disappointed, but then continues to read. A little while later, when he comes across another interesting bit, he tries again: "You *have* to read this, Mother!"

Mother sits on the folding bed, either reading, sewing, knitting or studying, whichever is next on her list. An idea suddenly occurs to her, and she quickly says, so as not to forget, "Anne, remember to . . . Margot, jot this down . . . ."

After a while it's quiet again. Margot slams her book shut; Father knits his forehead, his eyebrows forming a funny curve and his wrinkle of concentration reappearing at the back of his head, and he buries himself in his book again; Mother starts chatting with Margot; and I get curious and listen too. Pim is drawn into the conversation . . . Nine o'clock. Breakfast!

*Dearest Kitty,*                    FRIDAY, SEPTEMBER 10, 1943

Every time I write to you, something special has happened, usually unpleasant rather than pleasant. This time, however, something wonderful is going on.

On Wednesday, September 8, we were listening to the seven o'clock news when we heard an announcement: "Here is some of the best news of the war so far: Italy has capitulated." Italy has unconditionally surrendered! The Dutch broadcast from England began at eight-fifteen with the news: "Listeners, an hour and fifteen minutes ago, just as I finished writing my daily report, we received the wonderful news of Italy's capitulation. I tell you, I never tossed my notes into the wastepaper basket with more delight than I did today!"

"God Save the King," the American national anthem and the Russian "Internationale" were played. As always, the Dutch program was uplifting without being too optimistic.

The British have landed in Naples. Northern Italy is occupied by the Germans. The truce was signed on Friday, September 3, the day the British landed in Italy. The Germans are ranting and raving in all the newspapers at the treachery of Badoglio and the Italian king.

Still, there's bad news as well. It's about Mr. Kleiman. As you know, we all like him very much. He's unfailingly cheerful and amazingly brave, despite the fact that he's always sick and in pain and can't eat much or do a lot of walking. "When Mr. Kleiman enters a room, the sun begins to shine," Mother said recently, and she's absolutely right.

Now it seems he has to go to the hospital for a very difficult operation on his stomach, and will have to stay there for at least four weeks. You should have seen him when he told us goodbye. He acted so normally, as though he were just off to do an errand.

*Yours, Anne*

THURSDAY, SEPTEMBER 16, 1943
*Dearest Kitty,*

Relationships here in the Annex are getting worse all the time. We don't dare open our mouths at mealtime (except to slip in a bite of food), because no matter what we say, someone is bound to resent it or take it the wrong way. Mr. Voskuijl occasionally comes to visit us. Unfortunately, he's not doing very well. He isn't making it any easier for his family, because his attitude seems to be: what do I care, I'm going to die anyway! When I think how touchy everyone is here, I can just imagine what it must be like at the Voskuijls'.

I've been taking valerian every day to fight the anxiety and depression, but it doesn't stop me from being even more miserable the next day. A good hearty laugh would help more than ten valerian drops, but we've almost forgotten how to laugh. Sometimes I'm afraid my face is going to sag with all this sorrow and that my mouth is going to permanently droop at the corners. The others aren't doing any better. Everyone here is dreading the great terror known as winter.

Another fact that doesn't exactly brighten up our days is that Mr. van Maaren, the man who works in the warehouse, is getting suspicious about the Annex. A person with any brains must have noticed by now that Miep sometimes says she's going to the lab,

Bep to the file room and Mr. Kleiman to the Opekta supplies, while Mr. Kugler claims the Annex doesn't belong to this building at all, but to the one next door.

We wouldn't care what Mr. van Maaren thought of the situation except that he's known to be unreliable and to possess a high degree of curiosity. He's not one who can be put off with a flimsy excuse.

One day Mr. Kugler wanted to be extra cautious, so at twenty past twelve he put on his coat and went to the drugstore around the corner. Less than five minutes later he was back, and he sneaked up the stairs like a thief to visit us. At one-fifteen he started to leave, but Bep met him on the landing and warned him that van Maaren was in the office. Mr. Kugler did an about-face and stayed with us until one-thirty. Then he took off his shoes and went in his stockinged feet (despite his cold) to the front attic and down the other stairway, taking one step at a time to avoid the creaks. It took him fifteen minutes to negotiate the stairs, but he wound up safely in the office after having entered from the outside.

In the meantime, Bep had gotten rid of van Maaren and come to get Mr. Kugler from the Annex. But he'd already left and at that moment was still tiptoeing down the stairs. What must the passersby have thought when they saw the manager putting on his shoes outside? Hey, you there, in the socks!

                                                                    *Yours, Anne*

*Dearest Kitty,*              WEDNESDAY, SEPTEMBER 29, 1943

It's Mrs. van Daan's birthday. Other than one ration stamp each for cheese, meat and bread, all she received from us was a jar of jam. Her husband, Dussel and the office staff gave her nothing but flowers and also food. Such are the times we live in!

Bep had a nervous fit last week because she had so many errands to do. Ten times a day people were sending her out for something, each time insisting she go right away or go again or that she'd done it all wrong. And when you think that she has her regular office work to do, that Mr. Kleiman is sick, that Miep is home with a cold and that Bep herself has a sprained ankle, boyfriend troubles and a grouchy father, it's no wonder she's at the end of her tether. We comforted her and told her that if she'd put her foot down once or twice and say she didn't have the time, the shopping lists would shrink of their own accord.

Saturday there was a big drama, the likes of which have never been seen here before. It started with a discussion of van Maaren and ended in a general argument and tears. Dussel complained to Mother that he was being treated like a leper, that no one was friendly to him and that, after all, he hadn't done anything to deserve it. This was followed by a lot of sweet talk, which luckily Mother didn't fall for this time. She told him we were disappointed in him and that, on more than one occasion, he'd been a source of great annoyance. Dussel promised her the moon, but, as usual, we haven't seen so much as a beam.

There's trouble brewing with the van Daans, I can tell! Father's furious because they're cheating us: they've been holding back meat and other things. Oh, what kind of bombshell is about to burst now? If only I weren't so involved in all these skirmishes! If only I could leave here! They're driving us crazy!

*Yours, Anne*

*Dearest Kitty,*                                      SUNDAY, OCTOBER 17, 1943

Mr. Kleiman is back, thank goodness! He looks a bit pale, and yet he cheerfully set off to sell some clothes for Mr. van Daan.

The disagreeable fact is that Mr. van Daan has run out of money. He lost his last hundred guilders in the warehouse, which is still creating trouble for us: the men are wondering how a hundred guilders could wind up in the warehouse on a Monday morning. Suspicion abounds. Meanwhile, the hundred guilders have been stolen. Who's the thief?

But I was talking about the money shortage. Mrs. van D. has scads of dresses, coats and shoes, none of which she feels she can do without. Mr. van D.'s suit is difficult to sell, and Peter's bike was put on the block, but is back again, since nobody wanted it. But the story doesn't end there. You see, Mrs. van D. is going to have to part with her fur coat. In her opinion, the firm should pay for our upkeep, but that's ridiculous. They just had a flaming row about it and have entered the "oh, my sweet Putti" and "darling Kerli" stage of reconciliation.

My mind boggles at the profanity this honorable house has had to endure in the past month. Father walks around with his lips pressed together, and whenever he hears his name, he looks up in alarm, as if he's afraid he'll be called upon to resolve another delicate problem. Mother's so wrought up her cheeks are blotched with red, Margot complains of headaches, Dussel can't sleep, Mrs. van D. frets and fumes all day long, and I've gone completely round the bend. To tell you the truth, I sometimes forget who we're at odds with and who we're not.

The only way to take my mind off it is to study, and I've been doing a lot of that lately.

*Yours, Anne*

FRIDAY, OCTOBER 29, 1943

*My dearest Kitty,*

Mr. Kleiman is out again; his stomach won't give him a moment's peace. He doesn't even know whether it's stopped bleeding. He came to tell us he wasn't feeling well and was going home, and for the first time he seemed really down.

Mr. and Mrs. van D. have had more raging battles. The reason is simple: they're broke. They wanted to sell an overcoat and a suit of Mr. van D.'s, but were unable to find any buyers. His prices were way too high.

Some time ago Mr. Kleiman was talking about a furrier he knows. This gave Mr. van D. the idea of selling his wife's fur coat. It's made of rabbit skin, and she's had it for seventeen years. Mrs. van D. got 325 guilders for it, an enormous amount. She wanted to keep the money herself to buy new clothes after the war, and it took some doing before Mr. van D. could make her understand that it was desperately needed to cover household expenses.

You can't imagine the screaming, shouting, stamping of feet and swearing that went on. It was terrifying. My family stood holding its breath at the bottom of the stairs, in case it might be necessary to drag them apart. All the bickering, tears and nervous tension have become such a stress and strain that I fall into my bed at night crying and thanking my lucky stars that I have half an hour to myself.

I'm doing fine, except I've got no appetite. I keep hearing: "Goodness, you look awful!" I must admit they're doing their best to keep me in condition: they're plying me with dextrose, cod-liver oil, brewer's yeast and calcium. My nerves often get the better of me, especially on Sundays; that's when I really feel miserable. The atmosphere is stifling, sluggish, leaden. Outside, you don't hear a single bird, and a deathly, oppressive silence hangs over the house and clings to me as if it were going to drag me into the deepest regions of the underworld. At times like these, Father, Mother and Margot don't matter to me in the least. I wander from room to room, climb up and down the stairs and feel like a songbird whose wings have been ripped off and who keeps hurling itself against the bars of its dark cage. "Let me out, where there's fresh air and laughter!" a voice within me cries. I don't even bother to reply anymore, but lie down on the divan. Sleep makes the silence and the terrible fear go by more quickly, helps pass the time, since it's impossible to kill it.

Yours, Anne

*Dearest Kitty,*                                     SATURDAY, OCTOBER 30, 1943

Mother's nerves are very much on edge, and that doesn't bode well for me. Is it just a coincidence that Father and Mother never scold Margot and always blame me for everything? Last night, for example, Margot was reading a book with beautiful illustrations; she got up and put the book aside for later. I wasn't doing anything, so I picked it up and began looking at the pictures. Margot came back, saw "her" book in my hands, knitted her brow and angrily demanded the book back. I wanted to look through it some more. Margot got madder by the minute, and Mother butted in: "Margot was reading that book; give it back to her."

Father came in, and without even knowing what was going on, saw that Margot was being wronged and lashed out at me: "I'd like to see what you'd do if Margot was looking at one of your books!"

I promptly gave in, put the book down and, according to them, left the room "in a huff." I was neither huffy nor cross, but merely sad.

It wasn't right of Father to pass judgment without knowing what the issue was. I would have given the book to Margot myself, and a lot sooner, if Father and Mother hadn't intervened and rushed to take Margot's part, as if she were suffering some great injustice.

Of course, Mother took Margot's side; they always take each other's sides. I'm so used to it that I've become completely indifferent to Mother's rebukes and Margot's moodiness. I love them, but only because they're Mother and Margot. I don't give a darn about them as people. As far as I'm concerned, they can go jump in a lake. It's different with Father. When I see him being partial to Margot, approving Margot's every action, praising her, hugging her, I feel a gnawing ache inside, because I'm crazy about him. I model myself after Father, and there's no one in the world I love more. He doesn't realize that he treats Margot differently than he does me: Margot just happens to be the smartest, the kindest, the prettiest and the best. But I have a right to be taken seriously too. I've always been the clown and mischief maker of the family; I've always had to pay double for my sins: once with scoldings and then again with my own sense of despair. I'm no longer satisfied with the meaningless affection or the supposedly serious talks. I long for something from Father that he's incapable of giving. I'm not jealous of Margot; I never have been. I'm not envious of her brains or her beauty. It's just that I'd like to feel that Father really loves me, not because I'm his child, but because I'm me, Anne.

I cling to Father because my contempt of Mother is growing daily and it's only through him that I'm able to retain the last ounce of family feeling I have left. He doesn't understand that I sometimes need to vent my feelings for Mother. He doesn't want to talk about it, and he avoids any discussion involving Mother's failings.

And yet Mother, with all her shortcomings, is tougher for me to deal with. I don't know how I should act. I can't very well confront her with her carelessness, her sarcasm and her hard-heartedness, yet I can't continue to take the blame for everything.

I'm the opposite of Mother, so of course we clash. I don't mean to judge her; I don't have that right. I'm simply looking at her as a mother. She's not a mother to me – I have to mother myself. I've cut myself adrift from them. I'm charting my own course, and we'll see where it leads me. I have no choice, because I can picture what a mother and a wife should be and can't seem to find anything of the sort in the woman I'm supposed to call "Mother."

I tell myself time and again to overlook Mother's bad example. I only want to see her good points, and to look inside myself for what's lacking in her. But it doesn't work, and the worst part is that Father and Mother don't realize their own inadequacies and how much I blame them for letting me down. Are there any parents who can make their children completely happy?

Sometimes I think God is trying to test me, both now and in the future. I'll have to become a good person on my own, without anyone to serve as a model or advise me, but it'll make me stronger in the end.

Who else but me is ever going to read these letters? Who else but me can I turn to for comfort? I'm frequently in need of consolation, I often feel weak, and more often than not, I fail to meet expectations. I know this, and every day I resolve to do better.

They aren't consistent in their treatment of me. One day they say that Anne's a sensible girl and entitled to know everything, and the next that Anne's a silly goose who doesn't know a thing and yet imagines she's learned all she needs to know from books! I'm no longer the baby and spoiled little darling whose every deed can be laughed at. I have my own ideas, plans and ideals, but am unable to articulate them yet.

Oh well. So much comes into my head at night when I'm alone, or during the day when I'm obliged to put up with people I can't abide or who invariably misinterpret my intentions. That's why I always wind up coming back to my diary – I start there and end there because Kitty's always patient. I promise her that, despite everything, I'll keep going, that I'll find my own way and choke back my tears. I only wish I could see some results or, just once, receive encouragement from someone who loves me.

Don't condemn me, but think of me as a person who sometimes reaches the bursting point!

*Yours, Anne*

*Dearest Kitty,*

To take our minds off matters as well as to develop them, Father ordered a catalog from a correspondence school. Margot pored through the thick brochure three times without finding anything to her liking and within her budget. Father was easier to satisfy and decided to write and ask for a trial lesson in "Elementary Latin." No sooner said than done. The lesson arrived, Margot set to work enthusiastically and decided to take the course, despite the expense. It's much too hard for me, though I'd really like to learn Latin.

To give me a new project as well, Father asked Mr. Kleiman for a children's Bible so I could finally learn something about the New Testament.

"Are you planning to give Anne a Bible for Hanukkah?" Margot asked, somewhat perturbed.

"Yes . . . Well, maybe St. Nicholas Day would be a better occasion," Father replied.

Jesus and Hanukkah don't exactly go together.

Since the vacuum cleaner's broken, I have to take an old brush to the rug every night. The window's closed, the light's on, the stove's burning, and there I am brushing away at the rug. "That's sure to be a problem," I thought to myself the first time. "There're bound to be complaints." I was right: Mother got a headache from the thick clouds of dust whirling around the room, Margot's new Latin dictionary was caked with dirt, and Pim grumbled that the floor didn't look any different anyway. Small thanks for my pains.

We've decided that from now on the stove is going to be lit at seven-thirty on Sunday mornings instead of five-thirty. I think it's risky. What will the neighbors think of our smoking chimney?

It's the same with the curtains. Ever since we first went into hiding, they've been tacked firmly to the windows. Sometimes one of the ladies or gentlemen can't resist the urge to peek outside. The result: a storm of reproaches. The response: "Oh, nobody will notice." That's how every act of carelessness begins and ends. No one will notice, no one will hear, no one will pay the least bit of attention. Easy to say, but is it true?

At the moment, the tempestuous quarrels have subsided; only Dussel and the van Daans are still at loggerheads. When Dussel is talking about Mrs. van D., he invariably calls her "that old bat" or "that stupid hag," and conversely, Mrs. van D. refers to our ever so learned gentleman as an "old maid" or a "touchy neurotic spinster," etc.

The pot calling the kettle black!

*Yours, Anne*

MONDAY EVENING, NOVEMBER 8, 1943

*Dearest Kitty,*

If you were to read all my letters in one sitting, you'd be struck by the fact that they were written in a variety of moods. It annoys me to be so dependent on the moods here in the Annex, but I'm not the only one: we're all subject to them. If I'm engrossed in a book, I have to rearrange my thoughts before I can mingle with other people, because otherwise they might think I was strange. As you can see, I'm currently in the middle of a depression. I couldn't really tell you what set it off, but I think it stems from my cowardice, which confronts me at every turn. This evening, when Bep was still here, the doorbell rang long and loud. I instantly turned white, my stomach churned, and my heart beat wildly – and all because I was afraid.

At night in bed I see myself alone in a dungeon, without Father and Mother. Or I'm roaming the streets, or the Annex is on fire, or they come in the middle of the night to take us away and I crawl under my bed in desperation. I see everything as if it were actually taking place. And to think it might all happen soon!

Miep often says she envies us because we have such peace and quiet here. That may be true, but she's obviously not thinking about our fear.

I simply can't imagine the world will ever be normal again for us. I do talk about "after the war," but it's as if I were talking about a castle in the air, something that can never come true.

I see the eight of us in the Annex as if we were a patch of blue sky surrounded by menacing black clouds. The perfectly round spot on which we're standing is still safe, but the clouds are moving in on us, and the ring between us and the approaching danger is being pulled tighter and tighter. We're surrounded by darkness and danger, and in our desperate search for a way out we keep bumping into each other. We look at the fighting down below and the peace and beauty up above. In the meantime, we've been cut off by the dark mass of clouds, so that we can go neither up nor down. It looms before us like an impenetrable wall, trying to crush us, but not yet able to. I can only cry out and implore, "Oh, ring, ring, open wide and let us out!"

*Yours, Anne*

THURSDAY, NOVEMBER 11, 1943

*Dearest Kitty,*
    I have a good title for this chapter:

*Ode to My Fountain Pen*
*In Memoriam*

My fountain pen was always one of my most prized possessions; I valued it highly, especially because it had a thick nib, and I can only write neatly with thick nibs. It has led a long and interesting fountain-pen life, which I will summarize below.

When I was nine, my fountain pen (packed in cotton) arrived as a "sample of no commercial value" all the way from Aachen, where my grandmother (the kindly donor) used to live. I lay in bed with the flu, while the February winds howled around the apartment house. This splendid fountain pen came in a red leather case, and I showed it to my girlfriends the first chance I got. Me, Anne Frank, the proud owner of a fountain pen.

When I was ten, I was allowed to take the pen to school, and to my surprise, the teacher even let me write with it. When I was eleven, however, my treasure had to be tucked away again, because my sixth-grade teacher allowed us to use only school pens and inkpots. When I was twelve, I started at the Jewish Lyceum and my fountain pen was given a new case in honor of the occasion. Not only did it have room for a pencil, it also had a zipper, which was much more impressive. When I was thirteen, the fountain pen went with me to the Annex, and together we've raced through countless diaries and compositions. I'd turned fourteen and my fountain pen was enjoying the last year of its life with me when . . .

It was just after five on Friday afternoon. I came out of my room and was about to sit down at the table to write when I was roughly pushed to one side to make room for Margot and Father, who wanted to practice their Latin. The fountain pen remained unused on the table, while its owner, sighing, was forced to make do with a very tiny corner of the table, where she began rubbing beans. That's how we remove mold from the beans and restore them to their original state. At a quarter to six I swept the floor, dumped the dirt into a newspaper, along with the rotten beans, and tossed it into the stove. A giant flame shot up, and I thought it was wonderful that the stove, which had been gasping its last breath, had made such a miraculous recovery.

All was quiet again. The Latin students had left, and I sat down at the table to pick up where I'd left off. But no matter where I looked, my fountain pen was nowhere in sight. I took another look. Margot looked, Mother looked, Father looked, Dussel looked. But it had vanished.

"Maybe it fell in the stove, along with the beans!" Margot suggested.

"No, it couldn't have!" I replied.

But that evening, when my fountain pen still hadn't turned up, we all assumed it had been burned, especially because celluloid is highly inflammable. Our darkest fears were confirmed the next day when Father went to empty the stove and discovered the clip, used to fasten it to a pocket, among the ashes. Not a trace of the gold nib was left. "It must have melted into stone," Father conjectured.

I'm left with one consolation, small though it may be: my fountain pen was cremated, just as I would like to be someday!

*Yours, Anne*

*Dearest Kitty,* WEDNESDAY, NOVEMBER 17, 1943

Recent events have the house rocking on its foundations. Owing to an outbreak of diphtheria at Bep's, she won't be allowed to come in contact with us for six weeks. Without her, the cooking and shopping will be very difficult, not to mention how much we'll miss her company. Mr. Kleiman is still in bed and has eaten nothing but gruel for three weeks. Mr. Kugler is up to his neck in work.

Margot sends her Latin lessons to a teacher, who corrects and then returns them. She's registered under Bep's name. The teacher's very nice, and witty too. I bet he's glad to have such a smart student.

Dussel is in a turmoil and we don't know why. It all began with Dussel's saying nothing when he was upstairs; he didn't exchange so much as a word with either Mr. or Mrs. van Daan. We all noticed it. This went on for a few days, and then Mother took the opportunity to warn him about Mrs. van D., who could make life miserable for him. Dussel said Mr. van Daan had started the silent treatment and he had no intention of breaking it. I should explain that yesterday was November 16, the first anniversary of his living in the Annex. Mother received a plant in honor of the occasion, but Mrs. van Daan, who had alluded to the date for weeks and made no bones about the fact that she thought Dussel should treat us to dinner, received nothing. Instead of making use of the opportunity to thank us – for the first time – for unselfishly taking him in, he didn't utter a word. And on the morning of the sixteenth, when I asked him whether I should offer him my congratulations or my condolences, he replied that either one would do. Mother, having cast herself in the role of peacemaker, made no headway whatsoever, and the situation finally ended in a draw.

I can say without exaggeration that Dussel has definitely got a screw loose. We often laugh to ourselves because he has no memory, no fixed opinions and no common sense. He's amused us more than once by trying to pass on the news he's just heard, since the message invariably gets garbled in transmission. Furthermore, he answers every reproach or accusation with a load of fine promises, which he never manages to keep.

"*Der Mann hat einen grossen Geist*
*Und ist so klein von Taten!*"*

                                                        *Yours, Anne*

---

*A well-known expression: 'The spirit of the man is great, / How puny are his deeds."

SATURDAY, NOVEMBER 27, 1943
*Dearest Kitty,*

Last night, just as I was falling asleep, Hanneli suddenly appeared before me.

I saw her there, dressed in rags, her face thin and worn. She looked at me with such sadness and reproach in her enormous eyes that I could read the message in them: "Oh, Anne, why have you deserted me? Help me, help me, rescue me from this hell!"

And I can't help her. I can only stand by and watch while other people suffer and die. All I can do is pray to God to bring her back to us. I saw Hanneli, and no one else, and I understood why. I misjudged her, wasn't mature enough to understand how difficult it was for her. She was devoted to her girlfriend, and it must have seemed as though I were trying to take her away. The poor thing, she must have felt awful! I know, because I recognize the feeling in myself! I had an occasional flash of understanding, but then got selfishly wrapped up again in my own problems and pleasures.

It was mean of me to treat her that way, and now she was looking at me, oh so helplessly, with her pale face and beseeching eyes. If only I could help her! Dear God, I have everything I could wish for, while fate has her in its deadly clutches. She was as devout as I am, maybe even more so, and she too wanted to do what was right. But then why have I been chosen to live, while she's probably going to die? What's the difference between us? Why are we now so far apart?

To be honest, I hadn't thought of her for months – no, for at least a year. I hadn't forgotten her entirely, and yet it wasn't until I saw her before me that I thought of all her suffering.

Oh, Hanneli, I hope that if you live to the end of the war and return to us, I'll be able to take you in and make up for the wrong I've done you.

But even if I were ever in a position to help, she wouldn't need it more than she does now. I wonder if she ever thinks of me; and what she's feeling?

Merciful God, comfort her, so that at least she won't be alone. Oh, if only You could tell her I'm thinking of her with compassion and love, it might help her go on.

I've got to stop dwelling on this. It won't get me anywhere. I keep seeing her enormous eyes, and they haunt me. Does Hanneli really and truly believe in God, or has religion merely been foisted upon her? I don't even know that. I never took the trouble to ask.

Hanneli, Hanneli, if only I could take you away, if only I could share everything I have with you. It's too late. I can't help, or undo the wrong I've done. But I'll never forget her again and I'll always pray for her!

*Yours, Anne*

MONDAY, DECEMBER 6, 1943

*Dearest Kitty,*

The closer it got to St. Nicholas Day, the more we all thought back to last year's festively decorated basket. More than anyone, I thought it would be terrible to skip a celebration this year. After long deliberation, I finally came up with an idea, something funny. I consulted Pim, and a week ago we set to work writing a verse for each person.

Sunday evening at a quarter to eight we trooped upstairs carrying the big laundry basket, which had been decorated with cutouts and bows made of pink and blue carbon paper. On top was a large piece of brown wrapping paper with a note attached. Everyone was rather amazed at the sheer size of the gift. I removed the note and read it aloud:

*"Once again St. Nicholas Day*
*Has even come to our hideaway;*
*It won't be quite as fun, I fear,*
*As the happy day we had last year.*
*Then we were hopeful, no reason to doubt*
*That optimism would win the bout,*
*And by the time this year came round,*
*We'd all be free, and safe and sound.*
*Still, let's not forget it's St. Nicholas Day,*
*Though we've nothing left to give away.*
*We'll have to find something else to do:*
*So everyone please look in their shoe!"*

As each person took their own shoe out of the basket, there was a roar of laughter. Inside each shoe was a little paper package addressed to its owner.

*Yours, Anne*

*Dearest Kitty,*

A bad case of flu has prevented me from writing to you until today. Being sick here is dreadful. With every cough, I had to duck under the blanket – once, twice, three times – and try to keep from coughing anymore. Most of the time the tickle refused to go away, so I had to drink milk with honey, sugar or cough drops. I get dizzy just thinking about all the cures I've been subjected to: sweating out the fever, steam treatment, wet compresses, dry compresses, hot drinks, swabbing my throat, lying still, heating pad, hot-water bottles, lemonade and, every two hours, the thermometer. Will these remedies really make you better? The worst part was when Mr. Dussel decided to play doctor and lay his pomaded head on my bare chest to listen to the sounds. Not only did his hair tickle, but I was embarrassed, even though he went to school thirty years ago and does have some kind of medical degree. Why should he lay his head on my heart? After all, he's not my boyfriend! For that matter, he wouldn't be able to tell a healthy sound from an unhealthy one. He'd have to have his ears cleaned first, since he's becoming alarmingly hard of hearing. But enough about my illness. I'm fit as a fiddle again. I've grown almost half an inch and gained two pounds. I'm pale, but itching to get back to my books.

*Ausnahmsweise** (the only word that will do here), we're all getting on well together. No squabbles, though that probably won't last long. There hasn't been such peace and quiet in this house for at least six months.

Bep is still in isolation, but any day now her sister will no longer be contagious.

For Christmas, we're getting extra cooking oil, candy and molasses. For Hanukkah, Mr. Dussel gave Mrs. van Daan and Mother a beautiful cake, which he'd asked Miep to bake. On top

*By way of exception.

of all the work she has to do! Margot and I received a brooch made out of a penny, all bright and shiny. I can't really describe it, but it's lovely.

I also have a Christmas present for Miep and Bep. For a whole month I've saved up the sugar I put on my hot cereal, and Mr. Kleiman has used it to have fondant made.

The weather is drizzly and overcast, the stove stinks, and the food lies heavily on our stomachs, producing a variety of rumbles.

The war is at an impasse, spirits are low.

*Yours, Anne*

*Dear Kitty,*
FRIDAY, DECEMBER 24, 1943

As I've written you many times before, moods have a tendency to affect us quite a bit here, and in my case it's been getting worse lately. *"Himmelhoch jauchzend, zu Tode betrübt"* * certainly applies to me. I'm "on top of the world" when I think of how fortunate we are and compare myself to other Jewish children, and "in the depths of despair" when, for example, Mrs. Kleiman comes by and talks about Jopie's hockey club, canoe trips, school plays and afternoon teas with friends.

I don't think I'm jealous of Jopie, but I long to have a really good time for once and to laugh so hard it hurts. We're stuck in this house like lepers, especially during winter and the Christmas and New Year's holidays. Actually, I shouldn't even be writing this, since it makes me seem so ungrateful, but I can't keep everything to myself, so I'll repeat what I said at the beginning: "Paper is more patient than people."

Whenever someone comes in from outside, with the wind in their clothes and the cold on their cheeks, I feel like burying my head under the blankets to keep from thinking, "When will we be allowed to breathe fresh air again?" I can't do that – on the contrary, I have to hold my head up high and put a bold face on things, but the thoughts keep coming anyway. Not just once, but over and over.

Believe me, if you've been shut up for a year and a half, it can

---

*A famous line from Goethe: "On top of the world, or in the depths of despair."

get to be too much for you sometimes. But feelings can't be ignored, no matter how unjust or ungrateful they seem. I long to ride a bike, dance, whistle, look at the world, feel young and know that I'm free, and yet I can't let it show. Just imagine what would happen if all eight of us were to feel sorry for ourselves or walk around with the discontent clearly visible on our faces. Where would that get us? I sometimes wonder if anyone will ever understand what I mean, if anyone will ever overlook my ingratitude and not worry about whether or not I'm Jewish and merely see me as a teenager badly in need of some good plain fun. I don't know, and I wouldn't be able to talk about it with anyone, since I'm sure I'd start to cry. Crying can bring relief, as long as you don't cry alone. Despite all my theories and efforts, I miss – every day and every hour of the day – having a mother who understands me. That's why with everything I do and write, I imagine the kind of mom I'd like to be to my children later on. The kind of mom who doesn't take everything people say too seriously, but who does take *me* seriously. I find it difficult to describe what I mean, but the word "mom" says it all. Do you know what I've come up with? In order to give me the feeling of calling my mother something that sounds like "Mom," I often call her "Momsy." Sometimes I shorten it to "Moms": an imperfect "Mom." I wish I could honor her by removing the "s." It's a good thing she doesn't realize this, since it would only make her unhappy.

Well, that's enough of that. My writing has raised me somewhat from "the depths of despair."

*Yours, Anne*

It's the day after Christmas, and I can't help thinking about Pim and the story he told me this time last year. I didn't understand the meaning of his words then as well as I do now. If only he'd bring it up again, I might be able to show him I understood what he meant!

I think Pim told me because he, who knows the "intimate secrets" of so many others, needed to express his own feelings for once; Pim never talks about himself, and I don't think Margot has any inkling of what he's been through. Poor Pim, he can't fool me into thinking he's forgotten that girl. He never will.

It's made him very accommodating, since he's not blind to
Mother's faults. I hope I'm going to be a little like him, without
having to go through what he has!

*Anne*


MONDAY, DECEMBER 27, 1943

Friday evening, for the first time in my life, I received a
Christmas present. Mr. Kleiman, Mr. Kugler and the girls had
prepared a wonderful surprise for us. Miep made a delicious
Christmas cake with "Peace 1944" written on top, and Bep
provided a batch of cookies that was up to prewar standards.

There was a jar of yogurt for Peter, Margot and me, and a
bottle of beer for each of the adults. And once again everything
was wrapped so nicely, with pretty pictures glued to the packages. For the rest, the holidays passed by quickly for us.

*Anne*


WEDNESDAY, DECEMBER 29, 1943

I was very sad again last night. Grandma and Hanneli came to
me once more. Grandma, oh, my sweet Grandma. How little we
understood what she suffered, how kind she always was and what
an interest she took in everything that concerned us. And to
think that all that time she was carefully guarding her terrible
secret.*

Grandma was always so loyal and good. She would never have
let any of us down. Whatever happened, no matter how much
I misbehaved, Grandma always stuck up for me. Grandma, did
you love me, or did you not understand me either? I don't know.
How lonely Grandma must have been, in spite of us. You can be
lonely even when you're loved by many people, since you're still
not anybody's "one and only."

And Hanneli? Is she still alive? What's she doing? Dear God,
watch over her and bring her back to us. Hanneli, you're a
reminder of what my fate might have been. I keep seeing myself
in your place. So why am I often miserable about what goes on
here? Shouldn't I be happy, contented and glad, except when I'm
thinking of Hanneli and those suffering along with her?
I'm selfish and cowardly. Why do I always think and dream the

* Anne's grandmother was terminally ill.

most awful things and want to scream in terror? Because, in spite of everything, I still don't have enough faith in God. He's given me so much, which I don't deserve, and yet each day I make so many mistakes!

Thinking about the suffering of those you hold dear can reduce you to tears; in fact, you could spend the whole day crying. The most you can do is pray for God to perform a miracle and save at least some of them. And I hope I'm doing enough of that!

*Anne*

*Dearest Kitty,*                              THURSDAY, DECEMBER 30, 1943

Since the last raging quarrels, things have settled down here, not only between ourselves, Dussel and "upstairs," but also between Mr. and Mrs. van D. Nevertheless, a few dark thunderclouds are heading this way, and all because of . . . food. Mrs. van D. came up with the ridiculous idea of frying fewer potatoes in the morning and saving them for later in the day. Mother and Dussel and the rest of us didn't agree with her, so now we're dividing up the potatoes as well. It seems the fats and oils aren't being doled out fairly, and Mother's going to have to put a stop to it. I'll let you know if there are any interesting developments. For the last few months now we've been splitting up the meat (theirs with fat, ours without), the soup (they eat it, we don't), the potatoes (theirs peeled, ours not), the extras and now the fried potatoes too.

If only we could split up completely!

*Yours, Anne*

PS. Bep had a picture postcard of the entire Royal Family copied for me. Juliana looks very young, and so does the Queen. The three little girls are adorable. It was incredibly nice of Bep, don't you think?

*Dearest Kitty,*                              SUNDAY, JANUARY 2, 1944

This morning, when I had nothing to do, I leafed through the pages of my diary and came across so many letters dealing with the subject of "Mother" in such strong terms that I was shocked. I said to myself, "Anne, is that really you talking about hate? Oh, Anne, how could you?"

I continued to sit with the open book in my hand and wonder why I was filled with so much anger and hate that I had to confide it all to you. I tried to understand the Anne of last year and make apologies for her, because as long as I leave you with these accusations and don't attempt to explain what prompted them, my conscience won't be clear. I was suffering then (and still do) from moods that kept my head under water (figuratively speaking) and allowed me to see things only from my own perspective, without calmly considering what the others – those whom I, with my mercurial temperament, had hurt or offended – had said, and then acting as they would have done.

I hid inside myself, thought of no one but myself and calmly wrote down all my joy, sarcasm and sorrow in my diary. Because this diary has become a kind of memory book, it means a great deal to me, but I could easily write "over and done with" on many of its pages.

I was furious at Mother (and still am a lot of the time). It's true, she didn't understand me, but I didn't understand her either. Because she loved me, she was tender and affectionate, but because of the difficult situations I put her in, and the sad circumstances in which she found herself, she was nervous and irritable, so I can understand why she was often short with me.

I was offended, took it far too much to heart and was insolent and beastly to her, which, in turn, made her unhappy. We were caught in a vicious circle of unpleasantness and sorrow. Not a very happy period for either of us, but at least it's coming to an end. I didn't want to see what was going on, and I felt very sorry for myself, but that's understandable too.

Those violent outbursts on paper are simply expressions of anger that, in normal life, I could have worked off by locking myself in my room and stamping my foot a few times or calling Mother names behind her back.

The period of tearfully passing judgment on Mother is over. I've grown wiser and Mother's nerves are a bit steadier. Most of the time I manage to hold my tongue when I'm annoyed, and she does too; so on the surface, we seem to be getting along better. But there's one thing I can't do, and that's to love Mother with the devotion of a child.

I soothe my conscience with the thought that it's better for unkind words to be down on paper than for Mother to have to carry them around in her heart.

*Yours, Anne*

*Dearest Kitty,*                       THURSDAY, JANUARY 6, 1944

Today I have two things to confess. It's going to take a long time, but I have to tell them to someone, and you're the most likely candidate, since I know you'll keep a secret, no matter what happens.

The first is about Mother. As you know, I've frequently complained about her and then tried my best to be nice. I've suddenly realized what's wrong with her. Mother has said that she sees us more as friends than as daughters. That's all very nice, of course, except that a friend can't take the place of a mother. I need my mother to set a good example and be a person I can respect, but in most matters she's an example of what *not* to do. I have the feeling that Margot thinks so differently about these things that she'd never be able to understand what I've just told you. And Father avoids all conversations having to do with Mother.

I imagine a mother as a woman who, first and foremost, possesses a great deal of tact, especially toward her adolescent children, and not one who, like Momsy, pokes fun at me when I cry. Not because I'm in pain, but because of other things.

This may seem trivial, but there's one incident I've never forgiven her for. It happened one day when I had to go to the dentist. Mother and Margot planned to go with me and agreed I should take my bicycle. When the dentist was finished and we were back outside, Margot and Mother very sweetly informed me that they were going downtown to buy or look at something, I don't remember what, and of course I wanted to go along. But they said I couldn't come because I had my bike with me. Tears of rage rushed to my eyes, and Margot and Mother began laughing at me. I was so furious that I stuck my tongue out at them, right there on the street. A little old lady happened to be passing by, and she looked terribly shocked. I rode my bike home and must have cried for hours. Strangely enough, even though

Mother has wounded me thousands of times, this particular wound still stings whenever I think of how angry I was.

I find it difficult to confess the second one because it's about myself. I'm not prudish, Kitty, and yet every time they give a blow-by-blow account of their trips to the bathroom, which they often do, my whole body rises in revolt.

Yesterday I read an article on blushing by Sis Heyster. It was as if she'd addressed it directly to me. Not that I blush easily, but the rest of the article did apply. What she basically says is that during puberty girls withdraw into themselves and begin thinking about the wondrous changes taking place in their bodies. I feel that too, which probably accounts for my recent embarrassment over Margot, Mother and Father. On the other hand, Margot is a lot shyer than I am, and yet she's not in the least embarrassed.

I think that what's happening to me is so wonderful, and I don't just mean the changes taking place on the outside of my body, but also those on the inside. I never discuss myself or any of these things with others, which is why I have to talk about them to myself. Whenever I get my period (and that's only been three times), I have the feeling that in spite of all the pain, discomfort and mess, I'm carrying around a sweet secret. So even though it's a nuisance, in a certain way I'm always looking forward to the time when I'll feel that secret inside me once again.

Sis Heyster also writes that girls my age feel very insecure about themselves and are just beginning to discover that they're individuals with their own ideas, thoughts and habits. I'd just turned thirteen when I came here, so I started thinking about myself and realized that I've become an "independent person" sooner than most girls. Sometimes when I lie in bed at night I feel a terrible urge to touch my breasts and listen to the quiet, steady beating of my heart.

Unconsciously, I had these feelings even before I came here. Once when I was spending the night at Jacque's, I could no longer restrain my curiosity about her body, which she'd always hidden from me and which I'd never seen. I asked her whether, as proof of our friendship, we could touch each other's breasts. Jacque refused. I also had a terrible desire to kiss her, which I did.

Every time I see a female nude, such as the Venus in my art history book, I go into ecstasy. Sometimes I find them so exquisite I have to struggle to hold back my tears. If only I had a girlfriend!

*Dearest Kitty,*

THURSDAY, JANUARY 6, 1944

My longing for someone to talk to has become so unbearable that I somehow took it into my head to select Peter for this role. On the few occasions when I have gone to Peter's room during the day, I've always thought it was nice and cozy. But Peter's too polite to show someone the door when they're bothering him, so I've never dared to stay long. I've always been afraid he'd think I was a pest. I've been looking for an excuse to linger in his room and get him talking without his noticing, and yesterday I got my chance. Peter, you see, is currently going through a crossword-puzzle craze, and he doesn't do anything else all day. I was helping him, and we soon wound up sitting across from each other at his table, Peter on the chair and me on the divan.

It gave me a wonderful feeling when I looked into his dark blue eyes and saw how bashful my unexpected visit had made him. I could read his innermost thoughts, and in his face I saw a look of helplessness and uncertainty as to how to behave, and at the same time a flicker of awareness of his masculinity. I saw his shyness, and I melted. I wanted to say, "Tell me about yourself. Look beneath my chatty exterior." But I found that it was easier to think up questions than to ask them.

The evening came to a close, and nothing happened, except that I told him about the article on blushing. Not what I wrote you, of course, just that he would grow more secure as he got older.

That night I lay in bed and cried my eyes out, all the while making sure no one could hear me. The idea that I had to beg Peter for favors was simply revolting. But people will do almost anything to satisfy their longings; take me, for example, I've made up my mind to visit Peter more often and, somehow, get him to talk to me.

You mustn't think I'm in love with Peter, because I'm not.

If the van Daans had had a daughter instead of a son, I'd have tried to make friends with her.

This morning I woke up just before seven and immediately remembered what I'd been dreaming about. I was sitting on a chair and across from me was Peter... Peter Schiff. We were looking at Mary Bos's sketchbook. The dream was so vivid I can even remember some of the drawings. But that wasn't all – the dream went on. Peter's eyes suddenly met mine, and I stared for a long time into those velvety brown eyes. Then he said very softly, "If I'd only known, I'd have come to you long ago!" I turned abruptly away, overcome by emotion. And then I felt a soft, oh-so-cool and gentle cheek against mine, and it felt so good, so good...

At that point I woke up, still feeling his cheek against mine and his brown eyes staring deep into my heart, so deep that he could read how much I'd loved him and how much I still do. Again my eyes filled with tears, and I was sad because I'd lost him once more, and yet at the same time glad because I knew with certainty that Peter is still the only one for me.

It's funny, but I often have such vivid images in my dreams. One night I saw Grammy* so clearly that I could even make out her skin of soft, crinkly velvet. Another time Grandma appeared to me as a guardian angel. After that it was Hanneli, who still symbolizes to me the suffering of my friends as well as that of Jews in general, so that when I'm praying for her, I'm also praying for all the Jews and all those in need.

And now Peter, my dearest Peter. I've never had such a clear mental image of him. I don't need a photograph, I can see him oh so well.

*Yours, Anne*

*Dearest Kitty,* FRIDAY, JANUARY 7, 1944

I'm such an idiot. I forgot that I haven't yet told you the story of my one true love.

When I was a little girl, way back in kindergarten, I took a liking to Sally Kimmel. His father was gone, and he and his

---

*Grammy is Anne's grandmother on her father's side, and Grandma her grandmother on her mother's side.

mother lived with an aunt. One of Sally's cousins was a good-looking, slender, dark-haired boy named Appy, who later turned out to look like a movie idol and aroused more admiration than the short, comical, chubby Sally. For a long time we went everywhere together, but aside from that, my love was unrequited until Peter crossed my path. I had an out-and-out crush on him. He liked me too, and we were inseparable for one whole summer. I can still see us walking hand in hand through our neighborhood, Peter in a white cotton suit and me in a short summer dress. At the end of the summer vacation he went to the seventh grade at the middle school, while I was in the sixth grade at the grammar school. He'd pick me up on the way home, or I'd pick him up. Peter was the ideal boy: tall, good-looking and slender, with a serious, quiet and intelligent face. He had dark hair, beautiful brown eyes, ruddy cheeks and a nicely pointed nose. I was crazy about his smile, which made him look so boyish and mischievous.

I'd gone away to the countryside during summer vacation, and when I came back, Peter was no longer at his old address; he'd moved and was living with a much older boy, who apparently told him I was just a kid, because Peter stopped seeing me. I loved him so much that I didn't want to face the truth. I kept clinging to him until the day I finally realized that if I continued to chase after him, people would say I was boy-crazy.

The years went by. Peter hung around with girls his own age and no longer bothered to say hello to me. I started school at the Jewish Lyceum, and several boys in my class were in love with me. I enjoyed it and felt honored by their attentions, but that was all. Later on, Hello had a terrible crush on me, but as I've already told you, I never fell in love again.

There's a saying: "Time heals all wounds." That's how it was with me. I told myself I'd forgotten Peter and no longer liked him in the least. But my memories of him were so strong that I had to admit to myself that the only reason I no longer liked him was that I was jealous of the other girls. This morning I realized that nothing has changed; on the contrary, as I've grown older and more mature, my love has grown along with me. I can understand now that Peter thought I was childish, and yet it still hurts to think he'd forgotten me completely. I saw his face so clearly; I knew for certain that no one but Peter could have stuck in my mind that way.

I've been in an utter state of confusion today. When Father kissed me this morning, I wanted to shout, "Oh, if only you were Peter!" I've been thinking of him constantly, and all day long I've been repeating to myself, "Oh, Petel, my darling, darling Petel . . ."

Where can I find help? I simply have to go on living and praying to God that, if we ever get out of here, Peter's path will cross mine and he'll gaze into my eyes, read the love in them and say, "Oh, Anne, if I'd only known, I'd have come to you long ago."

Once when Father and I were talking about sex, he said I was too young to understand that kind of desire. But I thought I did understand it, and now I'm sure I do. Nothing is as dear to me now as my darling Petel!

I saw my face in the mirror, and it looked so different. My eyes were clear and deep, my cheeks were rosy, which they hadn't been in weeks, my mouth was much softer. I looked happy, and yet there was something so sad in my expression that the smile immediately faded from my lips. I'm not happy, since I know Petel's not thinking of me, and yet I can still feel his beautiful eyes gazing at me and his cool, soft cheek against mine . . . Oh, Petel, Petel, how am I ever going to free myself from your image? Wouldn't anyone who took your place be a poor substitute? I love you, with a love so great that it simply couldn't keep growing inside my heart, but had to leap out and reveal itself in all its magnitude.

A week ago, even a day ago, if you'd asked me, "Which of your friends do you think you'd be most likely to marry?" I'd have answered, "Sally, since he makes me feel good, peaceful and safe!" But now I'd cry, "Petel, because I love him with all my heart and all my soul. I surrender myself completely!" Except for that one thing: he may touch my face, but that's as far as it goes.

This morning I imagined I was in the front attic with Petel, sitting on the floor by the windows, and after talking for a while, we both began to cry. Moments later I felt his mouth and his wonderful cheek! Oh, Petel, come to me. Think of me, my dearest Petel!

*Dearest Kitty,*                               WEDNESDAY, JANUARY 12, 1944

Bep's been back for the last two weeks, though her sister won't be allowed back at school until next week. Bep herself spent two days in bed with a bad cold. Miep and Jan were also out for two days, with upset stomachs.

I'm currently going through a dance and ballet craze and am diligently practicing my dance steps every evening. I've made an ultramodern dance costume out of a lacy lavender slip belonging to Momsy. Bias tape is threaded through the top and tied just above the bust. A pink corded ribbon completes the ensemble. I tried to turn my tennis shoes into ballet slippers, but with no success. My stiff limbs are well on the way to becoming as limber as they used to be. A terrific exercise is to sit on the floor, place a heel in each hand and raise both legs in the air. I have to sit on a cushion, because otherwise my poor backside really takes a beating.

Everyone here is reading a book called *Salute to Freedom*. Mother thought it was extremely good because it describes a number of adolescent problems. I thought to myself, a bit ironically, "Why don't you take more interest in your own adolescents first!"

I think Mother believes that Margot and I have a better relationship with our parents than anyone in the whole wide world, and that no mother is more involved in the lives of her children than she is. She must have my sister in mind, since I don't believe Margot has the same problems and thoughts as I do. Far be it from me to point out to Mother that one of her daughters is not at all what she imagines. She'd be completely bewildered, and anyway, she'd never be able to change; I'd like to spare her that grief, especially since I know that everything would remain the same. Mother does sense that Margot loves her much more than I do, but she thinks I'm just going through a phase.

Margot's gotten much nicer. She seems a lot different than she used to be. She's not nearly as catty these days and is becoming a real friend. She no longer thinks of me as a little kid who doesn't count.

It's funny, but I can sometimes see myself as others see me. I take a leisurely look at the person called "Anne Frank" and browse through the pages of her life as though she were a stranger.

Before I came here, when I didn't think about things as much as I do now, I occasionally had the feeling that I didn't belong to Momsy, Pim and Margot and that I would always be an outsider. I sometimes went around for six months at a time pretending I was an orphan. Then I'd chastise myself for playing the victim, when really, I'd always been so fortunate. After that I'd force myself to be friendly for a while. Every morning when I heard footsteps on the stairs, I hoped it would be Mother coming to say good morning. I'd greet her warmly, because I honestly did look forward to her affectionate glance. But then she'd snap at me for having made some comment or other and I'd go off to school feeling completely discouraged. On the way home I'd make excuses for her, telling myself that she had so many worries. I'd arrive home in high spirits, chatting nineteen to the dozen, until the events of the morning would repeat themselves and I'd leave the room with my schoolbag in my hand and a pensive look on my face. Sometimes I'd decide to stay angry, but then I always had so much to talk about after school that I'd forget my resolution and want Mother to stop whatever she was doing and lend a willing ear. Then the time would come once more when I no longer listened for the steps on the stairs and felt lonely and cried into my pillow every night.

Everything has gotten much worse here. But you already knew that. Now God has sent someone to help me: Peter. I fondle my pendant, press it to my lips and think, "What do I care! Petel is mine and nobody knows it!" With this in mind, I can rise above every nasty remark. Which of the people here would suspect that so much is going on in the mind of a teenage girl?

*My dearest Kitty,*                          SATURDAY, JANUARY 15, 1944

There's no reason for me to go on describing all our quarrels and arguments down to the last detail. It's enough to tell you that we've divided many things like meat and fats and oils and are frying our own potatoes. Recently we've been eating a little extra rye bread because by four o'clock we're so hungry for dinner we can barely control our rumbling stomachs.

Mother's birthday is rapidly approaching. She received some extra sugar from Mr. Kugler, which sparked off jealousy on the part of the van Daans, because Mrs. van D. didn't receive any on her birthday. But what's the point of boring you with harsh words, spiteful conversations and tears when you know they bore us even more?

Mother has expressed a wish, which isn't likely to come true any time soon: not to have to see Mr. van Daan's face for two whole weeks. I wonder if everyone who shares a house sooner or later ends up at odds with their fellow residents. Or have we just had a stroke of bad luck? At mealtime, when Dussel helps himself to a quarter of the half-filled gravy boat and leaves the rest of us to do without, I lose my appetite and feel like jumping to my feet, knocking him off his chair and throwing him out the door.

Are most people so stingy and selfish? I've gained some insight into human nature since I came here, which is good, but I've had enough for the present. Peter says the same.

The war is going to go on despite our quarrels and our longing for freedom and fresh air, so we should try to make the best of our stay here.

I'm preaching, but I also believe that if I live here much longer, I'll turn into a dried-up old beanstalk. And all I really want is to be an honest-to-goodness teenager!

Yours, Anne

WEDNESDAY EVENING, JANUARY 19, 1944
Dearest Kitty,

I (there I go again!) don't know what's happened, but since my dream I keep noticing how I've changed. By the way, I dreamed about Peter again last night and once again I felt his eyes penetrate mine, but this dream was less vivid and not quite as beautiful as the last.

You know that I always used to be jealous of Margot's relationship with Father. There's not a trace of my jealousy left now; I still feel hurt when Father's nerves cause him to be unreasonable toward me, but then I think, "I can't blame you for being the way you are. You talk so much about the minds of children and adolescents, but you don't know the first thing about them!" I long for more than Father's affection, more than his hugs and kisses. Isn't it awful of me to be so preoccupied with myself? Shouldn't I, who want to be good and kind, forgive them first? I forgive Mother too, but every time she makes a sarcastic remark or laughs at me, it's all I can do to control myself.

I know I'm far from being what I should; will I ever be?

*Anne Frank*

PS. Father asked if I told you about the cake. For Mother's birthday, she received a real mocha cake, prewar quality, from the office. It was a really nice day! But at the moment, there's no room in my head for things like that.

SATURDAY, JANUARY 22, 1944

*Dearest Kitty,*

Can you tell me why people go to such lengths to hide their real selves? Or why I always behave very differently when I'm in the company of others? Why do people have so little trust in one another? I know there must be a reason, but sometimes I think it's horrible that you can't ever confide in anyone, not even those closest to you.

It seems as if I've grown up since the night I had that dream, as if I've become more independent. You'll be amazed when I tell you that even my attitude toward the van Daans has changed. I've stopped looking at all the discussions and arguments from my family's biased point of view. What's brought on such a radical change? Well, you see, I suddenly realized that if Mother had been different, if she'd been a real mom, our relationship would have been very, very different. Mrs. van Daan is by no means a wonderful person, yet half the arguments could have been avoided if Mother hadn't been so hard to deal with every time they got onto a tricky subject. Mrs. van Daan does have one good point, though: you can talk to her. She may be selfish, stingy and underhanded, but she'll readily back down as long as you don't provoke her and make her unreasonable. This tactic doesn't work every time, but if you're patient, you can keep trying and see how far you get.

All the conflicts about our upbringing, about not pampering children, about the food – about everything, absolutely everything – might have taken a different turn if we'd remained open and on friendly terms instead of always seeing the worst side.

I know exactly what you're going to say, Kitty. "But, Anne, are these words really coming from your lips? From you, who have had to put up with so many unkind words from upstairs? From you, who are aware of all the injustices?"

And yet they are coming from me. I want to take a fresh look at things and form my own opinion, not just ape my parents, as in the proverb "The apple never falls far from the tree." I want to reexamine the van Daans and decide for myself what's true and what's been blown out of proportion. If I wind up being disappointed in them, I can always side with Father and Mother. But if not, I can try to change their attitude. And if that doesn't work, I'll have to stick with my own opinions and judgment. I'll take every opportunity to speak openly to Mrs. van D. about our many differences and not be afraid – despite my reputation as a smart aleck – to offer my impartial opinion. I won't say anything negative about my own family, though that doesn't mean I won't defend them if somebody else does, and as of today, my gossiping is a thing of the past.

Up to now I was absolutely convinced that the van Daans were entirely to blame for the quarrels, but now I'm sure the fault was largely ours. We were right as far as the issues were concerned, but intelligent people (such as ourselves!) should have more insight into how to deal with others.

I hope I've got at least a touch of that insight, and that I'll find an occasion to put it to good use.

*Yours, Anne*

*Dearest Kitty,*                                    MONDAY, JANUARY 24, 1944

A very strange thing has happened to me. (Actually, "happened" isn't quite the right word.)

Before I came here, whenever anyone at home or at school talked about sex, they were either secretive or disgusting. Any words having to do with sex were spoken in a low whisper, and kids who weren't in the know were often laughed at. That struck me as odd, and I often wondered why people were so mysterious or obnoxious when they talked about this subject. But because I couldn't change things, I said as little as possible or asked my girlfriends for information.

After I'd learned quite a lot, Mother once said to me, "Anne, let me give you some good advice. Never discuss this with boys, and if they bring it up, don't answer them."

I still remember my exact reply. "No, of course not," I exclaimed. "Imagine!" And nothing more was said.

When we first went into hiding, Father often told me about things I'd rather have heard from Mother, and I learned the rest from books or things I picked up in conversations.

Peter van Daan wasn't ever as obnoxious about this subject as the boys at school. Or maybe just once or twice, in the beginning, though he wasn't trying to get me to talk. Mrs. van Daan once told us she'd never discussed these matters with Peter, and as far as she knew, neither had her husband. Apparently she didn't even know how much Peter knew or where he got his information.

Yesterday, when Margot, Peter and I were peeling potatoes, the conversation somehow turned to Boche. "We're still not sure whether Boche is a boy or a girl, are we?" I asked.

"Yes we are," he answered. "Boche is a tomcat."

I began to laugh. "Some tomcat if he's pregnant."

Peter and Margot joined in the laughter. You see, a month or two ago Peter informed us that Boche was sure to have kittens before long, because her stomach was rapidly swelling. However, Boche's fat tummy turned out to be due to a bunch of stolen bones. No kittens were growing inside, much less about to be born.

Peter felt called upon to defend himself against my accusation. "Come with me. You can see for yourself. I was horsing around with the cat one day, and I could definitely see it was a 'he.' "

Unable to restrain my curiosity, I went with him to the warehouse. Boche, however, wasn't receiving visitors at that hour, and was nowhere in sight. We waited for a while, but when it got cold, we went back upstairs.

Later that afternoon I heard Peter go downstairs for the second time. I mustered the courage to walk through the silent house by myself and reached the warehouse. Boche was on the packing table, playing with Peter, who was getting ready to put him on the scale and weigh him.

"Hi, do you want to have a look?" Without any preliminaries, he picked up the cat, turned him over on his back, deftly held his head and paws and began the lesson. "This is the male sexual organ, these are a few stray hairs, and that's his backside."

The cat flipped himself over and stood up on his little white feet.

If any other boy had pointed out the "male sexual organ" to me, I would never have given him a second glance. But Peter went on talking in a normal voice about what is otherwise a very awkward subject. Nor did he have any ulterior motives. By the time he'd finished, I felt so much at ease that I started acting normally too. We played with Boche, had a good time, chatted a bit and finally sauntered through the long warehouse to the door.

"Were you there when Mouschi was fixed?"

"Yeah, sure. It doesn't take long. They give the cat an anesthetic, of course."

"Do they take something out?"

"No, the vet just snips the tube. There's nothing to see on the outside."

I had to get up my nerve to ask a question, since it wasn't as "normal" as I thought. "Peter, the German word *Geschlechtsteil* means 'sexual organ,' doesn't it? But then the male and female ones have different names."

"I know that."

"The female one is a vagina, that I know, but I don't know what it's called in males."

"Hmm."

"Oh well," I said. "How are we supposed to know these words? Most of the time you just come across them by accident."

"Why wait? I'll ask my parents. They know more than I do and they've had more experience."

We were already on the stairs, so nothing more was said.

Yes, it really did happen. I'd never have talked to a girl about this in such a normal tone of voice. I'm also certain that this isn't what Mother meant when she warned me about boys.

All the same, I wasn't exactly my usual self for the rest of the day. When I thought back to our talk, it struck me as odd. But I've learned at least one thing: there are young people, even those of the opposite sex, who can discuss these things naturally, without cracking jokes.

Is Peter really going to ask his parents a lot of questions? Is he really the way he seemed yesterday?

Oh, what do I know?!!!

*Yours, Anne*

*Dearest Kitty,*                              FRIDAY, JANUARY 28, 1944

In recent weeks I've developed a great liking for family trees and the genealogical tables of royal families. I've come to the conclusion that once you begin your search, you have to keep digging deeper and deeper into the past, which leads you to even more interesting discoveries.

Although I'm extremely diligent when it comes to my school-work and can pretty much follow the BBC Home Service on the radio, I still spend many of my Sundays sorting out and looking over my movie-star collection, which has grown to a very respectable size. Mr. Kugler makes me happy every Monday by bringing me a copy of *Cinema & Theater* magazine. The less worldly members of our household often refer to this small indulgence as a waste of money, yet they never fail to be surprised at how accurately I can list the actors in any given movie, even after a year. Bep, who often goes to the movies with her boyfriend on her day off, tells me on Saturday the name of the show they're going to see, and I then proceed to rattle off the names of the leading actors and actresses and the reviews. Moms recently remarked that I wouldn't need to go to the movies later on, because I know all the plots, the names of the stars and the reviews by heart.

Whenever I come sailing in with a new hairstyle, I can read the disapproval on their faces, and I can be sure someone will ask which movie star I'm trying to imitate. My reply, that it's my own invention, is greeted with skepticism. As for the hairdo, it doesn't hold its set for more than half an hour. By that time I'm so sick and tired of their remarks that I race to the bathroom and restore my hair to its normal mass of curls.

*Yours, Anne*

*Dearest Kitty,*                          FRIDAY, JANUARY 28, 1944

This morning I was wondering whether you ever felt like a cow, having to chew my stale news over and over again until you're so fed up with the monotonous fare that you yawn and secretly wish Anne would dig up something new.

Sorry, I know you find it dull as ditchwater, but imagine how sick and tired I am of hearing the same old stuff. If the talk at mealtime isn't about politics or good food, then Mother or Mrs. van D. trot out stories about their childhood that we've heard a thousand times before, or Dussel goes on and on about beautiful racehorses, his Charlotte's extensive wardrobe, leaky rowboats, boys who can swim at the age of four, aching muscles and frightened patients. It all boils down to this: whenever one of the eight of us opens his mouth, the other seven can finish the story for him. We know the punch line of every joke before it gets told, so that whoever's telling it is left to laugh alone. The various milkmen, grocers and butchers of the two former housewives have been praised to the skies or run into the ground so many times that in our imaginations they've grown as old as Methuselah; there's absolutely no chance of anything new or fresh being brought up for discussion in the Annex.

Still, all this might be bearable if only the grown-ups weren't in the habit of repeating the stories we hear from Mr. Kleiman, Jan or Miep, each time embellishing them with a few details of their own, so that I often have to pinch my arm under the table to keep myself from setting the enthusiastic storyteller on the right track. Little children, such as Anne, must never, ever correct their elders, no matter how many blunders they make or how often they let their imaginations run away with them.

Jan and Mr. Kleiman love talking about people who have gone underground or into hiding; they know we're eager to hear about others in our situation and that we truly sympathize with the sorrow of those who've been arrested as well as the joy of prisoners who've been freed.

Going underground or into hiding has become as routine as the proverbial pipe and slippers that used to await the man of the house after a long day at work. There are many resistance groups, such as Free Netherlands, that forge identity cards, provide financial support to those in hiding, organize hiding places and find work for young Christians who go underground. It's amazing how much these generous and unselfish people do, risking their own lives, to help and save others.

The best example of this is our own helpers, who have managed to pull us through so far and will hopefully bring us safely to shore, because otherwise they'll find themselves sharing the fate of those they're trying to protect. Never have they uttered a single word about the burden we must be, never have they complained that we're too much trouble. They come upstairs every day and talk to the men about business and politics, to the women about food and wartime difficulties and to the children about books and newspapers. They put on their most cheerful expressions, bring flowers and gifts for birthdays and holidays and are always ready to do what they can. That's something we should never forget; while others display their heroism in battle or against the Germans, our helpers prove theirs every day by their good spirits and affection.

The most bizarre stories are making the rounds, yet most of them are really true. For instance, Mr. Kleiman reported this week that a soccer match was held in the province of Gelderland; one team consisted entirely of men who had gone underground, and the other of eleven Military Policemen. In Hilversum, new registration cards were issued. In order for the many people in hiding to get their rations (you have to show this card to obtain your ration book or else pay 60 guilders a book), the registrar asked all those hiding in that district to pick up their cards at a specified hour, when the documents could be collected at a separate table.

All the same, you have to be careful that stunts like these don't reach the ears of the Germans.

                                                              *Yours, Anne*

*My dearest Kit,*                                   SUNDAY, JANUARY 30, 1944

Another Sunday has rolled around; I don't mind them as much as I did in the beginning, but they're boring enough.

I still haven't gone to the warehouse yet, but maybe sometime soon. Last night I went downstairs in the dark, all by myself, after having been there with Father a few nights before. I stood at the top of the stairs while German planes flew back and forth, and I knew I was on my own, that I couldn't count on others for support. My fear vanished. I looked up at the sky and trusted in God.

I have an intense need to be alone. Father has noticed I'm not my usual self, but I can't tell him what's bothering me. All I want to do is scream "Let me be, leave me alone!"

Who knows, perhaps the day will come when I'm left alone more than I'd like!

*Anne Frank*

*Dearest Kitty,*                                   THURSDAY, FEBRUARY 3, 1944

Invasion fever is mounting daily throughout the country. If you were here, I'm sure you'd be as impressed as I am at the many preparations, though you'd no doubt laugh at all the fuss we're making. Who knows, it may all be for nothing!

The papers are full of invasion news and are driving everyone insane with such statements as: "In the event of a British landing in Holland, the Germans will do what they can to defend the country, even flooding it, if necessary." They've published maps of Holland with the potential flood areas marked. Since large portions of Amsterdam were shaded in, our first question was what we should do if the water in the streets rose to above our waists. This tricky question elicited a variety of responses:

"It'll be impossible to walk or ride a bike, so we'll have to wade through the water."

"Don't be silly. We'll have to try and swim. We'll all put on our bathing suits and caps and swim underwater as much as we can, so nobody can see we're Jews."

"Oh, baloney! I can just imagine the ladies swimming with the rats biting their legs!" (That was a man, of course; we'll see who screams loudest!)

"We won't even be able to leave the house. The warehouse is so unstable it'll collapse if there's a flood."

"Listen, everyone, all joking aside, we really ought to try and get a boat."

"Why bother? I have a better idea. We can each take a packing crate from the attic and row with a wooden spoon."

"I'm going to walk on stilts. I used to be a whiz at it when I was young."

"Jan Gies won't need to. He'll let his wife ride piggyback, and then Miep will be on stilts."

So now you have a rough idea of what's going on, don't you, Kit? This lighthearted banter is all very amusing, but reality will prove otherwise. The second question about the invasion was bound to arise: what should we do if the Germans evacuate Amsterdam?

"Leave the city along with the others. Disguise ourselves as well as we can."

"Whatever happens, don't go outside! The best thing to do is to stay put! The Germans are capable of herding the entire population of Holland into Germany, where they'll all die."

"Of course we'll stay here. This is the safest place. We'll try to talk Kleiman and his family into coming here to live with us. We'll somehow get hold of a bag of wood shavings, so we can sleep on the floor. Let's ask Miep and Kleiman to bring some blankets, just in case. And we'll order some extra cereal grains to supplement the sixty-five pounds we already have. Jan can try to find some more beans. At the moment we've got about sixty-five pounds of beans and ten pounds of split peas. And don't forget the fifty cans of vegetables."

"What about the rest, Mother? Give us the latest figures."

"Ten cans of fish, forty cans of milk, twenty pounds of powdered milk, three bottles of oil, four crocks of butter, four jars of meat, two big jars of strawberries, two jars of raspberries, twenty jars of tomatoes, ten pounds of oatmeal, nine pounds of rice. That's it."

Our provisions are holding out fairly well. All the same, we have to feed the office staff, which means dipping into our stock every week, so it's not as much as it seems. We have enough coal and firewood, candles too.

"Let's all make little moneybags to hide in our clothes so we can take our money with us if we need to leave here."

"We can make lists of what to take first in case we have to run for it, and pack our knapsacks in advance."

"When the time comes, we'll put two people on the lookout, one in the loft at the front of the house and one in the back."

"Hey, what's the use of so much food if there isn't any water, gas or electricity?"

"We'll have to cook on the wood stove. Filter the water and boil it. We should clean some big jugs and fill them with water. We can also store water in the three kettles we use for canning, and in the washtub."

"Besides, we still have about two hundred and thirty pounds of winter potatoes in the spice storeroom."

All day long that's all I hear. Invasion, invasion, nothing but invasion. Arguments about going hungry, dying, bombs, fire extinguishers, sleeping bags, identity cards, poison gas, etc., etc. Not exactly cheerful.

A good example of the explicit warnings of the male contingent is the following conversation with Jan:

Annex: "We're afraid that when the Germans retreat, they'll take the entire population with them."

Jan: "That's impossible. They haven't got enough trains."

Annex: "Trains? Do you really think they'd put civilians on trains? Absolutely not. Everyone would have to hoof it." (Or, as Dussel always says, *per pedes apostolorum*.)

Jan: "I can't believe that. You're always looking on the dark side. What reason would they have to round up all the civilians and take them along?"

Annex: "Don't you remember Goebbels saying that if the Germans have to go, they'll slam the doors to all the occupied territories behind them?"

Jan: "They've said a lot of things."

Annex: "Do you think the Germans are too noble or humane

to do it? Their reasoning is: if we go under, we'll drag everyone else down with us."

Jan: "You can say what you like, I just don't believe it."

Annex: "It's always the same old story. No one wants to see the danger until it's staring them in the face."

Jan: "But you don't know anything for sure. You're just making an assumption."

Annex: "Because we've already been through it all ourselves. First in Germany and then here. What do you think's happening in Russia?"

Jan: "You shouldn't include the Jews. I don't think anyone knows what's going on in Russia. The British and the Russians are probably exaggerating for propaganda purposes, just like the Germans."

Annex: "Absolutely not. The BBC has always told the truth. And even if the news is slightly exaggerated, the facts are bad enough as they are. You can't deny that millions of peace-loving citizens in Poland and Russia have been murdered or gassed."

I'll spare you the rest of our conversations. I'm very calm and take no notice of all the fuss. I've reached the point where I hardly care whether I live or die. The world will keep on turning without me, and I can't do anything to change events anyway. I'll just let matters take their course and concentrate on studying and hope that everything will be all right in the end.

*Yours, Anne*

TUESDAY, FEBRUARY 8, 1944*
*Dear Kitty,*

I can't tell you how I feel. One minute I'm longing for peace and quiet, and the next for a little fun. We've forgotten how to laugh – I mean, laughing so hard you can't stop.

This morning I had "the giggles"; you know, the kind we used to have at school. Margot and I were giggling like real teenagers.

Last night there was another scene with Mother. Margot was tucking her wool blanket around her when suddenly she leapt out of bed and carefully examined the blanket. What do you think she found? A pin! Mother had patched the blanket and

---

* The last four paragraphs of this entry have never been published before. For a further explanation, see page 4 of the Foreword.

forgotten to take it out. Father shook his head meaningfully and made a comment about how careless Mother is. Soon afterward Mother came in from the bathroom, and just to tease her I said, "*Du bist doch eine echte Rabenmutter.*"*

Of course, she asked me why I'd said that, and we told her about the pin she'd overlooked. She immediately assumed her haughtiest expression and said, "You're a fine one to talk. When you're sewing, the entire floor is covered with pins. And look, you've left the manicure set lying around again. You never put that away either!"

I said I hadn't used it, and Margot backed me up, since she was the guilty party.

Mother went on talking about how messy I was until I got fed up and said, rather curtly, "I wasn't even the one who said you were careless. I'm always getting blamed for other people's mistakes!"

Mother fell silent, and less than a minute later I was obliged to kiss her good-night. This incident may not have been very important, but these days everything gets on my nerves.

As I seem to be going through a period of reflection at the moment and letting my mind range over anything and everything, my thoughts have naturally turned to Father and Mother's marriage. It has always been presented to me as an ideal marriage. Never a quarrel, no angry faces, perfect harmony, etc., etc.

I know a few things about Father's past, and what I don't know, I've made up; I have the impression that Father married Mother because he felt she would be a suitable wife. I have to admit I admire Mother for the way she assumed the role of his wife and has never, as far as I know, complained or been jealous. It can't be easy for a loving wife to know she'll never be first in her husband's affections, and Mother did know that. Father certainly admired Mother's attitude and thought she had an excellent character. Why marry anyone else? His ideals had been shattered and his youth was over. What kind of marriage has it turned out to be? No quarrels or differences of opinion – but hardly an ideal marriage. Father respects Mother and loves

*Oh, you *are* cruel.

her, but not with the kind of love I envision for a marriage. Father accepts Mother as she is, is often annoyed, but says as little as possible, because he knows the sacrifices Mother has had to make.

Father doesn't always ask her opinion – about the business, about other matters, about people, about all kinds of things. He doesn't tell her everything, because he knows she's far too emotional, far too critical, and often far too biased. Father's not in love. He kisses her the way he kisses us. He never holds her up as an example, because he can't. He looks at her teasingly, or mockingly, but never lovingly. It may be that Mother's great sacrifice has made her harsh and disagreeable toward those around her, but it's guaranteed to take her even farther from the path of love, to arouse even less admiration, and one day Father is bound to realize that while, on the outside, she has never demanded his total love, on the inside, she has slowly but surely been crumbling away. She loves him more than anyone, and it's hard to see this kind of love not being returned.

So should I actually feel more sympathy for Mother? Should I help her? And Father? – I can't, I'm always imagining another mother. I just can't. – How could I? She hasn't told me anything about herself, and I've never asked her to. What do we know of each other's thoughts? I can't talk to her, I can't look lovingly into those cold eyes, I can't. Not ever! – If she had even one quality an understanding mother is supposed to have, gentleness or friendliness or patience or *some*thing, I'd keep trying to get closer to her. But as for loving this insensitive person, this mocking creature – it's becoming more and more impossible every day!

*Yours, Anne*

*Dearest Kitty,*                         SATURDAY, FEBRUARY 12, 1944

The sun is shining, the sky is deep blue, there's a magnificent breeze, and I'm longing – really longing – for everything: conversation, freedom, friends, being alone. I long . . . to cry! I feel as if I were about to explode. I know crying would help, but I can't cry. I'm restless. I walk from one room to another, breathe through the crack in the window frame, feel my heart beating as if to say, "Fulfill my longing at last..."

I think spring is inside me. I feel spring awakening, I feel it in my entire body and soul. I have to force myself to act normally. I'm in a state of utter confusion, don't know what to read, what to write, what to do. I only know that I'm longing for something...

*Yours, Anne*

MONDAY, FEBRUARY 14, 1944

*Dearest Kitty,*

A lot has changed for me since Saturday. What's happened is this: I was longing for something (and still am), but . . . a small, a very small, part of the problem has been resolved.

On Sunday morning I noticed, to my great joy (I'll be honest with you), that Peter kept looking at me. Not in the usual way. I don't know, I can't explain it, but I suddenly had the feeling he wasn't as in love with Margot as I used to think. All day long I tried not to look at him too much, because whenever I did, I caught him looking at me and then — well, it made me feel wonderful inside, and that's not a feeling I should have too often.

Sunday evening everyone, except Pim and me, was clustered around the radio, listening to the "Immortal Music of the German Masters." Dussel kept twisting and turning the knobs, which annoyed Peter, and the others too. After restraining himself for half an hour, Peter asked somewhat irritably if he would stop fiddling with the radio. Dussel replied in his haughtiest tone, "*Ich mach' das schon!*"* Peter got angry and made an insolent remark. Mr. van Daan sided with him, and Dussel had to back down. That was it.

The reason for the disagreement wasn't particularly interesting in and of itself, but Peter has apparently taken the matter very much to heart, because this morning, when I was rummaging around in the crate of books in the attic, Peter came up and began telling me what had happened. I didn't know anything about it, but Peter soon realized he'd found an attentive listener and started warming up to his subject.

*I'll decide that.

"Well, it's like this," he said. "I don't usually talk much, since I know beforehand I'll just be tongue-tied. I start stuttering and blushing and I twist my words around so much I finally have to stop, because I can't find the right words. That's what happened yesterday. I meant to say something entirely different, but once I started, I got all mixed up. It's awful. I used to have a bad habit, and sometimes I wish I still did: whenever I was mad at someone, I'd beat them up instead of arguing with them. I know this method won't get me anywhere, and that's why I admire you. You're never at a loss for words: you say exactly what you want to say and aren't in the least bit shy."

"Oh, you're wrong about that," I replied. "Most of what I say comes out very differently from the way I'd planned. Plus I talk too much and too long, and that's just as bad."

"Maybe, but you have the advantage that no one can see you're embarrassed. You don't blush or go to pieces."

I couldn't help being secretly amused at his words. However, since I wanted him to go on talking quietly about himself, I hid my laughter, sat down on a cushion on the floor, wrapped my arms around my knees and gazed at him intently.

I'm glad there's someone else in this house who flies into the same rages as I do. Peter seemed relieved that he could criticize Dussel without being afraid I'd tell. As for me, I was pleased too, because I sensed a strong feeling of fellowship, which I only remember having had with my girlfriends.

Yours, Anne

TUESDAY, FEBRUARY 15, 1944

The minor run-in with Dussel had several repercussions, for which he had only himself to blame. Monday evening Dussel came in to see Mother and told her triumphantly that Peter had asked him that morning if he'd slept well, and then added how sorry he was about what had happened Sunday evening – he hadn't really meant what he'd said. Dussel assured him he hadn't taken it to heart. So everything was right as rain again. Mother passed this story on to me, and I was secretly amazed that Peter, who'd been so angry at Dussel, had humbled himself, despite all his assurances to the contrary.

I couldn't refrain from sounding Peter out on the subject,

and he instantly replied that Dussel had been lying. You should have seen Peter's face. I wish I'd had a camera. Indignation, rage, indecision, agitation and much more crossed his face in rapid succession.

That evening Mr. van Daan and Peter really told Dussel off. But it couldn't have been all that bad, since Peter had another dental appointment today.

Actually, they never wanted to speak to each other again.

WEDNESDAY, FEBRUARY 16, 1944

Peter and I hadn't talked to each other all day, except for a few meaningless words. It was too cold to go up to the attic, and anyway, it was Margot's birthday. At twelve thirty he came to look at the presents and hung around chatting longer than was strictly necessary, something he'd never have done otherwise. But I got my chance in the afternoon. Since I felt like spoiling Margot on her birthday, I went to get the coffee, and after that the potatoes. When I came to Peter's room, he immediately took his papers off the stairs, and I asked if I should close the trapdoor to the attic.

"Sure," he said, "go ahead. When you're ready to come back down, just knock and I'll open it for you."

I thanked him, went upstairs and spent at least ten minutes searching around in the barrel for the smallest potatoes. My back started aching, and the attic was cold. Naturally, I didn't bother to knock but opened the trapdoor myself. But he obligingly got up and took the pan out of my hands.

"I did my best, but I couldn't find any smaller ones."

"Did you look in the big barrel?"

"Yes, I've been through them all."

By this time I was at the bottom of the stairs, and he examined the pan of potatoes he was still holding. "Oh, but these are fine," he said, and added, as I took the pan from him, "My compliments!"

As he said this, he gave me such a warm, tender look that I started glowing inside. I could tell he wanted to please me, but since he couldn't make a long complimentary speech, he said everything with his eyes. I understood him so well and was very grateful. It still makes me happy to think back to those words and that look!

When I went downstairs, Mother said she needed more potatoes, this time for dinner, so I volunteered to go back up. When I entered Peter's room, I apologized for disturbing him again. As I was going up the stairs, he stood up, went over to stand between the stairs and the wall, grabbed my arm and tried to stop me.

"I'll go," he said. "I have to go upstairs anyway."

I replied that it wasn't really necessary, that I didn't have to get only the small ones this time. Convinced, he let go of my arm. On my way back, he opened the trapdoor and once again took the pan from me. Standing by the door, I asked, "What are you working on?"

"French," he replied.

I asked if I could take a look at his lessons. Then I went to wash my hands and sat down across from him on the divan.

After I'd explained some French to him, we began to talk. He told me that after the war he wanted to go to the Dutch East Indies and live on a rubber plantation. He talked about his life at home, the black market and how he felt like a worthless bum. I told him he had a big inferiority complex. He talked about the war, saying that Russia and England were bound to go to war against each other, and about the Jews. He said life would have been much easier if he'd been a Christian or could become one after the war. I asked if he wanted to be baptized, but that wasn't what he meant either. He said he'd never be able to feel like a Christian, but that after the war he'd make sure nobody would know he was Jewish. I felt a momentary pang. It's such a shame he still has a touch of dishonesty in him.

Peter added, "The Jews have been and always will be the chosen people!"

I answered, "Just this once, I hope they'll be chosen for something good!"

But we went on chatting very pleasantly, about Father, about judging human character and all sorts of things, so many that I can't even remember them all.

I left at a quarter past five, because Bep had arrived.

That evening he said something else I thought was nice. We were talking about the picture of a movie star I'd once given him, which has been hanging in his room for at least a year and a half. He liked it so much that I offered to give him a few more.

"No," he replied, "I'd rather keep the one I've got. I look at it every day, and the people in it have become my friends."

I now have a better understanding of why he always hugs Mouschi so tightly. He obviously needs affection too. I forgot to mention something else he was talking about. He said, "No, I'm not afraid, except when it comes to things about myself, but I'm working on that."

Peter has a huge inferiority complex. For example, he always thinks he's so stupid and we're so smart. When I help him with French, he thanks me a thousand times. One of these days I'm going to say, "Oh, cut it out! You're much better at English and geography!"

Anne Frank

THURSDAY, FEBRUARY 17, 1944
Dear Kitty,

I was upstairs this morning, since I promised Mrs. van D. I'd read her some of my stories. I began with "Eva's Dream," which she liked a lot, and then I read a few passages from "The Secret Annex," which had her in stitches. Peter also listened for a while (just the last part) and asked if I'd come to his room sometime to read more. I decided I had to take a chance right then and there, so I got my notebook and let him read that bit where Cady and Hans talk about God. I can't really tell what kind of impression it made on him. He said something I don't quite remember, not about whether it was good, but about the idea behind it. I told him I just wanted him to see that I didn't write only amusing things. He nodded, and I left the room. We'll see if I hear anything more!

Yours, Anne Frank

FRIDAY, FEBRUARY 18, 1944
My dearest Kitty,

Whenever I go upstairs, it's alway so I can see "him." Now that I have something to look forward to, my life here has improved greatly.

At least the object of my friendship is always here, and I don't have to be afraid of rivals (except for Margot). Don't think I'm in love, because I'm not, but I do have the feeling that something beautiful is going to develop between Peter and me, a kind of friendship and a feeling of trust. I go see him whenever I get the chance, and it's not the way it used to be, when he didn't know what to make of me. On the contrary, he's still talking away as I'm heading out the door. Mother doesn't like me going upstairs. She always says I'm bothering Peter and that I should leave him alone. Honestly, can't she credit me with some intuition? She always looks at me so oddly when I go to Peter's room. When I come down again, she asks me where I've been. It's terrible, but I'm beginning to hate her!

Yours, Anne M. Frank

SATURDAY, FEBRUARY 19, 1944

*Dearest Kitty,*

It's Saturday again, and that should tell you enough. This morning all was quiet. I spent nearly an hour upstairs making meatballs, but I only spoke to "him" in passing.

When everyone went upstairs at two-thirty to either read or take a nap, I went downstairs, with blanket and all, to sit at the desk and read or write. Before long I couldn't take it anymore. I put my head in my arms and sobbed my heart out. The tears streamed down my cheeks, and I felt desperately unhappy. Oh, if only "he" had come to comfort me.

It was past four by the time I went upstairs again. At five o'clock I set off to get some potatoes, hoping once again that we'd meet, but while I was still in the bathroom fixing my hair, he went to see Boche.

I wanted to help Mrs. van D. and went upstairs with my book and everything, but suddenly I felt the tears coming again. I raced downstairs to the bathroom, grabbing the hand mirror on the way. I sat there on the toilet, fully dressed, long after I was through, my tears leaving dark spots on the red of my apron, and I felt utterly dejected.

Here's what was going through my mind: "Oh, I'll never reach Peter this way. Who knows, maybe he doesn't even like me and he doesn't need anyone to confide in. Maybe he only thinks of me in a casual sort of way. I'll have to go back to being alone, without anyone to confide in and without Peter, without hope, comfort or anything to look forward to. Oh, if only I could rest my head on his shoulder and not feel so hopelessly alone and deserted! Who knows, maybe he doesn't care for me at all and looks at the others in the same tender way. Maybe I only imagined it was especially for me. Oh, Peter, if only you could hear me or see me. If the truth is disappointing, I won't be able to bear it."

A little later I felt hopeful and full of expectation again, though my tears were still flowing – on the inside.

*Yours, Anne M. Frank*

SUNDAY, FEBRUARY 20, 1944

What happens in other people's houses during the rest of the week happens here in the Annex on Sundays. While other people put on their best clothes and go strolling in the sun, we scrub, sweep and do the laundry.

*Eight o'clock.* Though the rest of us prefer to sleep in, Dussel gets up at eight. He goes to the bathroom, then downstairs, then up again and then to the bathroom, where he devotes a whole hour to washing himself.

*Nine-thirty.* The stoves are lit, the blackout screen is taken down, and Mr. van Daan heads for the bathroom. One of my Sunday morning ordeals is having to lie in bed and look at Dussel's back when he's praying. I know it sounds strange, but a praying Dussel is a terrible sight to behold. It's not that he cries or gets sentimental, not at all, but he does spend a quarter of an hour – an entire fifteen minutes – rocking from his toes to his heels. Back and forth, back and forth. It goes on forever, and if I don't shut my eyes tight, my head starts to spin.

*Ten-fifteen.* The van Daans whistle; the bathroom's free. In the Frank family quarters, the first sleepy faces are beginning to emerge from their pillows. Then everything happens fast, fast, fast. Margot and I take turns doing the laundry. Since it's quite cold downstairs, we put on pants and head scarves. Meanwhile, Father is busy in the bathroom. Either Margot or I have a turn in the bathroom at eleven, and then we're all clean.

*Eleven-thirty.* Breakfast. I won't dwell on this, since there's enough talk about food without my bringing the subject up as well.

*Twelve-fifteen.* We each go our separate ways. Father, clad in overalls, gets down on his hands and knees and brushes the rug so vigorously that the room is enveloped in a cloud of dust. Mr. Dussel makes the beds (all wrong, of course), always whistling the same Beethoven violin concerto as he goes about his work. Mother can be heard shuffling around the attic as she hangs up the washing. Mr. van Daan puts on his hat and disappears into the lower regions, usually followed by Peter and Mouschi. Mrs. van D. dons a long apron, a black wool jacket and overshoes, winds a red wool scarf around her head, scoops up a bundle of dirty laundry and, with a well-rehearsed washerwoman's nod, heads downstairs. Margot and I do the dishes and straighten up the room.

*My dearest Kitty,*                    WEDNESDAY, FEBRUARY 23, 1944

The weather's been wonderful since yesterday, and I've perked up quite a bit. My writing, the best thing I have, is coming along well. I go to the attic almost every morning to get the stale air out of my lungs. This morning when I went there, Peter was busy cleaning up. He finished quickly and came over to where I was sitting on my favorite spot on the floor. The two of us looked out at the blue sky, the bare chestnut tree glistening with dew, the seagulls and other birds glinting with silver as they swooped through the air, and we were so moved and entranced that we couldn't speak. He stood with his head against a thick beam, while I sat. We breathed in the air, looked outside and both felt that the spell shouldn't be broken with words. We remained like this for a long while, and by the time he had to go to the loft to chop wood, I knew he was a good, decent boy. He climbed the ladder to the loft, and I followed; during the fifteen minutes he was chopping wood, we didn't say a word either. I watched him from where I was standing, and could see he was obviously doing his best to chop the right way and show off his strength. But I also looked out the open window, letting my eyes roam over a large part of Amsterdam, over the rooftops and on to the horizon, a strip of blue so pale it was almost invisible.

"As long as this exists," I thought, "this sunshine and this cloudless sky, and as long as I can enjoy it, how can I be sad?"

The best remedy for those who are frightened, lonely or unhappy is to go outside, somewhere they can be alone, alone with the sky, nature and God. For then and only then can you feel that everything is as it should be and that God wants people to be happy amid nature's beauty and simplicity.

As long as this exists, and that should be forever, I know that there will be solace for every sorrow, whatever the circumstances. I firmly believe that nature can bring comfort to all who suffer.

Oh, who knows, perhaps it won't be long before I can share this overwhelming feeling of happiness with someone who feels the same as I do.

*Yours, Anne*

PS. Thoughts: To Peter.

We've been missing out on so much here, so very much, and for such a long time. I miss it just as much as you do. I'm not talking about external things, since we're well provided for in that sense; I mean the internal things. Like you, I long for freedom and fresh air, but I think we've been amply compensated for their loss. On the inside, I mean.

This morning, when I was sitting in front of the window and taking a long, deep look outside at God and nature, I was happy, just plain happy. Peter, as long as people feel that kind of happiness within themselves, the joy of nature, health and much more besides, they'll always be able to recapture that happiness.

Riches, prestige, everything can be lost. But the happiness in your own heart can only be dimmed; it will always be there, as long as you live, to make you happy again.

Whenever you're feeling lonely or sad, try going to the loft on a beautiful day and looking outside. Not at the houses and the rooftops, but at the sky. As long as you can look fearlessly at the sky, you'll know that you're pure within and will find happiness once more.

*My dearest Kitty,*                      SUNDAY, FEBRUARY 27, 1944

From early in the morning to late at night, all I do is think about Peter. I fall asleep with his image before my eyes, dream about him and wake up with him still looking at me.

I have the strong feeling that Peter and I aren't really as different as we may seem on the surface, and I'll explain why: neither Peter nor I have a mother. His is too superficial, likes to flirt and doesn't concern herself much with what goes on in his head. Mine takes an active interest in my life, but has no tact, sensitivity or motherly understanding.

Both Peter and I are struggling with our innermost feelings. We're still unsure of ourselves and are too vulnerable, emotionally, to be dealt with so roughly. Whenever that happens, I want to run outside or hide my feelings. Instead, I bang the pots and pans, splash the water and am generally noisy, so that everyone wishes I were miles away. Peter's reaction is to shut himself up, say little, sit quietly and daydream, all the while carefully hiding his true self.

But how and when will we finally reach each other?

I don't know how much longer I can continue to keep this yearning under control.

*Yours, Anne M. Frank*


*My dearest Kitty,*                      MONDAY, FEBRUARY 28, 1944

It's like a nightmare, one that goes on long after I'm awake. I see him nearly every hour of the day and yet I can't be with him, I can't let the others notice, and I have to pretend to be cheerful, though my heart is aching.

Peter Schiff and Peter van Daan have melted into one Peter, who's good and kind and whom I long for desperately. Mother's horrible, Father's nice, which makes him even more exasperating, and Margot's the worst, since she takes advantage of my smiling face to claim me for herself, when all I want is to be left alone.

Peter didn't join me in the attic, but went up to the loft to do some carpentry work. At every rasp and bang, another chunk of my courage broke off and I was even more unhappy.

In the distance a clock was tolling "Be pure in heart, be pure in mind!"

I'm sentimental, I know. I'm despondent and foolish, I know that too.

Oh, help me!

*Yours, Anne M. Frank*

*Dearest Kitty,*

WEDNESDAY, MARCH 1, 1944

My own affairs have been pushed to the background by . . . a break in. I'm boring you with all my break-ins, but what can I do when burglars take such pleasure in honoring Gies & Co. with their presence? This incident is much more complicated than the last one, in July 1943.

Last night at seven-thirty Mr. van Daan was heading, as usual, for Mr. Kugler's office when he saw that both the glass door and the office door were open. He was surprised, but he went on through and was even more astonished to see that the alcove doors were open as well and that there was a terrible mess in the front office. "There's been a burglary" flashed through his mind. But just to make sure, he went downstairs to the front door, checked the lock and found everything closed. "Bep and Peter must just have been very careless this evening," Mr. van. D. concluded. He remained for a while in Mr. Kugler's office, switched off the lamp and went upstairs without worrying much about the open doors or the messy office.

Early this morning Peter knocked at our door to tell us that the front door was wide open and that the projector and Mr. Kugler's new briefcase had disappeared from the closet. Peter was instructed to lock the door. Mr. van Daan told us his discoveries of the night before, and we were extremely worried.

The only explanation is that the burglar must have had a duplicate key, since there were no signs of a forced entry. He must have sneaked in early in the evening, shut the door behind him, hidden himself when he heard Mr. van Daan, fled with the loot after Mr. van Daan went upstairs and, in his hurry, not bothered to shut the door.

Who could have our key? Why didn't the burglar go to the warehouse? Was it one of our own warehouse employees, and will he turn us in, now that he's heard Mr. van Daan and maybe even seen him?

It's really scary, since we don't know whether the burglar will take it into his head to try and get in again. Or was he so startled when he heard someone else in the building that he'll stay away?

*Yours, Anne*

PS. We'd be delighted if you could hunt up a good detective for us. Obviously, there's one condition: he must be relied upon not to inform on people in hiding.

THURSDAY, MARCH 2, 1944

*Dearest Kitty,*

Margot and I were in the attic together today. I can't enjoy being there with her the way I imagine it'd be with Peter (or someone else). I know she feels the same about most things as I do!

While doing the dishes, Bep began talking to Mother and Mrs. van Daan about how discouraged she gets. What help did those two offer her? Our tactless mother, especially, only made things go from bad to worse. Do you know what her advice was? That she should think about all the other people in the world who are suffering! How can thinking about the misery of others help if you're miserable yourself? I said as much. Their response, of course, was that I should stay out of conversations of this sort.

The grown-ups are such idiots! As if Peter, Margot, Bep and I didn't all have the same feelings. The only thing that helps is a mother's love, or that of a very, very close friend. But these two mothers don't understand the first thing about us! Perhaps Mrs. van Daan does, a bit more than Mother. Oh, I wish I could have said something to poor Bep, something that I know from my own experience would have helped. But Father came between us, pushing me roughly aside. They're all so stupid!

I also talked to Margot about Father and Mother, about how nice it could be here if they weren't so aggravating. We'd be able to organize evenings in which everyone could take turns discussing a given subject. But we've already been through all that. It's impossible for me to talk here! Mr. van Daan goes on the offensive, Mother gets sarcastic and can't say *anything* in a normal voice, Father doesn't feel like taking part, nor does Mr. Dussel, and Mrs. van D. is attacked so often that she just sits there with a red face, hardly able to put up a fight anymore. And what about us? We aren't allowed to have an opinion! My, my, aren't they progressive! Not have an opinion! People can tell you to shut up, but they can't keep you from having an opinion. You can't forbid someone to have an opinion, no matter how young they are! The only thing that would help Bep, Margot, Peter and me would be great love and devotion, which we don't get here. And no one, especially not the idiotic sages around here, is capable of understanding us, since we're more sensitive and much more advanced in our thinking than any of them ever suspect!

*Love, what is love? I don't think you can really put it into words. Love is understanding someone, caring for him, sharing his joys and sorrows. This eventually includes physical love. You've shared something, given something away and received something in return, whether or not you're married, whether or not you have a baby. Losing your virtue doesn't matter, as long as you know that for as long as you live you'll have someone at your side who understands you, and who doesn't have to be shared with anyone else!*

Yours, Anne M. Frank

At the moment, Mother's grouching at me again, she's clearly jealous because I talk to Mrs. van Daan more than to her. What do I care!

I managed to get hold of Peter this afternoon, and we talked for at least forty-five minutes. He wanted to tell me something about himself, but didn't find it easy. He finally got it out, though it took a long time. I honestly didn't know whether it was better for me to stay or to go. But I wanted so much to help him! I told him about Bep and how tactless our mothers are. He told me that his parents fight constantly, about politics and cigarettes and all kinds of things. As I've told you before, Peter's very shy, but not too shy to admit that he'd be perfectly happy not to see his parents for a year or two "My father isn't as nice as he looks," he said. "But in the matter of the cigarettes, Mother's absolutely right."

I also told him about my mother. But he came to Father's defense. He thought he was a "terrific guy."

Tonight when I was hanging up my apron after doing the dishes, he called me over and asked me not to say anything downstairs about his parents' having had another argument and not being on speaking terms. I promised, though I'd already told Margot. But I'm sure Margot won't pass it on.

"Oh no, Peter," I said, "you don't have to worry about me. I've learned not to blab everything I hear. I never repeat what you tell me."

He was glad to hear that. I also told him what terrible gossips we are, and said, "Margot's quite right, of course, when she says I'm not being honest, because as much as I want to stop gossiping, there's nothing I like better than discussing Mr. Dussel."

"It's good that you admit it," he said. He blushed, and his sincere compliment almost embarrassed me too.

Then we talked about "upstairs" and "downstairs" some more. Peter was really rather surprised to hear that we don't like his parents. "Peter," I said, "you know I'm always honest, so why shouldn't I tell you this as well? We can see their faults too."

I added, "Peter, I'd really like to help you. Will you let me? You're caught in an awkward position, and I know, even though you don't say anything, that it upsets you."

"Oh, your help is always welcome!"

"Maybe it'd be better for you to talk to Father. You can tell him anything, he won't pass it on."

"I know, he's a real pal."

"You like him a lot, don't you?"

Peter nodded, and I continued, "Well, he likes you too, you know!"

He looked up quickly and blushed. It was really touching to see how happy these few words made him. "You think so?" he asked.

"Yes," I said. "You can tell from the little things he lets slip now and then."

Then Mr. van Daan came in to do some dictating. Peter's a "terrific guy," just like Father!

*Yours, Anne M. Frank*

FRIDAY, MARCH 3, 1944

*My dearest Kitty,*

When I looked into the candle tonight, I felt calm and happy again. It seems Grandma is in that candle, and it's Grandma who watches over and protects me and makes me feel happy again. But ... there's someone else who governs all my moods and that's ... Peter. I went to get the potatoes today, and while I was standing on the stairway with my pan full, he asked, "What did you do during the lunch break?"

I sat down on the stairs, and we began to talk. The potatoes didn't make it to the kitchen until five-fifteen (an hour after I'd gone to get them). Peter didn't say anything more about his parents; we just talked about books and about the past. Oh, he gazes at me with such warmth in his eyes; I don't think it will take much for me to fall in love with him.

He brought the subject up this evening. I went to his room after peeling potatoes and remarked on how hot it was. "You can tell the temperature by looking at Margot and me, because we turn white when it's cold and red when it's hot," I said.

"In love?" he asked.

"Why should I be in love?" It was a pretty silly answer (or, rather, question).

"Why not?" he said, and then it was time for dinner.

What did he mean? Today I finally managed to ask him whether my chatter bothered him. All he said was, "Oh, it's fine with me!" I can't tell how much of his reply was due to shyness.

Kitty, I sound like someone who's in love and can talk about nothing but her dearest darling. And Peter is a darling. Will I ever be able to tell him that? Only if he thinks the same of me, but I'm the kind of person you have to treat with kid gloves, I know that all too well. And he likes to be left alone, so I don't know how much he likes me. In any case, we're getting to know each other a little better. I wish we dared to say more. But who knows, maybe that time will come sooner than I think! Once or twice a day he gives me a knowing glance, I wink back, and we're both happy. It seems crazy to talk about his being happy, and yet I have the overwhelming feeling he thinks the same way I do.

*Yours, Anne M. Frank*

*Dear Kitty,*                          SATURDAY, MARCH 4, 1944

This is the first Saturday in months that hasn't been tiresome, dreary and boring. The reason is Peter. This morning as I was on my way to the attic to hang up my apron, Father asked whether I wanted to stay and practice my French, and I said yes. We spoke French together for a while and I explained something to Peter, and then we worked on our English. Father read aloud from Dickens, and I was in seventh heaven, since I was sitting on father's chair, close to Peter.

I went downstairs at quarter to eleven. When I went back up at eleven-thirty, Peter was already waiting for me on the stairs. We talked until quarter to one. Whenever I leave the room, for example after a meal, and Peter has a chance and no one else can hear, he says, "Bye, Anne, see you later."

Oh, I'm so happy! I wonder if he's going to fall in love with me after all? In any case, he's a nice boy, and you have no idea how good it is to talk to him!

Mrs. van D. thinks it's all right for me to talk to Peter, but today she asked me teasingly, "Can I trust you two up there?"

"Of course," I protested. "I take that as an insult!" Morning, noon and night, I look forward to seeing Peter.

*Yours, Anne M. Frank*

PS. Before I forget, last night everything was blanketed in snow. Now it's thawed and there's almost nothing left.

*Dearest Kitty,*                        MONDAY, MARCH 6, 1944

Ever since Peter told me about his parents, I've felt a certain sense of responsibility toward him – don't you think that's strange? It's as though their quarrels were just as much my business as his, and yet I don't dare bring it up anymore, because I'm afraid it makes him uncomfortable. I wouldn't want to intrude, not for all the money in the world.

I can tell by Peter's face that he ponders things just as deeply as I do. Last night I was annoyed when Mrs. van D. scoffed, "The thinker!" Peter flushed and looked embarrassed, and I nearly blew my top.

Why don't these people keep their mouths shut? You can't

imagine what it's like to have to stand on the sidelines and see how lonely he is, without being able to do anything. I can imagine, as if I were in his place, how despondent he must sometimes feel at the quarrels. And about love. Poor Peter, he needs to be loved so much!

It sounded so cold when he said he didn't need any friends. Oh, he's so wrong! I don't think he means it. He clings to his masculinity, his solitude and his feigned indifference so he can maintain his role, so he'll never, ever have to show his feelings. Poor Peter, how long can he keep it up? Won't he explode from this superhuman effort?

Oh, Peter, if only I could help you, if only you would let me! Together we could banish our loneliness, yours and mine!

I've been doing a great deal of thinking, but not saying much. I'm happy when I see him, and happier still if the sun shines when we're together. I washed my hair yesterday, and because I knew he was next door, I was very rambunctious. I couldn't help it; the more quiet and serious I am on the inside, the noisier I get on the outside! Who will be the first to discover the chink in my armor?

It's just as well that the van Daans don't have a daughter. My conquest could never be so challenging, so beautiful and so nice with someone of the same sex!

                                        Yours, Anne M. Frank

PS. You know I'm always honest with you, so I think I should tell you that I live from one encounter to the next. I keep hoping to discover that he's dying to see me, and I'm in raptures when I notice his bashful attempts. I think he'd like to be able to express himself as easily as I do; little does he know it's his awkwardness that I find so touching.

Dearest Kitty,                   TUESDAY, MARCH 7, 1944

When I think back to my life in 1942, it all seems so unreal. The Anne Frank who enjoyed that heavenly existence was completely different from the one who has grown wise within these walls. Yes, it was heavenly. Five admirers on every street corner, twenty or so friends, the favorite of most of my teachers, spoiled

rotten by Father and Mother, bags full of candy and a big allow-
ance. What more could anyone ask for?

You're probably wondering how I could have charmed all
those people. Peter says it's because I'm "attractive," but that isn't
it entirely. The teachers were amused and entertained by my
clever answers, my witty remarks, my smiling face and my critical
mind. That's all I was: a terrible flirt, coquettish and amusing.
I had a few plus points, which kept me in everybody's good
graces: I was hardworking, honest and generous. I would never
have refused anyone who wanted to peek at my answers, I was
magnanimous with my candy, and I wasn't stuck-up.

Would all that admiration eventually have made me overconfident? It's a good thing that, at the height of my glory, I was
suddenly plunged into reality. It took me more than a year to get
used to doing without admiration.

How did they see me at school? As the class comedian, the
eternal ringleader, never in a bad mood, never a crybaby. Was it
any wonder that everyone wanted to bicycle to school with me
or do me little favors?

I look back at that Anne Frank as a pleasant, amusing, but
superficial girl, who has nothing to do with me. What did Peter
say about me? "Whenever I saw you, you were surrounded by a
flock of girls and at least two boys, you were always laughing, and
you were always the center of attention!" He was right.

What's remained of that Anne Frank? Oh, I haven't forgotten
how to laugh or toss off a remark, I'm just as good, if not better,
at raking people over the coals, and I can still flirt and be amusing,
if I want to be . . .

But there's the catch. I'd like to live that seemingly carefree
and happy life for an evening, a few days, a week. At the end of
that week I'd be exhausted, and would be grateful to the first
person to talk to me about something meaningful. I want
friends, not admirers. People who respect me for my character
and my deeds, not my flattering smile. The circle around me
would be much smaller, but what does that matter, as long as
they're sincere?

In spite of everything, I wasn't altogether happy in 1942;
I often felt I'd been deserted, but because I was on the go all day

long, I didn't think about it. I enjoyed myself as much as I could, trying consciously or unconsciously to fill the void with jokes.

Looking back, I realize that this period of my life has irrevocably come to a close; my happy-go-lucky, carefree schooldays are gone forever. I don't even miss them. I've outgrown them. I can no longer just kid around, since my serious side is always there.

I see my life up to New Year's 1944 as if I were looking through a powerful magnifying glass. When I was at home, my life was filled with sunshine. Then, in the middle of 1942, everything changed overnight. The quarrels, the accusations — I couldn't take it all in. I was caught off guard, and the only way I knew to keep my bearings was to talk back.

The first half of 1943 brought crying spells, loneliness and the gradual realization of my faults and shortcomings, which were numerous and seemed even more so. I filled the day with chatter, tried to draw Pim closer to me and failed. This left me on my own to face the difficult task of improving myself so I wouldn't have to hear their reproaches, because they made me so despondent.

The second half of the year was slightly better. I became a teenager, and was treated more like a grown-up. I began to think about things and to write stories, finally coming to the conclusion that the others no longer had anything to do with me. They had no right to swing me back and forth like a pendulum on a clock. I wanted to change myself in my own way. I realized I could manage without my mother, completely and totally, and that hurt. But what affected me even more was the realization that I was never going to be able to confide in Father. I didn't trust anyone but myself.

After New Year's the second big change occurred: my dream, through which I discovered my longing for . . . a boy; not for a girlfriend, but for a boyfriend. I also discovered an inner happiness underneath my superficial and cheerful exterior. From time to time I was quiet. Now I live only for Peter, since what happens to me in the future depends largely on him!

I lie in bed at night, after ending my prayers with the words *"Ich danke dir für all das Gute und Liebe und Schöne,"* * and I'm filled

* Thank you, God, for all that is good and dear and beautiful.

with joy. I think of going into hiding, my health and my whole being as *das Gute*; Peter's love (which is still so new and fragile and which neither of us dares to say aloud), the future, happiness and love as *das Liebe*; the world, nature and the tremendous beauty of everything, all that splendor, as *das Schöne*.

At such moments I don't think about all the misery, but about the beauty that still remains. This is where Mother and I differ greatly. Her advice in the face of melancholy is: "Think about all the suffering in the world and be thankful you're not part of it." My advice is: "Go outside, to the country, enjoy the sun and all nature has to offer. Go outside and try to recapture the happiness within yourself; think of all the beauty in yourself and in everything around you and be happy."

I don't think Mother's advice can be right, because what are you supposed to do if you become part of the suffering? You'd be completely lost. On the contrary, beauty remains, even in misfortune. If you just look for it, you discover more and more happiness and regain your balance. A person who's happy will make others happy; a person who has courage and faith will never die in misery!

*Yours, Anne M. Frank*

WEDNESDAY, MARCH 8, 1944

Margot and I have been writing each other notes, just for fun, of course.

> Anne: It's strange, but I can only remember the day after what has happened the night before. For example, I suddenly remembered that Mr. Dussel was snoring loudly last night. (It's now quarter to three on Wednesday afternoon and Mr. Dussel is snoring again, which is why it flashed through my mind, of course.) When I had to use the potty, I deliberately made more noise to get the snoring to stop.

> Margot: Which is better, the snoring or the gasping for air?

> Anne: The snoring's better, because it stops when I make noise, without waking the person in question.

What I didn't write to Margot, but what I'll confess to you, dear Kitty, is that I've been dreaming of Peter a great deal. The night before last I dreamed I was skating right here in our living room with that little boy from the Apollo ice-skating rink; he was with his sister, the girl with the spindly legs who always wore the same blue dress. I introduced myself, overdoing it a bit, and asked him his name. It was Peter. In my dream I wondered just how many Peters I actually knew!

Then I dreamed we were standing in Peter's room, facing each other beside the stairs. I said something to him; he gave me a kiss, but replied that he didn't love me all that much and that I shouldn't flirt. In a desperate and pleading voice I said, "I'm not flirting, Peter!"

When I woke up, I was glad Peter hasn't said it after all.

Last night I dreamed we were kissing each other, but Peter's cheeks were very disappointing: they weren't as soft as they looked. They were more like Father's cheeks — the cheeks of a man who already shaves.

*My dearest Kitty,*                    FRIDAY, MARCH 10, 1944

The proverb "Misfortunes never come singly" definitely applies to today. Peter just got through saying it. Let me tell you all the awful things that have happened and that are still hanging over our heads.

First, Miep is sick, as a result of Henk and Aagje's wedding yesterday. She caught cold in the Westerkerk, where the service was held. Second, Mr. Kleiman hasn't returned to work since the last time his stomach started bleeding, so Bep's been left to hold down the fort alone. Third, the police have arrested a man (whose name I won't put in writing). It's terrible not only for him, but for us as well, since he's been supplying us with potatoes, butter and jam. Mr. M., as I'll call him, has five children under the age of thirteen, and another on the way.

Last night we had another little scare: we were in the middle of dinner when suddenly someone knocked on the wall next door. For the rest of the evening we were nervous and gloomy.

Lately I haven't been at all in the mood to write down what's been going on here. I've been more wrapped up in myself. Don't get me wrong, I'm terribly upset about what's happened to poor, good-hearted Mr. M., but there's not much room for him in my diary.

Tuesday, Wednesday and Thursday I was in Peter's room from four-thirty to five-fifteen. We worked on our French and chatted about one thing and another. I really look forward to that hour or so in the afternoon, but best of all is that I think Peter's just as pleased to see me.

*Yours, Anne M. Frank*

*Dearest Kitty,*                     SATURDAY, MARCH 11, 1944

I haven't been able to sit still lately. I wander upstairs and down and then back again. I like talking to Peter, but I'm always afraid of being a nuisance. He's told me a bit about the past, about his parents and about himself, but it's not enough, and every five minutes I wonder why I find myself longing for more. He used to think I was a real pain in the neck, and the feeling was mutual. I've changed my mind, but how do I know he's changed his? I think he has, but that doesn't necessarily mean we have to become the best of friends, although as far as I'm concerned, it would make our time here more bearable. But I won't let this drive me crazy. I spend enough time thinking about him and don't have to get you all worked up as well, simply because I'm so miserable!

*Dearest Kitty,*                     SUNDAY, MARCH 12, 1944

Things are getting crazier here as the days go by. Peter hasn't looked at me since yesterday. He's been acting as if he's mad at me. I'm doing my best not to chase after him and to talk to him as little as possible, but it's not easy! What's going on, what makes him keep me at arm's length one minute and rush back to my side the next? Perhaps I'm imagining that it's worse than it really is. Perhaps he's just moody like me, and tomorrow everything will be all right again!

I have the hardest time trying to maintain a normal facade when I'm feeling so wretched and sad. I have to talk, help around the house, sit with the others and, above all, act cheerful! Most of all I miss the outdoors and having a place where I can be alone for as long as I want! I think I'm getting everything all mixed up,

Kitty, but then, I'm in a state of utter confusion: on the one hand, I'm half crazy with desire for him, can hardly be in the same room without looking at him; and on the other hand, I wonder why he should matter to me so much and why I can't be calm again!

Day and night, during every waking hour, I do nothing but ask myself, "Have you given him enough chance to be alone? Have you been spending too much time upstairs? Do you talk too much about serious subjects he's not yet ready to talk about? Maybe he doesn't even like you? Has it all been your imagination? But then why has he told you so much about himself? Is he sorry he did?" And a whole lot more.

Yesterday afternoon I was so worn out by the sad news from the outside that I lay down on my divan for a nap. All I wanted was to sleep and not have to think. I slept until four, but then I had to go next door. It wasn't easy, answering all Mother's questions and inventing an excuse to explain my nap to Father. I pleaded a headache, which wasn't a lie, since I did have one . . . on the inside!

Ordinary people, ordinary girls, teenagers like myself, would think I'm a little nuts with all my self-pity. But that's just it. I pour my heart out to you, and the rest of the time I'm as impudent, cheerful and self-confident as possible to avoid questions and keep from getting on my own nerves.

Margot is very kind and would like me to confide in her, but I can't tell her everything. She takes me too seriously, far too seriously, and spends a lot of time thinking about her loony sister, looking at me closely whenever I open my mouth and wondering, "Is she acting, or does she really mean it?"

It's because we're always together. I don't want the person I confide in to be around me all the time.

When will I untangle my jumbled thoughts? When will I find inner peace again?

Yours, Anne

TUESDAY, MARCH 14, 1944

*Dearest Kitty,*

It might be amusing for you (though not for me) to hear what we're going to eat today. The cleaning lady is working downstairs, so at the moment I'm seated at the van Daans' oilcloth-covered

table with a handkerchief sprinkled with fragrant prewar per-
fume pressed to my nose and mouth. You probably don't have
the faintest idea what I'm talking about, so let me "begin at the
beginning." The people who supply us with food coupons have
been arrested, so we have just our five black-market ration books
– no coupons, no fats and oils. Since Miep and Mr. Kleiman are
sick again, Bep can't manage the shopping. The food is
wretched, and so are we. As of tomorrow, we won't have a scrap
of fat, butter or margarine. We can't eat fried potatoes for breakfast (which we've been doing to save on bread), so we're having
hot cereal instead, and because Mrs. van D. thinks we're starving,
we bought some half-and-half. Lunch today consists of mashed
potatoes and pickled kale. This explains the precautionary measure with the handkerchief. You wouldn't believe how much
kale can stink when it's a few years old! The kitchen smells like
a mixture of spoiled plums, rotten eggs and brine. Ugh, just the
thought of having to eat that muck makes me want to throw up!
Besides that, our potatoes have contracted such strange diseases
that one out of every two buckets of *pommes de terre* winds up in
the garbage. We entertain ourselves by trying to figure out which
disease they've got, and we've reached the conclusion that they
suffer from cancer, smallpox and measles. Honestly, being in
hiding during the fourth year of the war is no picnic. If only the
whole stinking mess were over!

To tell you the truth, the food wouldn't matter so much to me
if life here were more pleasant in other ways. But that's just it:
this tedious existence is starting to make us all disagreeable. Here
are the opinions of the five grown-ups on the present situation
(children aren't allowed to have opinions, and for once I'm stick-
ing to the rules):

Mrs. van Daan: "I'd stopped wanting to be queen of the
kitchen long ago. But sitting around doing nothing was boring,
so I went back to cooking. Still, I can't help complaining: it's
impossible to cook without oil, and all those disgusting smells
make me sick to my stomach. Besides, what do I get in return
for my efforts? Ingratitude and rude remarks. I'm always the
black sheep; I get blamed for everything. What's more, it's my
opinion that the war is making very little progress. The Germans

will win in the end. I'm terrified that we're going to starve, and when I'm in a bad mood, I snap at everyone who comes near."

Mr. van Daan: "I just smoke and smoke and smoke. Then the food, the political situation and Kerli's moods don't seem so bad. Kerli's a sweetheart. If I don't have anything to smoke, I get sick, then I need to eat meat, life becomes unbearable, nothing's good enough, and there's bound to be a flaming row. My Kerli's an idiot."

Mrs. Frank: "Food's not very important, but I'd love a slice of rye bread right now, because I'm so hungry. If I were Mrs. van Daan, I'd have put a stop to Mr. van Daan's smoking long ago. But I desperately need a cigarette now, because my head's in such a whirl. The van Daans are horrible people; the English may make a lot of mistakes, but the war is progressing. I should keep my mouth shut and be grateful I'm not in Poland."

Mr. Frank: "Everything's fine, I don't need a thing. Stay calm, we've got plenty of time. Just give me my potatoes, and I'll be quiet. Better set aside some of my rations for Bep. The political situation is improving, I'm extremely optimistic."

Mr. Dussel: "I must complete the task I've set for myself, everything must be finished on time. The political situation is looking 'gut,' it's 'eempossible' for us to get caught. Me, me, me . . . !"

Yours, Anne

THURSDAY, MARCH 16, 1944

Dearest Kitty,

Whew! Released from the gloom and doom for a few moments! All I've been hearing today is: "If this and that happens, we're in trouble, and if so-and-so gets sick, we'll be left to fend for ourselves, and if . . ."

Well, you know the rest, or at any rate I assume you're familiar enough with the residents of the Annex to guess what they'd be talking about.

The reason for all the "ifs" is that Mr. Kugler has been called up for a six-day work detail, Bep is down with a bad cold and will probably have to stay home tomorrow, Miep hasn't gotten over her flu, and Mr. Kleiman's stomach bled so much he lost consciousness. What a tale of woe!

We think Mr. Kugler should go directly to a reliable doctor for a medical certificate of ill health, which he can present to the City Hall in Hilversum. The warehouse employees have been given a day off tomorrow, so Bep will be alone in the office. If (there's another "if") Bep has to stay home, the door will remain locked and we'll have to be as quiet as mice so the Keg Company won't hear us. At one o'clock Jan will come for half an hour to check on us poor forsaken souls, like a zookeeper.

This afternoon, for the first time in ages, Jan gave us some news of the outside world. You should have seen us gathered around him; it looked exactly like a print: "At Grandmother's Knee."

He regaled his grateful audience with talk of – what else? – food. Mrs. P., a friend of Miep's, has been cooking his meals. The day before yesterday Jan ate carrots with green peas, yesterday he had the leftovers, today she's cooking marrowfat peas, and tomorrow she's planning to mash the remaining carrots with potatoes.

We asked about Miep's doctor.

"Doctor?" said Jan. "What doctor? I called him this morning and got his secretary on the line. I asked for a flu prescription and was told I could come pick it up tomorrow morning between eight and nine. If you've got a particularly bad case of flu, the doctor himself comes to the phone and says, 'Stick out your tongue and say "Aah." Oh, I can hear it, your throat's infected. I'll write out a prescription and you can bring it to the pharmacy. Good day.' And that's that. Easy job he's got, diagnosis by phone. But I shouldn't blame the doctors. After all, a person has only two hands, and these days there're too many patients and too few doctors."

Still, we all had a good laugh at Jan's phone call. I can just imagine what a doctor's waiting room looks like these days. Doctors no longer turn up their noses at the poorer patients, but at those with minor illnesses. "Hey, what are you doing here?" they think. "Go to the end of the line; real patients have priority!"

                                                              *Yours, Anne*

*Dearest Kitty,*                                   THURSDAY, MARCH 16, 1944

The weather is gorgeous, indescribably beautiful; I'll be going up to the attic in a moment.

I now know why I'm so much more restless than Peter. He has his own room, where he can work, dream, think and sleep. I'm constantly being chased from one corner to another. I'm never alone in the room I share with Dussel, though I long to be so much. That's another reason I take refuge in the attic. When I'm there, or with you, I can be myself, at least for a little while. Still, I don't want to moan and groan. On the contrary, I want to be brave!

Thank goodness the others notice nothing of my innermost feelings, except that every day I'm growing cooler and more contemptuous of Mother, less affectionate to Father and less willing to share a single thought with Margot; I'm closed up tighter than a drum. Above all, I have to maintain my air of confidence. No one must know that my heart and mind are constantly at war with each other. Up to now reason has always won the battle, but will my emotions get the upper hand? Sometimes I fear they will, but more often I actually hope they do!

Oh, it's so terribly hard not to talk to Peter about these things, but I know I have to let him begin; it's so hard to act during the daytime as if everything I've said and done in my dreams had never taken place! Kitty, Anne is crazy, but then these are crazy times and even crazier circumstances.

The nicest part is being able to write down all my thoughts and feelings; otherwise, I'd absolutely suffocate. I wonder what Peter thinks about all these things? I keep thinking I'll be able to talk to him about them one day. He must have guessed something about the inner me, since he couldn't possibly love the outer Anne he's known so far! How could someone like Peter, who loves peace and quiet, possibly stand my bustle and noise? Will he be the first and only person to see what's beneath my granite mask? Will it take him long? Isn't there some old saying about love being akin to pity? Isn't that what's happening here as well? Because I often pity him as much as I do myself!

I honestly don't know how to begin, I really don't, so how can I

expect Peter to when talking is so much harder for him? If only
I could write to him, then at least he'd know what I was trying
to say, since it's so hard to say it out loud! *Yours, Anne M. Frank*

*My dearest darling,*                    FRIDAY, MARCH 17, 1944

Everything turned out all right after all; Bep just had a sore
throat, not the flu, and Mr. Kugler got a medical certificate to
excuse him from the work detail. The entire Annex breathed a
huge sigh of relief. Everything's fine here! Except that Margot
and I are rather tired of our parents.

Don't get me wrong. I still love Father as much as ever and
Margot loves both Father and Mother, but when you're as old as
we are, you want to make a few decisions for yourself, get out
from under their thumb. Whenever I go upstairs, they ask what
I'm going to do, they won't let me salt my food, Mother asks me
every evening at eight-fifteen if it isn't time for me to change
into my nighty, and they have to approve every book I read.
I must admit, they're not at all strict about that and let me read
nearly everything, but Margot and I are sick and tired of having
to listen to their comments and questions all day long.

There's something else that displeases them: I no longer feel
like giving them little kisses morning, noon and night. All those
cute nicknames seem so affected, and Father's fondness for talking about farting and going to the bathroom is disgusting. In
short, I'd like nothing better than to do without their company
for a while, and they don't understand that. Not that Margot and
I have ever said any of this to them. What would be the point?
They wouldn't understand anyway.

Margot said last night, "What really bothers me is that if you
happen to put your head in your hands and sigh once or twice,
they immediately ask whether you have a headache or don't feel
well."

For both of us, it's been quite a blow to suddenly realize that
very little remains of the close and harmonious family we used
to be at home! This is mostly because everything's out of kilter
here. By that I mean that we're treated like children when it
comes to external matters, while, inwardly, we're much older

than other girls our age. Even though I'm only fourteen, I know what I want, I know who's right and who's wrong, I have my own opinions, ideas and principles, and though it may sound odd coming from a teenager, I feel I'm more of a person than a child – I feel I'm completely independent of others. I know I'm better at debating or carrying on a discussion than Mother, I know I'm more objective, I don't exaggerate as much, I'm much tidier and better with my hands, and because of that I feel (this may make you laugh) that I'm superior to her in many ways. To love someone, I have to admire and respect the person, but I feel neither respect nor admiration for Mother!

Everything would be all right if only I had Peter, since I admire him in many ways. He's so decent and clever!

*Yours, Anne M. Frank*

SATURDAY, MARCH 18, 1944

*Dearest Kitty,*

I've told you more about myself and my feelings than I've ever told a living soul, so why shouldn't that include sex?

Parents, and people in general, are very peculiar when it comes to sex. Instead of telling their sons and daughters everything at the age of twelve, they send the children out of the room the moment the subject arises and leave them to find out everything on their own. Later on, when parents notice that their children have, somehow, come by their information, they assume they know more (or less) than they actually do. So why don't they try to make amends by asking them what's what?

A major stumbling block for the adults – though in my opinion it's no more than a pebble – is that they're afraid their children will no longer look upon marriage as sacred and pure once they realize that, in most cases, this purity is a lot of nonsense. As far as I'm concerned, it's not wrong for a man to bring a little experience to a marriage. After all, it has nothing to do with the marriage itself, does it?

Soon after I turned eleven, they told me about menstruation. But even then, I had no idea where the blood came from or what it was for. When I was twelve and a half, I learned some more from Jacque, who wasn't as ignorant as I was. My own intuition told me what a man and a woman do when they're together;

it seemed like a crazy idea at first, but when Jacque confirmed it, I was proud of myself for having figured it out!

It was also Jacque who told me that children didn't come out of their mothers' tummies. As she put it, "Where the ingredients go in is where the finished product comes out!" Jacque and I found out about the hymen, and quite a few other details, from a book on sex education. I also knew that you could keep from having children, but how that worked inside your body remained a mystery. When I came here, Father told me about prostitutes, etc., but all in all there are still unanswered questions.

If mothers don't tell their children everything, they hear it in bits and pieces, and that can't be right.

Even though it's Saturday, I'm not bored! That's because I've been up in the attic with Peter. I sat there dreaming with my eyes closed, and it was wonderful.

Yours, Anne M. Frank

SUNDAY, MARCH 19, 1944

*Dearest Kitty,*

Yesterday was a very important day for me. After lunch everything was as usual. At five I put on the potatoes, and Mother gave me some blood sausage to take to Peter. I didn't want to at first, but I finally went. He wouldn't accept the sausage, and I had the dreadful feeling it was still because of that argument we'd had about distrust. Suddenly I couldn't bear it a moment longer and my eyes filled with tears. Without another word, I returned the platter to Mother and went to the bathroom to have a good cry. Afterward I decided to talk things out with Peter. Before dinner, the four of us were helping him with a crossword puzzle, so I couldn't say anything. But as we were sitting down to eat, I whispered to him, "Are you going to practice your shorthand tonight, Peter?"

"No," was his reply.

"I'd like to talk to you later on."

He agreed.

After the dishes were done, I went to his room and asked if he'd refused the sausage because of our last quarrel. Luckily, that wasn't the reason; he just thought it was bad manners to seem so eager. It had been very hot downstairs and my face was as red as a lobster. So after taking down some water for Margot, I went back up to get a little fresh air. For the sake of appearances, I first went and stood beside the van Daans' window before going to Peter's room. He was standing on the left side of the open window, so I went over to the right side. It's much easier to talk next to an open window in semidarkness than in broad daylight, and I think Peter felt the same way. We told each other so much, so very much, that I can't repeat it all. But it felt good; it was the most wonderful evening I've ever had in the Annex. I'll give you a brief description of the various subjects we touched on.

First we talked about the quarrels and how I see them in a very different light these days, and then about how we've become alienated from our parents. I told Peter about Mother and Father and Margot and myself. At one point he asked, "You always give each other a good-night kiss, don't you?"

"One? Dozens of them. You don't, do you?"

"No, I've never really kissed anyone."

"Not even on your birthday?"

"Yeah, on my birthday I have."

We talked about how neither of us really trusts our parents, and how his parents love each other a great deal and wish he'd confide in them, but that he doesn't want to. How I cry my heart out in bed and he goes up to the loft and swears. How Margot and I have only recently gotten to know each other and yet still tell each other very little, since we're always together. We talked about every imaginable thing, about trust, feelings and ourselves. Oh, Kitty, he was just as I thought he would be.

Then we talked about the year 1942, and how different we were back then; we don't even recognize ourselves from that period. How we couldn't stand each other at first. He'd thought I was a noisy pest, and I'd quickly concluded that he was nothing special. I didn't understand why he didn't flirt with me, but now I'm glad. He also mentioned how he often used to retreat to his room. I said that my noise and exuberance and his silence were two sides of the same coin, and that I also liked peace and quiet but don't have anything for myself alone, except my diary, and that everyone would rather see the back of me, starting with Mr. Dussel, and that I don't always want to sit with my parents.

We discussed how glad he is that my parents have children and how glad I am that he's here. How I now understand his need to withdraw and his relationship to his parents, and how much I'd like to help him when they argue.

"But you're always a help to me!" he said.

"How?" I asked, greatly surprised.

"By being cheerful."

That was the nicest thing he said all evening. He also told me that he didn't mind my coming to his room the way he used to; in fact, he liked it. I also told him that all of Father's and Mother's pet names were meaningless, that a kiss here and there didn't automatically lead to trust. We also talked about doing things your own way, the diary, loneliness, the difference between everyone's inner and outer selves, my mask, etc.

It was wonderful. He must have come to love me as a friend, and, for the time being, that's enough. I'm so grateful and happy, I can't find the words. I must apologize, Kitty, since my style is not up to my usual standard today. I've just written whatever came into my head!

I have the feeling that Peter and I share a secret. Whenever he looks at me with those eyes, with that smile and that wink, it's as if a light goes on inside me. I hope things will stay like this and that we'll have many, many more happy hours together.

*Your grateful and happy Anne*

*Dearest Kitty,*                    MONDAY, MARCH 20, 1944

This morning Peter asked me if I'd come again one evening. He swore I wouldn't be disturbing him, and said that where there was room for one, there was room for two. I said I couldn't see him every evening, since my parents didn't think it was a good idea, but he thought I shouldn't let that bother me. So I told him I'd like to come some Saturday evening and also asked him if he'd let me know when you could see the moon.

"Sure," he said, "maybe we can go downstairs and look at the moon from there." I agreed; I'm not really so scared of burglars.

In the meantime, a shadow has fallen on my happiness. For a long time I've had the feeling that Margot likes Peter. Just how much I don't know, but the whole situation is very unpleasant.

Now every time I go see Peter I'm hurting her, without meaning to. The funny thing is that she hardly lets it show. I know I'd be insanely jealous, but Margot just says I shouldn't feel sorry for her.

"I think it's so awful that you've become the odd one out," I added.

"I'm used to that," she replied, somewhat bitterly.

I don't dare tell Peter. Maybe later on, but he and I need to discuss so many other things first.

Mother gave me a warning tap last night, which I deserved. I mustn't carry my indifference and contempt for her too far. In spite of everything, I should try once again to be friendly and keep my remarks to myself!

Even Pim isn't as nice as he used to be. He's been trying not to treat me like a child, but now he's much too cold. We'll just have to see what comes of it! He's warned me that if I don't do my algebra, I won't get any tutoring after the war. I could simply wait and see what happens, but I'd like to start again, provided I get a new book.

That's enough for now. I do nothing but gaze at Peter, and I'm filled to overflowing!

*Yours, Anne M. Frank*

Evidence of Margot's goodness. I received this today, March 20, 1944:

Anne, yesterday when I said I wasn't jealous of you, I wasn't being entirely honest. The situation is this: I'm not jealous of either you or Peter. I'm just sorry I haven't found anyone with whom to share my thoughts and feelings, and I'm not likely to in the near future. But that's why I wish, from the bottom of my heart, that you will both be able to place your trust in each other. You're already missing out on so much here, things other people take for granted.

On the other hand, I'm certain I'd never have gotten as far with Peter, because I think I'd need to feel very close to a person before I could share my thoughts. I'd want to have the feeling that he understood me through and through, even if I didn't say much. For this reason it would have to be someone I felt was intellectually superior to me, and that isn't the case with Peter. But I can imagine your feeling close to him.

So there's no need for you to reproach yourself because you think you're taking something I was entitled to; nothing could be further from the truth. You and Peter have everything to gain by your friendship.

My answer:

Dearest Margot,

Your letter was extremely kind, but I still don't feel completely happy about the situation, and I don't think I ever will.

At the moment, Peter and I don't trust each other as much as you seem to think. It's just that when you're standing beside an open window at twilight, you can say more to each other than in bright sunshine. It's also easier to whisper your feelings than to shout them from the rooftops. I think you've begun to feel a kind of sisterly affection for Peter and would like to help him, just as much as I would. Perhaps you'll be able to do that someday, though that's not the kind of trust we have in mind. I believe that trust has to come from both sides; I also think that's the reason why Father and I have never really grown so close. But let's not talk about it anymore. If there's anything you still want to discuss, please write, because it's easier for me to say what I mean on paper than face-to-face. You know how much I admire you, and only hope that some of your goodness and Father's goodness will rub off on me, because, in that sense, you two are a lot alike.

Yours, Anne

WEDNESDAY, MARCH 22, 1944

Dearest Kitty,

I received this letter last night from Margot:

Dear Anne,

After your letter of yesterday I have the unpleasant feeling that your conscience bothers you whenever you go to Peter's to work or talk; there's really no reason for that. In my heart, I know there's someone who deserves my trust (as I do his), and I wouldn't be able to tolerate Peter in his place.

However, as you wrote, I do think of Peter as a kind of brother ... a younger brother; we've been sending out feelers, and a brotherly and sisterly affection may or may not develop at some later date, but it's certainly not reached that stage yet. So there's no need for you to feel sorry for me. Now that you've found companionship, enjoy it as much as you can.

In the meantime, things are getting more and more wonderful here. I think, Kitty, that true love may be developing in the Annex. All those jokes about marrying Peter if we stayed here long enough weren't so silly after all. Not that I'm thinking of marrying him, mind you. I don't even know what he'll be like when he grows up. Or if we'll even love each other enough to get married.

I'm sure now that Peter loves me too; I just don't know in what way. I can't figure out if he wants only a good friend, or if he's attracted to me as a girl or as a sister. When he said I always helped him when his parents were arguing, I was tremendously happy; it was one step toward making me believe in his friendship. I asked him yesterday what he'd do if there were a dozen Annes who kept popping in to see him. His answer was: "If they were all like you, it wouldn't be so bad." He's extremely hospitable, and I think he really likes to see me. Meanwhile, he's been working hard at learning French, even studying in bed until ten-fifteen.

Oh, when I think back to Saturday night, to our words, our voices, I feel satisfied with myself for the very first time; what I mean is, I'd still say the same and wouldn't want to change a thing, the way I usually do. He's so handsome, whether he's smiling or just sitting still. He's so sweet and good and beautiful. I think what surprised him most about me was when he discovered that I'm not at all the superficial, worldly Anne I appear to be, but a dreamer, like he is, with just as many troubles!

Last night after the dinner dishes, I waited for him to ask me to stay upstairs. But nothing happened; I went away. He came downstairs to tell Dussel it was time to listen to the radio and hung around the bathroom for a while, but when Dussel took too long, he went back upstairs. He paced up and down his room and went to bed early.

The entire evening I was so restless I kept going to the bathroom to splash cold water on my face. I read a bit, daydreamed some more, looked at the clock and waited, waited, waited, all the while listening to his footsteps. I went to bed early, exhausted.

Tonight I have to take a bath, and tomorrow? Tomorrow's so far away!

*Yours, Anne M. Frank*

My answer:

Dearest Margot,

I think the best thing is simply to wait and see what happens. It can't be much longer before Peter and I will have to decide whether to go back to the way we were or do something else. I don't know how it'll turn out; I can't see any farther than the end of my nose.

But I'm certain of one thing: if Peter and I do become friends, I'm going to tell him you're also very fond of him and are prepared to help him if he needs you. You wouldn't want me to, I'm sure, but I don't care; I don't know what Peter thinks of you, but I'll ask him when the time comes. It's certainly nothing bad – on the contrary! You're welcome to join us in the attic, or wherever we are. You won't be disturbing us, because we have an unspoken agreement to talk only in the evenings when it's dark.

Keep your spirits up! I'm doing my best, though it's not always easy. Your time may come sooner than you think.

*Yours, Anne*

THURSDAY, MARCH 23, 1944

*Dearest Kitty,*

Things are more or less back to normal here. Our coupon men have been released from prison, thank goodness!

Miep's been back since yesterday, but today it was her husband's turn to take to his bed – chills and fever, the usual flu symptoms. Bep is better, though she still has a cough, and Mr. Kleiman will have to stay home for a long time.

Yesterday a plane crashed nearby. The crew was able to parachute out in time. It crashed on top of a school, but luckily there were no children inside. There was a small fire and a couple of people were killed. As the airmen made their descent, the Germans sprayed them with bullets. The Amsterdammers who saw it seethed with rage at such a dastardly deed. We – by which I mean the ladies – were also scared out of our wits. Brrr, I hate the sound of gunfire.

Now about myself.

I was with Peter yesterday and, somehow, I honestly don't know how, we wound up talking about sex. I'd made up my mind a long time ago to ask him a few things. He knows everything; when I said that Margot and I weren't very well informed, he was amazed. I told him a lot about Margot and me and Mother and Father and said that lately I didn't dare ask them anything. He offered to enlighten me, and I gratefully accepted: he described how contraceptives work, and I asked him very boldly how boys could tell they were grown up. He had to think about that one; he said he'd tell me tonight. I told him what had happened to Jacque, and said that girls are defenseless against strong boys. "Well, you don't have to be afraid of me," he said.

When I came back that evening, he told me how it is with boys. Slightly embarrassing, but still awfully nice to be able to discuss it with him. Neither he nor I had ever imagined we'd be able to talk so openly to a girl or a boy, respectively, about such intimate matters. I think I know everything now. He told me a lot about what he called *Präsentivmitteln** in German.

That night in the bathroom Margot and I were talking about Bram and Trees, two friends of hers.

This morning I was in for a nasty surprise: after breakfast Peter beckoned me upstairs. "That was a dirty trick you played on me," he said. "I heard what you and Margot were saying in the bathroom last hight. I think you just wanted to find out how much Peter knew and then have a good laugh!"

*Should be *Präservativmitteln*: prophylactics.

I was stunned! I did everything I could to talk him out of that outrageous idea; I could understand how he must have felt, but it just wasn't true!

"Oh no, Peter," I said. "I'd never be so mean. I told you I wouldn't pass on anything you said to me and I won't. To put on an act like that and then deliberately be so mean . . . No, Peter, that's not my idea of a joke. It wouldn't be fair. I didn't say anything, honest. Won't you believe me?" He assured me he did, but I think we'll have to talk about it again sometime. I've done nothing all day but worry about it. Thank goodness he came right out and said what was on his mind. Imagine if he'd gone around thinking I could be that mean. He's so sweet!

Now I'll have to tell him everything!

Yours, Anne

FRIDAY, MARCH 24, 1944

*Dear Kitty,*

I often go up to Peter's room after dinner nowadays to breathe in the fresh evening air. You can get around to meaningful conversations more quickly in the dark than with the sun tickling your face. It's cozy and snug sitting beside him on a chair and looking outside. The van Daans and Dussel make the silliest remarks when I disappear into his room. "*Annes zweite Heimat,*" * they say, or "Is it proper for a gentleman to receive young girls in his room at night with the lights out?" Peter has amazing presence of mind in the face of these so-called witticisms. My mother, incidentally, is also bursting with curiosity and simply dying to ask what we talk about, only she's secretly afraid I'd refuse to answer. Peter says the grown-ups are just jealous because we're young and that we shouldn't take their obnoxious comments to heart.

Sometimes he comes downstairs to get me, but that's awkward too, because in spite of all his precautions his face turns bright red and he can hardly get the words out of his mouth. I'm glad I don't blush; it must be extremely unpleasant.

Besides, it bothers me that Margot has to sit downstairs all by herself, while I'm upstairs enjoying Peter's company. But what

---

*Anne's second home.

can I do about it? I wouldn't mind it if she came, but she'd just be the odd one out, sitting there like a lump on a log.

I've had to listen to countless remarks about our sudden friendship. I can't tell you how often the conversation at meals has been about an Annex wedding, should the war last another five years. Do we take any notice of this parental chitchat? Hardly, since it's all so silly. Have my parents forgotten that they were young once? Apparently they have. At any rate, they laugh at us when we're serious, and they're serious when we're joking.

I don't know what's going to happen next, or whether we'll run out of things to say. But if it goes on like this, we'll eventually be able to be together without talking. If only his parents would stop acting so strangely. It's probably because they don't like seeing me so often; Peter and I certainly never tell them what we talk about. Imagine if they knew we were discussing such intimate things.

I'd like to ask Peter whether he knows what girls look like down there. I don't think boys are as complicated as girls. You can easily see what boys look like in photographs or pictures of male nudes, but with women it's different. In women, the genit-als, or whatever they're called, are hidden between their legs. Peter has probably never seen a girl up close. To tell you the truth, neither have I. Boys are a lot easier. How on earth would I go about describing a girl's parts? I can tell from what he said that he doesn't know exactly how it all fits together. He was talking about the "*Muttermund*,"* but that's on the inside, where you can't see it. Everything's pretty well arranged in us women. Until I was eleven or twelve, I didn't realize there was a second set of labia on the inside, since you couldn't see them. What's even funnier is that I thought urine came out of the clitoris. I asked Mother one time what that little bump was, and she said she didn't know. She can really play dumb when she wants to!

But to get back to the subject. How on earth can you explain what it all looks like without any models? Shall I try anyway? Okay, here goes!

When you're standing up, all you see from the front is hair.

* Cervix.

Between your legs there are two soft, cushiony things, also covered with hair, which press together when you're standing, so you can't see what's inside. They separate when you sit down, and they're very red and quite fleshy on the inside. In the upper part, between the outer labia, there's a fold of skin that, on second thought, looks like a kind of blister. That's the clitoris. Then come the inner labia, which are also pressed together in a kind of crease. When they open up, you can see a fleshy little mound, no bigger than the top of my thumb. The upper part has a couple of small holes in it, which is where the urine comes out. The lower part looks as if it were just skin, and yet that's where the vagina is. You can barely find it, because the folds of skin hide the opening. The hole's so small I can hardly imagine how a man could get in there, much less how a baby could come out. It's hard enough trying to get your index finger inside. That's all there is, and yet it plays such an important role!

                                               *Yours, Anne M. Frank*

*Dearest Kitty,*                      SATURDAY, MARCH 25, 1944

You never realize how much you've changed until after it's happened. I've changed quite drastically, everything about me is different: my opinions, ideas, critical outlook. Inwardly, outwardly, nothing's the same. And, I might safely add, since it's true, I've changed for the better. I once told you that, after years of being adored, it was hard for me to adjust to the harsh reality of grown-ups and rebukes. But Father and Mother are largely to blame for my having to put up with so much. At home they wanted me to enjoy life, which was fine, but here they shouldn't have encouraged me to agree with them and only shown me "their" side of all the quarrels and gossip. It was a long time before I discovered the score was fifty-fifty. I now know that many blunders have been committed here, by young and old alike. Father and Mother's biggest mistake in dealing with the van Daans is that they're never candid and friendly (admittedly, the friendliness might have to be feigned). Above all, I want to keep the peace, and to neither quarrel nor gossip. With Father and Margot that's not difficult, but it is with Mother, which is why I'm glad she gives me an occasional rap on the knuckles.

You can win Mr. van Daan to your side by agreeing with him, listening quietly, not saying much and most of all . . . responding to his teasing and his corny jokes with a joke of your own. Mrs. van D. can be won over by talking openly to her and admitting when you're wrong. She also frankly admits her faults, of which she has many. I know all too well that she doesn't think as badly of me as she did in the beginning. And that's simply because I'm honest and tell people right to their faces what I think, even when it's not very flattering. I want to be honest; I think it gets you further and also makes you feel better about yourself.

Yesterday Mrs. van D. was talking about the rice we gave Mr. Kleiman. "All we do is give, give, give. But at a certain point I think that enough is enough. If he'd only take the trouble, Mr. Kleiman could scrounge up his own rice. Why should we give away all our supplies? We need them just as badly."

"No, Mrs. van Daan," I replied. "I don't agree with you. Mr. Kleiman may very well be able to get hold of a little rice, but he doesn't like having to worry about it. It's not our place to criticize the people who are helping us. We should give them whatever they need if we can possibly spare it. One less plate of rice a week won't make that much difference; we can always eat beans."

Mrs. van D. didn't see it my way, but she added that, even though she disagreed, she was willing to back down, and that was an entirely different matter.

Well, I've said enough. Sometimes I know what my place is and sometimes I have my doubts, but I'll eventually get where I want to be! I know I will! Especially now that I have help, since Peter helps me through many a rough patch and rainy day!

I honestly don't know how much he loves me and whether we'll ever get as far as a kiss; in any case, I don't want to force the issue! I told Father I often go see Peter and asked if he approved, and of course he did!

It's much easier now to tell Peter things I'd normally keep to myself; for example, I told him I want to write later on, and if I can't be a writer, to write in addition to my work.

I don't have much in the way of money or worldly possessions, I'm not beautiful, intelligent or clever, but I'm happy, and I intend to stay that way! I was born happy, I love people, I have a trusting nature, and I'd like everyone else to be happy too.

*Your devoted friend, Anne M. Frank*

> *An empty day, though clear and bright,*
> *Is just as dark as any night.*

(I wrote this a few weeks ago and it no longer holds true, but I included it because my poems are so few and far between.)

MONDAY, MARCH 27, 1944
*Dearest Kitty,*

At least one long chapter on our life in hiding should be about politics, but I've been avoiding the subject, since it interests me so little. Today, however, I'll devote an entire letter to politics.

Of course, there are many different opinions on this topic, and it's not surprising to hear it frequently discussed in times of war, but ... arguing so much about politics is just plain stupid! Let them laugh, swear, make bets, grumble and do whatever they want as long as they stew in their own juice. But don't let them argue, since that only makes things worse. The people who come from outside bring us a lot of news that later proves to be untrue; however, up to now our radio has never lied. Jan, Miep, Mr. Kleiman, Bep and Mr. Kugler go up and down in their political moods, though Jan least of all.

Here in the Annex the mood never varies. The endless debates over the invasion, air raids, speeches, etc., etc., are accompanied by countless exclamations such as "Eempossible!, *Um Gottes Willen*,* If they're just getting started now, how long is it going to last!, It's going splendidly, *gut*, great!"

Optimists and pessimists – not to mention the realists – air their opinions with unflagging energy, and as with everything else, they're all certain that they have a monopoly on the truth. It annoys a certain lady that her spouse has such supreme faith in the British, and a certain husband attacks his wife because of her teasing and disparaging remarks about his beloved nation!

And so it goes from early in the morning to late at night; the funny part is that they never get tired of it. I've discovered a trick,

* Oh, for heaven's sake.

and the effect is overwhelming, just like pricking someone with a pin and watching them jump. Here's how it works: I start talking about politics. All it takes is a single question, a word or a sentence, and before you know it, the entire family is involved!

As if the German "Wehrmacht News" and the English BBC weren't enough, they've now added special air-raid announcements. In a word, splendid. But the other side of the coin is that the British Air Force is operating around the clock. Not unlike the German propaganda machine, which is cranking out lies twenty-four hours a day!

So the radio is switched on every morning at eight (if not earlier) and is listened to every hour until nine, ten or even eleven at night. This is the best evidence yet that the adults have infinite patience, but also that their brains have turned to mush (some of them, I mean, since I wouldn't want to insult anyone). One broadcast, two at the most, should be enough to last the entire day. But no, those old nincompoops . . . never mind, I've already said it all! "Music While You Work," the Dutch broadcast from England, Frank Phillips or Queen Wilhelmina, they each get a turn and find a willing listener. If the adults aren't eating or sleeping, they're clustered around the radio talking about eating, sleeping and politics. Whew! It's getting to be a bore, and it's all I can do to keep from turning into a dreary old crone myself! Though with all the old folks around me, that might not be such a bad idea!

Here's a shining example, a speech made by our beloved Winston Churchill.

Nine o'clock, Sunday evening. The teapot, under its cozy, is on the table, and the guests enter the room. Dussel sits to the left of the radio, Mr. van D. in front of it and Peter to the side. Mother is next to Mr. van D., with Mrs. van D. behind them. Margot and I are sitting in the last row and Pim at the table. I realize this isn't a very clear description of our seating arrangements, but it doesn't matter. The men smoke, Peter's eyes close from the strain of listening, Mama is dressed in her long, dark negligee, Mrs. van D. is trembling because of the planes, which take no notice of the speech but fly blithely on toward Essen, Father is slurping his tea, and Margot and I are united in a sisterly way by the sleeping Mouschi, who has taken possession of both our knees. Margot's hair is in curlers and my nightgown is too small, too tight and too short. It all looks so intimate, cozy and peaceful, and for once it really is. Yet I await the end of the speech with dread. They're impatient, straining at the leash to start another argument! Pst, pst, like a cat luring a mouse from its hole, they goad each other into quarrels and dissent.

*Yours, Anne*

*My dearest Kitty,*                    TUESDAY, MARCH 28, 1944

As much as I'd like to write more on politics, I have lots of other news to report today. First, Mother has virtually forbidden me to go up to Peter's, since, according to her, Mrs. van Daan is jealous. Second, Peter's invited Margot to join us upstairs. Whether he really means it or is just saying it out of politeness, I don't know. Third, I asked Father if he thought I should take any notice of Mrs. van Daan's jealousy and he said I didn't have to.

What should I do now? Mother's angry, doesn't want me going upstairs, wants me to go back to doing my homework in the room I share with Dussel. She may be jealous herself. Father doesn't begrudge us those few hours and thinks it's nice we get along so well. Margot likes Peter too, but feels that three people can't talk about the same things as two.

Furthermore, Mother thinks Peter's in love with me. To tell you the truth, I wish he were. Then we'd be even, and it'd be a lot easier to get to know each other. She also claims he's always looking at me. Well, I suppose we do give each other the occasional wink. But I can't help it if he keeps admiring my dimples, can I?

I'm in a very difficult position. Mother's against me and I'm against her. Father turns a blind eye to the silent struggle between Mother and me. Mother is sad, because she still loves me, but I'm not at all unhappy, because she no longer means anything to me.

As for Peter . . . I don't want to give him up. He's so sweet and I admire him so much. He and I could have a really beautiful relationship, so why are the old folks poking their noses into our business again? Fortunately, I'm used to hiding my feelings, so

I manage not to show how crazy I am about him. Is he ever going to say anything? Am I ever going to feel his cheek against mine, the way I felt Petel's cheek in my dream? Oh, Peter and Petel, you're one and the same! They don't understand us; they'd never understand that we're content just to sit beside each other and not say a word. They have no idea of what draws us together! Oh, when will we overcome all these difficulties? And yet it's good that we have to surmount them, since it makes the end that much more beautiful. When he lays his head on his arms and closes his eyes, he's still a child; when he plays with Mouschi or talks about her, he's loving; when he carries the potatoes or other heavy loads, he's strong; when he goes to watch the gunfire or walks through the dark house to look for burglars, he's brave; and when he's so awkward and clumsy, he's hopelessly endearing. It's much nicer when he explains something to me than when I have to teach him. I wish he were superior to me in nearly every way!

What do we care about our two mothers? Oh, if only he'd say something.

Father always says I'm conceited, but I'm not, I'm merely vain! I haven't had many people tell me I was pretty, except for a boy at school who said I looked so cute when I smiled. Yesterday Peter paid me a true compliment, and just for fun I'll give you a rough idea of our conversation.

Peter often says, "Smile!" I thought it was strange, so yesterday I asked him, "Why do you always want me to smile?"

"Because you get dimples in your cheeks. How do you do that?"

"I was born with them. There's also one in my chin. It's the only mark of beauty I possess."

"No, no, that's not true!"

"Yes it is. I know I'm not beautiful. I never have been and I never will be!"

"I don't agree. I think you're pretty."

"I am not."

"I say you are, and you'll have to take my word for it!"

So of course I then said the same about him.

*Yours, Anne M. Frank*

*Dearest Kitty,*                    WEDNESDAY, MARCH 29, 1944

Mr. Bolkestein, the Cabinet Minister, speaking on the Dutch broadcast from London, said that after the war a collection would be made of diaries and letters dealing with the war. Of course, everyone pounced on my diary. Just imagine how interesting it would be if I were to publish a novel about the Secret Annex. The title alone would make people think it was a detective story.

Seriously, though, ten years after the war people would find it very amusing to read how we lived, what we ate and what we talked about as Jews in hiding. Although I tell you a great deal about our lives, you still know very little about us. How frightened the women are during air raids; last Sunday, for instance, when 350 British planes dropped 550 tons of bombs on IJmuiden, so that the houses trembled like blades of grass in the wind. Or how many epidemics are raging here.

You know nothing of these matters, and it would take me all day to describe everything down to the last detail. People have to stand in line to buy vegetables and all kinds of goods; doctors can't visit their patients, since their cars and bikes are stolen the moment they turn their backs; burglaries and thefts are so common that you ask yourself what's suddenly gotten into the Dutch to make them so light-fingered. Little children, eight- and eleven-year-olds, smash the windows of people's homes and steal whatever they can lay their hands on. People don't dare leave the house for even five minutes, since they're liable to come back and find all their belongings gone. Every day the newspapers are filled with reward notices for the return of stolen typewriters, Persian rugs, electric clocks, fabrics, etc. The electric clocks on street corners are dismantled, public phones are stripped down to the last wire.

Morale among the Dutch can't be good. Everyone's hungry; except for the ersatz coffee, a week's food ration doesn't last two days. The invasion's long in coming, the men are being shipped off to Germany, the children are sick or undernourished, every-one's wearing worn-out clothes and run-down shoes. A new sole costs 7.50 guilders on the black market. Besides, few shoe-makers will do repairs, or if they do, you have to wait four months for your shoes, which might very well have disappeared in the meantime.

One good thing has come out of this: as the food gets worse and the decrees more severe, the acts of sabotage against the authorities are increasing. The ration board, the police, the officials — they're all either helping their fellow citizens or denouncing them and sending them off to prison. Fortunately, only a small percentage of Dutch people are on the wrong side.

                                                                Yours, Anne


*Dearest Kitty,*                                    FRIDAY, MARCH 31, 1944

Just imagine, it's still fairly cold, and yet most people have been without coal for nearly a month. Sounds awful, doesn't it? There's a general mood of optimism about the Russian front, because that's going great guns! I don't often write about the political situation, but I must tell you where the Russians are at the moment. They've reached the Polish border and the Prut River in Romania. They're close to Odessa, and they've surrounded Ternopol. Every night we're expecting an extra communiqué from Stalin.

They're firing off so many salutes in Moscow, the city must be rumbling and shaking all day long. Whether they like to pretend the fighting's nearby or they simply don't have any other way to express their joy, I don't know!

Hungary has been occupied by German troops. There are still a million Jews living there; they too are doomed.

Nothing special is happening here. Today is Mr. van Daan's birthday. He received two packets of tobacco, one serving of coffee, which his wife had managed to save, lemon punch from Mr. Kugler, sardines from Miep, eau de cologne from us, lilacs, tulips and, last but not least, a cake with raspberry filling, slightly gluey because of the poor quality of the flour and the lack of butter, but delicious anyway.

All that talk about Peter and me has died down a bit. He's coming to pick me up tonight. Pretty nice of him, don't you think, since he hates doing it! We're very good friends. We spend a lot of time together and talk about every imaginable subject. It's so nice not having to hold back when we come to a delicate topic, the way I would with other boys. For example, we were talking about blood and somehow the conversation turned to menstruation, etc. He thinks we women are quite tough to be able to withstand the loss of blood, and that I am too. I wonder why?

My life here has gotten better, much better. God has not forsaken me, and He never will.

Yours, Anne M. Frank

SATURDAY, APRIL 1, 1944

*My dearest Kitty,*

And yet everything is still so difficult. You do know what I mean, don't you? I long so much for him to kiss me, but that kiss is taking its own sweet time. Does he still think of me as a friend? Don't I mean anything more?

You and I both know that I'm strong, that I can carry most burdens alone. I've never been used to sharing my worries with anyone, and I've never clung to a mother, but I'd love to lay my head on his shoulder and just sit there quietly.

I can't, I simply can't forget that dream of Peter's cheek, when everything was so good! Does he have the same longing? Is he just too shy to say he loves me? Why does he want me near him so much? Oh, why doesn't he say something?

I've got to stop, I've got to be calm. I'll try to be strong again, and if I'm patient, the rest will follow. But – and this is the worst part – I seem to be chasing him. I'm always the one who has to go upstairs; *he* never comes to *me*. But that's because of the rooms, and he understands why I object. Oh, I'm sure he understands more than I think.

Yours, Anne M. Frank

MONDAY, APRIL 3, 1944

*My dearest Kitty,*

Contrary to my usual practice, I'm going to write you a detailed description of the food situation, since it's become a matter of some difficulty and importance, not only here in the Annex, but in all of Holland, all of Europe and even beyond.

In the twenty-one months we've lived here, we've been through a good many "food cycles" – you'll understand what that means in a moment. A "food cycle" is a period in which we have only one particular dish or type of vegetable to eat. For a long time we ate nothing but endive. Endive with sand, endive without sand, endive with mashed potatoes, endive-and-mashed potato casserole. Then it was spinach, followed by kohlrabi, salsify, cucumbers, tomatoes, sauerkraut, etc., etc.

It's not much fun when you have to eat, say, sauerkraut every day for lunch and dinner, but when you're hungry enough, you do a lot of things. Now, however, we're going through the most delightful period so far, because there are no vegetables at all.

Our weekly lunch menu consists of brown beans, split-pea soup, potatoes with dumplings, potato kugel and, by the grace of God, turnip greens or rotten carrots, and then it's back to brown beans. Because of the bread shortage, we eat potatoes at every meal, starting with breakfast, but then we fry them a little. To make soup we use brown beans, navy beans, potatoes, packages of vegetable soup, packages of chicken soup and packages of bean soup. There are brown beans in everything, including the bread. For dinner we always have potatoes with imitation gravy and – thank goodness we've still got it – beet salad. I must tell you about the dumplings. We make them with government-issue flour, water and yeast. They're so gluey and tough that it feels as if you have rocks in your stomach, but oh well!

The high point is our weekly slice of liverwurst, and the jam on our unbuttered bread. But we're still alive, and much of the time it still tastes good too!

*Yours, Anne M. Frank*

WEDNESDAY, APRIL 5, 1944

*My dearest Kitty,*

For a long time now I didn't know why I was bothering to do any schoolwork. The end of the war still seemed so far away, so unreal, like a fairy tale. If the war isn't over by September, I won't go back to school, since I don't want to be two years behind.

Peter filled my days, nothing but Peter, dreams and thoughts until Saturday night, when I felt so utterly miserable; oh, it was awful. I held back my tears when I was with Peter, laughed uproariously with the van Daans as we drank lemon punch and was cheerful and excited, but the minute I was alone I knew I was going to cry my eyes out. I slid to the floor in my nightgown and began by saying my prayers, very fervently. Then I drew my knees to my chest, lay my head on my arms and cried, all huddled up on the bare floor. A loud sob brought me back down to earth, and I choked back my tears, since I didn't want anyone next door to hear me. Then I tried to pull myself together, saying over and over, "I must, I must, I must ..." Stiff from sitting in such an unusual position, I fell back against the side of the bed and kept up my struggle until just before ten-thirty, when I climbed back into bed. It was over!

And now it's really over. I finally realized that I must do my schoolwork to keep from being ignorant, to get on in life, to become a journalist, because that's what I want! I know I can write. A few of my stories are good, my descriptions of the Secret Annex are humorous, much of my diary is vivid and alive, but ... it remains to be seen whether I really have talent.

"Eva's Dream" is my best fairy tale, and the odd thing is that I don't have the faintest idea where it came from. Parts of "Cady's Life" are also good, but as a whole it's nothing special. I'm my best and harshest critic. I know what's good and what isn't. Unless you write yourself, you can't know how wonderful it is; I always used to bemoan the fact that I couldn't draw, but now I'm overjoyed that at least I can write. And if I don't have the talent to write books or newspaper articles, I can always write for myself. But I want to achieve more than that. I can't imagine having to live like Mother, Mrs. van Daan and all the women who go about their work and are then forgotten. I need to have something besides a husband and children to devote myself to! I don't want to have lived in vain like most people. I want to be useful or bring enjoyment to all people, even those I've never met. I want to go on living even after my death! And that's why I'm so grateful to God for having given me this gift, which I can use to develop myself and to express all that's inside me!

When I write I can shake off all my cares. My sorrow disappears, my spirits are revived! But, and that's a big question, will I ever be able to write something great, will I ever become a journalist or a writer?

I hope so, oh, I hope so very much, because writing allows me to record everything, all my thoughts, ideals and fantasies.

I haven't worked on "Cady's Life" for ages. In my mind I've worked out exactly what happens next, but the story doesn't seem to be coming along very well. I might never finish it, and it'll wind up in the wastepaper basket or the stove. That's a horrible thought, but then I say to myself, "At the age of fourteen and with so little experience, you can't write about philosophy."

So onward and upward, with renewed spirits. It'll all work out, because I'm determined to write!

*Yours, Anne M. Frank*

THURSDAY, APRIL 6, 1944

*Dearest Kitty,*

You asked me what my hobbies and interests are and I'd like to answer, but I'd better warn you, I have lots of them, so don't be surprised.

First of all: writing, but I don't really think of that as a hobby.

Number two: genealogical charts. I'm looking in every newspaper, book and document I can find for the family trees of the French, German, Spanish, English, Austrian, Russian, Norwegian and Dutch royal families. I've made great progress with many of them, because for a long time I've been taking notes while reading biographies or history books. I even copy out many of the passages on history.

So my third hobby is history, and Father's already bought me numerous books. I can hardly wait for the day when I'll be able to go to the public library and ferret out the information I need.

Number four is Greek and Roman mythology. I have various books on this subject too. I can name the nine Muses and the seven loves of Zeus. I have the wives of Hercules, etc., etc., down pat.

My other hobbies are movie stars and family photographs. I'm crazy about reading and books. I adore the history of the arts, especially when it concerns writers, poets and painters; musicians may come later. I loathe algebra, geometry and arithmetic. I enjoy all my other school subjects, but history's my favorite!

*Yours, Anne M. Frank*

*My dearest Kitty,*                      TUESDAY, APRIL II, 1944

My head's in a whirl, I really don't know where to begin. Thursday (the last time I wrote you) everything was as usual. Friday afternoon (Good Friday) we played Monopoly; Saturday afternoon too. The days passed very quickly. Around two o'clock on Saturday, heavy firing began – machine guns, according to the men. For the rest, everything was quiet.

Sunday afternoon Peter came to see me at four-thirty, at my invitation. At five-fifteen we went to the front attic, where we stayed until six. There was a beautiful Mozart concert on the radio from six to seven-fifteen; I especially enjoyed the *Kleine Nachtmusik*. I can hardly bear to listen in the kitchen, since beautiful music stirs me to the very depths of my soul. Sunday evening Peter couldn't take his bath, because the washtub was down in the office kitchen, filled with laundry. The two of us went to the front attic together, and in order to be able to sit comfortably, I took along the only cushion I could find in my room. We seated ourselves on a packing crate. Since both the crate and the cushion were very narrow, we were sitting quite close, leaning against two other crates; Mouschi kept us company, so we weren't without a chaperon. Suddenly, at a quarter to nine, Mr. van Daan whistled and asked if we had Mr. Dussel's cushion. We jumped up and went downstairs with the cushion, the cat and Mr. van Daan. This cushion was the source of much misery. Dussel was angry because I'd taken the one he uses as a pillow, and he was afraid it might be covered with fleas; he had the entire house in an uproar because of this one cushion. In revenge, Peter and I stuck two hard brushes in his bed, but had to take them out again when Dussel unexpectedly decided to go sit in his room. We had a really good laugh at this little intermezzo.

But our fun was short-lived. At nine-thirty Peter knocked gently on the door and asked Father to come upstairs and help him with a difficult English sentence.

"That sounds fishy," I said to Margot. "It's obviously a pretext. You can tell by the way the men are talking that there's been a break-in!" I was right. The warehouse was being broken into at that very moment. Father, Mr. van Daan and Peter were downstairs in a flash. Margot, Mother, Mrs. van D. and I waited. Four frightened women need to talk, so that's what we did until we heard a bang downstairs. After that all was quiet. The clock struck quarter to ten. The color had drained from our faces, but we remained calm, even though we were afraid. Where were the men? What was that bang? Were they fighting with the burglars? We were too scared to think; all we could do was wait.

Ten o'clock, footsteps on the stairs. Father, pale and nervous, came inside, followed by Mr. van Daan. "Lights out, tiptoe upstairs, we're expecting the police!"

There wasn't time to be scared. The lights were switched off, I grabbed a jacket, and we sat down upstairs.

"What happened? Tell us quickly!"

There was no one to tell us; the men had gone back downstairs. The four of them didn't come back up until ten past ten. Two of them kept watch at Peter's open window. The door to the landing was locked, the bookcase shut. We draped a sweater over our night-light, and then they told us what had happened:

Peter was on the landing when he heard two loud bangs. He went downstairs and saw that a large panel was missing from the left half of the warehouse door. He dashed upstairs, alerted the "Home Guard," and the four of them went downstairs. When they entered the warehouse, the burglars were going about their business. Without thinking, Mr. van Daan yelled "Police!" Hurried footsteps outside; the burglars had fled. The board was put back in the door so the police wouldn't notice the gap, but then a swift kick from outside sent it flying to the floor. The men were amazed at the burglars' audacity. Both Peter and Mr. van Daan felt a murderous rage come over them. Mr. van Daan slammed an ax against the floor, and all was quiet again. Once more the panel was replaced, and once more the attempt was foiled. Outside, a man and a woman shone a glaring flashlight through the opening, lighting up the entire warehouse. "What the . . ." mumbled one of the men, but now their roles had been reversed. Instead of policemen, they were now burglars. All four of them raced upstairs. Dussel and Mr. van Daan snatched up Dussel's books, Peter opened the doors and windows in the kitchen and private office, hurled the phone to the ground, and the four of them finally ended up behind the bookcase.

END OF PART ONE

In all probability the man and woman with the flashlight had alerted the police. It was Sunday night, Easter Sunday. The next day, Easter Monday, the office was going to be closed, which meant we wouldn't be able to move around until Tuesday morning. Think of it, having to sit in such terror for a day and two nights! We thought of nothing, but simply sat there in pitch darkness – in her fear, Mrs. van D. had switched off the lamp. We whispered, and every time we heard a creak, someone said, "Shh, shh."

It was ten-thirty, then eleven. Not a sound. Father and Mr. van Daan took turns coming upstairs to us. Then, at eleven-fifteen, a noise below. Up above you could hear the whole family breathing. For the rest, no one moved a muscle. Footsteps in the house, the private office, the kitchen, then . . . on the staircase. All sounds of breathing stopped, eight hearts pounded. Footsteps on the stairs, then a rattling at the bookcase. This moment is indescribable.

"Now we're done for," I said, and I had visions of all fifteen of us being dragged away by the Gestapo that very night.

More rattling at the bookcase, twice. Then we heard a can fall, and the footsteps receded. We were out of danger, so far! A shiver went though everyone's body, I heard several sets of teeth chattering, no one said a word. We stayed like this until eleven-thirty.

There were no more sounds in the house, but a light was shining on our landing, right in front of the bookcase. Was that because the police thought it looked so suspicious or because they simply forgot? Was anyone going to come back and turn it off? We found our tongues again. There were no longer any people inside the building, but perhaps someone was standing guard outside. We then did three things: tried to guess what was going on, trembled with fear and went to the bathroom. Since the buckets were in the attic, all we had was Peter's metal waste-paper basket. Mr. van Daan went first, then Father, but Mother was too embarrassed. Father brought the wastebasket to the next room, where Margot, Mrs. van Daan and I gratefully made use of it. Mother finally gave in. There was a great demand for paper, and luckily I had some in my pocket.

The wastebasket stank, everything went on in a whisper, and we were exhausted. It was midnight.

"Lie down on the floor and go to sleep!" Margot and I were each given a pillow and a blanket. Margot lay down near the food cupboard, and I made my bed between the table legs. The smell wasn't quite so bad when you were lying on the floor, but Mrs. van Daan quietly went and got some powdered bleach and draped a dish towel over the potty as a further precaution.

Talk, whispers, fear, stench, farting and people continually going to the bathroom; try sleeping through that! By two-thirty, however, I was so tired I dozed off and didn't hear a thing until three-thirty. I woke up when Mrs. van D. lay her head on my feet.

"For heaven's sake, give me something to put on!" I said. I was handed some clothes, but don't ask what: a pair of wool slacks over my pajamas, a red sweater and a black skirt, white understockings and tattered kneesocks.

Mrs. van D. sat back down on the chair, and Mr. van D. lay down with his head on my feet. From three-thirty onward I was engrossed in thought, and still shivering so much that Mr. van Daan couldn't sleep. I was preparing myself for the return of the police. We'd tell them we were in hiding; if they were good people, we'd be safe, and if they were Nazi sympathizers, we could try to bribe them!

"We should hide the radio!" moaned Mrs. van D.

"Sure, in the stove," answered Mr. van D. "If they find us, they might as well find the radio!"

"Then they'll also find Anne's diary," added Father.

"So burn it," suggested the most terrified of the group.

This and the police rattling on the bookcase were the moments when I was most afraid. Oh, not my diary; if my diary goes, I go too! Thank goodness Father didn't say anything more.

There's no point in recounting all the conversations; so much was said. I comforted Mrs. van Daan, who was very frightened. We talked about escaping, being interrogated by the Gestapo, phoning Mr. Kleiman and being courageous.

"We must behave like soldiers, Mrs. van Daan. If our time has come, well then, it'll be for Queen and Country, for freedom, truth and justice, as they're always telling us on the radio. The only bad thing is that we'll drag the others down with us!"

After an hour Mr. van Daan switched places with his wife again, and Father came and sat beside me. The men smoked one cigarette after another, an occasional sigh was heard, somebody made another trip to the potty, and then everything began all over again.

Four o'clock, five, five-thirty. I went and sat with Peter by his window and listened, so close we could feel each other's bodies trembling; we spoke a word or two from time to time and listened intently. Next door they took down the blackout screen. They made a list of everything they were planning to tell Mr. Kleiman over the phone, because they intended to call him at seven and ask him to send someone over. They were taking a big chance, since the police guard at the door or in the warehouse might hear them calling, but there was an even greater risk that the police would return.

I'm enclosing their list, but for the sake of clarity, I'll copy it here.

> *Burglary:* Police in building, up to *bookcase*, but no farther.
> Burglars apparently interrupted, forced warehouse door,
> fled through garden. Main entrance bolted; Kugler *must*
> have left through second door.
> Typewriter and adding machine safe in black chest in
> private office.
> Miep's or Bep's laundry in washtub in kitchen.
> Only Bep or Kugler have key to second door; lock may be
> broken.
> Try to warn Jan and get key, look around office; also feed cat.

*The Frank family, Amsterdam, 1941.*

*Anne, Amsterdam, 1935-42 (left to right: May 1935, December 1935, May 1936, May 1937, May 1938, May 1939, May 1940, May 1941, May 1942).*

*263 Prinsengracht, Amsterdam, front view.*

*263 Prinsengracht, Amsterdam, rear view. The Secret Annex*
*(top two floors and attic) as seen from the courtyard garden.*

*Johannes Kleiman next to the bookcase, after the war.*

*Peter van Daan*
*(date and place unknown).*

*Albert Dussel*
*(date and place unknown).*

*Miep Gies and Bep Voskuijl, Amsterdam, 1945.*

*Johannes Kleiman and Victor Kugler, Amsterdam, 1945.*

*Margot and
Anne with
their father,
Frankfurt,
Germany,
1930.*

*Anne (right)
and her
friend Sanne
Ledermann,
Amsterdam,
1935.*

*Anne,
Aachen, Germany,
1934.*

*Edith Frank,
May 1935.*

*Otto Frank
May 1936.*

*Brothers Robert and Otto Frank in the German Army, 1916.*

*Wedding of Edith and Otto Frank, Aachen, Germany, 1925.*

*Anne,*
*Amsterdam, 1941.*

*Mrs. van Daan, Mr. van Daan*
*and Victor Kugler, Amsterdam, 1941.*

*Otto, Anne and Margot Frank walking along with other guests to the*
*wedding of Jan and Miep Gies, Amsterdam, June 1941.*

*Anne's tenth birthday, Amsterdam, June 12, 1939*
*(left to right: Lucie van Dijk, Anne, Sanne Ledermann, Hanneli*
*Goslar, Juultje Ketellapper, Käthe Egyedie, Mary Bos, Ietje Swillens,*
*Martha van den Berg).*

*Margot, Anne and Grandma Holländer, Zandvoort, Holland, 1939.*

For the rest, everything went according to plan. Mr. Kleiman was phoned, the poles were removed from the doors, the typewriter was put back in the chest. Then we all sat around the table again and waited for either Jan or the police.

Peter had dropped off to sleep and Mr. van Daan and I were lying on the floor when we heard loud footsteps below. I got up quietly. "It's Jan!"

"No, no, it's the police!" they all said.

There was a knocking at our bookcase. Miep whistled. This was too much for Mrs. van Daan, who sank limply in her chair, white as a sheet. If the tension had lasted another minute, she would have fainted.

Jan and Miep came in and were met with a delightful scene. The table alone would have been worth a photograph: a copy of *Cinema & Theater*, opened to a page of dancing girls and smeared with jam and pectin, which we'd been taking to combat the diarrhea, two jam jars, half a bread roll, a quarter of a bread roll, pectin, a mirror, a comb, matches, ashes, cigarettes, tobacco, an ashtray, books, a pair of underpants, a flashlight, Mrs. van Daan's comb, toilet paper, etc.

Jan and Miep were of course greeted with shouts and tears. Jan nailed a pinewood board over the gap in the door and went off again with Miep to inform the police of the break-in. Miep had also found a note under the warehouse door from Sleegers, the night watchman, who had noticed the hole and alerted the police. Jan was also planning to see Sleegers.

So we had half an hour in which to put the house and ourselves to rights. I've never seen such a transformation as in those thirty minutes. Margot and I got the beds ready downstairs, went to the bathroom, brushed our teeth, washed our hands and combed our hair. Then I straightened up the room a bit and went back upstairs. The table had already been cleared, so we got some water, made coffee and tea, boiled the milk and set the table. Father and Peter emptied our improvised potties and rinsed them with warm water and powdered bleach. The largest one was filled to the brim and was so heavy they had a hard time lifting it. To make things worse, it was leaking, so they had to put it in a bucket.

At eleven o'clock Jan was back and joined us at the table, and gradually everyone began to relax. Jan had the following story to tell:

Mr. Sleegers was asleep, but his wife told Jan that her husband had discovered the hole in the door while making his rounds. He called in a policeman, and the two of them searched the building. Mr. Sleegers, in his capacity as night watchman, patrols the area every night on his bike, accompanied by his two dogs. His wife said he would come on Tuesday and tell Mr. Kugler the rest. No one at the police station seemed to know anything about the break-in, but they made a note to come first thing Tuesday morning to have a look.

On the way back Jan happened to run into Mr. van Hoeven, the man who supplies us with potatoes, and told him of the break-in. "I know," Mr. van Hoeven calmly replied. "Last night when my wife and I were walking past your building, I saw a gap in the door. My wife wanted to walk on, but I peeked inside with a flashlight, and that's when the burglars must have run off. To be on the safe side, I didn't call the police. I thought it wouldn't be wise in your case. I don't know anything, but I have my suspicions." Jan thanked him and went on. Mr. van Hoeven obviously suspects we're here, because he always delivers the potatoes at lunchtime. A decent man!

It was one o'clock by the time Jan left and we'd done the dishes. All eight of us went to bed. I woke up at quarter to three and saw that Mr. Dussel was already up. My face rumpled with sleep, I happened to run into Peter in the bathroom, just after he'd come downstairs. We agreed to meet in the office. I freshened up a bit and went down.

"After all this, do you still dare go to the front attic?" he asked. I nodded, grabbed my pillow, with a cloth wrapped around it, and we went up together. The weather was gorgeous, and even though the air-raid sirens soon began to wail, we stayed where we were. Peter put his arm around my shoulder, I put mine around his, and we sat quietly like this until four o'clock, when Margot came to get us for coffee.

We ate our bread, drank our lemonade and joked (we were finally able to again), and for the rest everything was back to normal. That evening I thanked Peter because he'd been the bravest of us all.

None of us have ever been in such danger as we were that night. God was truly watching over us. Just think — the police were right at the bookcase, the light was on, and still no one had discovered our hiding place! "Now we're done for!" I'd whispered at that moment, but once again we were spared. When the invasion comes and the bombs start falling, it'll be every man for himself, but this time we feared for those good, innocent Christians who are helping us.

"We've been saved, keep on saving us!" That's all we can say.

This incident has brought about a whole lot of changes. As of now, Dussel will be doing his work in the bathroom, and Peter will be patrolling the house between eight-thirty and nine-thirty. Peter isn't allowed to open his window anymore, since one of the Keg people noticed it was open. We can no longer flush the toilet after nine-thirty at night. Mr. Sleegers has been hired as night watchman, and tonight a carpenter from the underground is coming to make a barricade out of our white Frankfurt bedsteads. Debates are going on left and right in the Annex. Mr. Kugler has reproached us for our carelessness. Jan also said we should never go downstairs. What we have to do now is find out whether Sleegers can be trusted, whether the dogs will bark if they hear someone behind the door, how to make the barricade, all sorts of things.

We've been strongly reminded of the fact that we're Jews in chains, chained to one spot, without any rights, but with a thousand obligations. We must put our feelings aside; we must be brave and strong, bear discomfort without complaint, do whatever is in our power and trust in God. One day this terrible war will be over. The time will come when we'll be people again and not just Jews!

Who has inflicted this on us? Who has set us apart from all the rest? Who has put us through such suffering? It's God who has made us the way we are, but it's also God who will lift us up again. In the eyes of the world, we're doomed, but if, after all this suffering, there are still Jews left, the Jewish people will be held up as an example. Who knows, maybe our religion will teach the world and all the people in it about goodness, and that's the reason, the only reason, we have to suffer. We can never be just Dutch, or just English, or whatever, we will always be Jews as well. And we'll have to keep on being Jews, but then, we'll want to be.

Be brave! Let's remember our duty and perform it without complaint. There will be a way out. God has never deserted our people. Through the ages Jews have had to suffer, but through the ages they've gone on living, and the centuries of suffering have only made them stronger. The weak shall fall and the strong shall survive and not be defeated!

That night I really thought I was going to die. I waited for the police and I was ready for death, like a soldier on a battlefield. I'd gladly have given my life for my country. But now, now that I've been spared, my first wish after the war is to become a Dutch citizen. I love the Dutch, I love this country, I love the language, and I want to work here. And even if I have to write to the Queen herself, I won't give up until I've reached my goal!

I'm becoming more and more independent of my parents. Young as I am, I face life with more courage and have a better and truer sense of justice than Mother. I know what I want, I have a goal, I have opinions, a religion and love. If only I can be myself, I'll be satisfied. I know that I'm a woman, a woman with inner strength and a great deal of courage!

If God lets me live, I'll achieve more than Mother ever did, I'll make my voice heard, I'll go out into the world and work for mankind!

I now know that courage and happiness are needed first!

Yours, Anne M. Frank

Dear Kitty,                              FRIDAY, APRIL 14, 1944

Everyone here is still very tense. Pim has nearly reached the boiling point; Mrs. van D. is lying in bed with a cold, grumbling; Mr. van D. is growing pale without his cigarettes; Dussel, who's having to give up many of his comforts, is carping at everyone; etc., etc. We seem to have run out of luck lately. The toilet's leaking, and the faucet's stuck. Thanks to our many connections, we'll soon be able to get these repaired.

I'm occasionally sentimental, as you know, but from time to time I have reason to be: when Peter and I are sitting close together on a hard wooden crate among the junk and dust, our arms around each other's shoulders, Peter toying with a lock of my hair; when the birds outside are trilling their songs, when the trees are in bud, when the sun beckons and the sky is so blue – oh, that's when I wish for so much!

All I see around me are dissatisfied and grumpy faces, all I hear are sighs and stifled complaints. You'd think our lives had taken a sudden turn for the worse. Honestly, things are only as bad as you make them. Here in the Annex no one even bothers to set a good example. We each have to figure out how to get the better of our own moods!

Every day you hear, "If only it were all over!"

*Work, love, courage and hope,*
*Make me good and help me cope!*

I really believe, Kit, that I'm a little nutty today, and I don't know why. My writing's all mixed up, I'm jumping from one thing to another, and sometimes I seriously doubt whether anyone will ever be interested in this drivel. They'll probably call it "The Musings of an Ugly Duckling." *My* diaries certainly won't be of much use to Mr. Bolkestein or Mr. Gerbrandy.*

*Yours, Anne M. Frank*

*Dearest Kitty,*                                    SATURDAY, APRIL 15, 1944

"There's just one bad thing after another. When will it all end?" You can sure say that again. Guess what's happened now? Peter forgot to unbolt the front door. As a result, Mr. Kugler and the warehouse employees couldn't get in. He went to Keg's,

*Gerrit Bolkestein was the Minister of Education and Pieter Gerbrandy was the Prime Minister of the Dutch government in exile in London. See Anne's letter of March 29, 1944.

smashed in our office kitchen window and got in that way. The windows in the Annex were open, and the Keg people saw that too. What must they be thinking? And van Maaren? Mr. Kugler's furious. We accuse him of not doing anything to reinforce the doors, and then we do a stupid thing like this! Peter's extremely upset. At the table, Mother said she felt more sorry for Peter than for anyone else, and he nearly began to cry. We're equally to blame, since we usually ask him every day if he's unbolted the door, and so does Mr. van Daan. Maybe I can go comfort him later on. I want to help him so much!

Here are the latest news bulletins about life in the Secret Annex over the last few weeks:

A week ago, on Saturday, Boche suddenly got sick. He sat quite still and started drooling. Miep immediately picked him up, rolled him in a towel, tucked him in her shopping bag and brought him to the dog-and-cat clinic. Boche had some kind of intestinal problem, so the vet gave him medicine. Peter gave it to him a few times, but Boche soon made himself scarce. I'll bet he was out courting his sweetheart. But now his nose is swollen and he meows whenever you pick him up – he was probably trying to steal food and somebody smacked him. Mouschi lost her voice for a few days. Just when we decided she had to be taken to the vet too, she started getting better.

We now leave the attic window open a crack every night. Peter and I often sit up there in the evening.

Thanks to rubber cement and oil paint, our toilet could quickly be repaired. The broken faucet has been replaced.

Luckily, Mr. Kleiman is feeling better. He's going to see a specialist soon. We can only hope he won't need an operation.

This month we received eight ration books. Unfortunately, for the next two weeks beans have been substituted for oatmeal or groats. Our latest delicacy is piccalilli. If you're out of luck, all you get is a jar full of cucumber and mustard sauce.

Vegetables are hard to come by. There's only lettuce, lettuce and more lettuce. Our meals consist entirely of potatoes and imitation gravy.

The Russians are in possession of more than half the Crimea. The British aren't advancing beyond Cassino. We'll have to count on the Western Wall. There have been a lot of unbelievably heavy air raids. The Registry of Births, Deaths and Marriages in The Hague was bombed. All Dutch people will be issued new ration registration cards.

Enough for today.

*Yours, Anne M. Frank*

*My dearest Kitty,*

SUNDAY, APRIL 16, 1944

Remember yesterday's date, since it was a red-letter day for me. Isn't it an important day for every girl when she gets her first kiss? Well then, it's no less important to me. The time Bram kissed me on my right cheek or Mr. Woudstra on my right hand doesn't count. How did I suddenly come by this kiss? I'll tell you.

Last night at eight I was sitting with Peter on his divan and it wasn't long before he put an arm around me. (Since it was Saturday, he wasn't wearing his overalls.) "Why don't we move over a little," I said, "so I won't keep bumping my head against the cupboard."

He moved so far over he was practically in the corner. I slipped my arm under his and across his back, and he put his arm around my shoulder, so that I was nearly engulfed by him. We've sat like this on other occasions, but never so close as we were last night. He held me firmly against him, my left side against his chest; my heart had already begun to beat faster, but there was more to come. He wasn't satisfied until my head lay on his shoulder, with his on top of mine. I sat up again after about five minutes, but before long he took my head in his hands and put it back next to his. Oh, it was so wonderful. I could hardly talk, my pleasure was too intense; he caressed my cheek and arm, a bit clumsily, and played with my hair. Most of the time our heads were touching.

I can't tell you, Kitty, the feeling that ran through me. I was too happy for words, and I think he was too.

At nine-thirty we stood up. Peter put on his tennis shoes so he wouldn't make much noise on his nightly round of the building, and I was standing next to him. How I suddenly made the right movement, I don't know, but before we went downstairs, he gave me a kiss, through my hair, half on my left cheek and half on my ear. I tore downstairs without looking back, and I long so much for today.

*Sunday morning, just before eleven.*

                                                    *Yours, Anne M. Frank*


*Dearest Kitty,*                         MONDAY, APRIL 17, 1944

Do you think Father and Mother would approve of a girl my age sitting on a divan and kissing a seventeen-and-a-half-year-old boy? I doubt they would, but I have to trust my own judgment in this matter. It's so peaceful and safe, lying in his arms and dreaming, it's so thrilling to feel his cheek against mine, it's so wonderful to know there's someone waiting for me. But, and there is a but, will Peter want to leave it at that? I haven't forgotten his promise, but . . . he is a boy!

I know I'm starting at a very young age. Not even fifteen and already so independent – that's a little hard for other people to understand. I'm pretty sure Margot would never kiss a boy unless there was some talk of an engagement or marriage. Neither Peter nor I has any such plans. I'm also sure that Mother never touched a man before she met Father. What would my girlfriends or Jacque say if they knew I'd lain in Peter's arms with my heart against his chest, my head on his shoulder and his head and face against mine!

Oh, Anne, how terribly shocking! But seriously, I don't think it's at all shocking; we're cooped up here, cut off from the world, anxious and fearful, especially lately. Why should we stay apart when we love each other? Why shouldn't we kiss each other in times like these? Why should we wait until we've reached a suitable age? Why should we ask anybody's permission?

I've decided to look out for my own interests. He'd never want to hurt me or make me unhappy. Why shouldn't I do what my heart tells me and makes both of us happy?

Yet I have a feeling, Kitty, that you can sense my doubt. It must be my honesty rising in revolt against all this sneaking around. Do you think it's my duty to tell Father what I'm up to? Do you think our secret should be shared with a third person? Much of the beauty would be lost, but would it make me feel better inside? I'll bring it up with *him*.

Oh, yes, I still have so much I want to discuss with him, since I don't see the point of just cuddling. Sharing our thoughts with each other requires a great deal of trust, but we'll both be stronger because of it!

*Yours, Anne M. Frank*

PS. We were up at six yesterday morning, because the whole family heard the sounds of a break-in again. It must have been one of our neighbors who was the victim this time. When we checked at seven o'clock, our doors were still shut tight, thank goodness!

TUESDAY, APRIL 18, 1944

*Dearest Kitty,*

Everything's fine here. Last night the carpenter came again to put some sheets of iron over the door panels. Father just got through saying he definitely expects large-scale operations in Russia and Italy, as well as in the West, before May 20; the longer the war lasts, the harder it is to imagine being liberated from this place.

Yesterday Peter and I finally got around to having the talk we've been postponing for the last ten days. I told him all about girls, without hesitating to discuss the most intimate matters. I found it rather amusing that he thought the opening in a woman's body was simply left out of illustrations. He couldn't imagine that it was actually located between a woman's legs. The evening ended with a mutual kiss, near the mouth. It's really a lovely feeling!

I might take my "favorite quotes notebook" up with me sometime so Peter and I can go into things more deeply. I don't think lying in each other's arms day in and day out is very satisfying, and I hope he feels the same.

After our mild winter we've been having a beautiful spring. April is glorious, not too hot and not too cold, with occasional light showers. Our chestnut tree is in leaf, and here and there you can already see a few small blossoms.

Bep presented us Saturday with four bouquets of flowers: three bouquets of daffodils, and one bouquet of grape hyacinths for me. Mr. Kugler is supplying us with more and more newspapers.

It's time to do my algebra, Kitty. Bye.

*Yours, Anne M. Frank*

WEDNESDAY, APRIL 19, 1944

*Dearest Darling,*

(That's the title of a movie with Dorit Kreysler, Ida Wüst and Harald Paulsen!)

What could be nicer than sitting before an open window, enjoying nature, listening to the birds sing, feeling the sun on your cheeks and holding a darling boy in your arms? I feel so peaceful and safe with his arm around me, knowing he's near and yet not having to speak; how can this be bad when it does me so much good? Oh, if only we were never disturbed again, not even by Mouschi.

*Yours, Anne M. Frank*

FRIDAY, APRIL 21, 1944

*My dearest Kitty,*

I stayed in bed yesterday with a sore throat, but since I was already bored the very first afternoon and didn't have a fever, I got up today. My sore throat has nearly *"verschwunden."* *

Yesterday, as you've probably already discovered, was our Führer's fifty-fifth birthday. Today is the eighteenth birthday of Her Royal Highness Princess Elizabeth of York. The BBC reported that she hasn't yet been declared of age, though royal children usually are. We've been wondering which prince they'll marry this beauty off to, but can't think of a suitable candidate; perhaps her sister, Princess Margaret Rose, can have Crown Prince Baudouin of Belgium!

Here we've been going from one disaster to the next. No sooner have the outside doors been reinforced than van Maaren rears his head again. In all likelihood he's the one who stole the potato flour, and now he's trying to pin the blame on Bep. Not surprisingly, the Annex is once again in an uproar. Bep is beside herself with rage. Perhaps Mr. Kugler will finally have this shady character tailed.

The appraiser from Beethovenstraat was here this morning. He offered us 400 guilders for our chest; in our opinion, the other estimates are also too low.

I want to ask the magazine *The Prince* if they'll take one of my

*Disappeared.

fairy tales, under a pseudonym, of course. But up to now all my fairy tales have been too long, so I don't think I have much of a chance.

Until the next time, darling.

*Yours, Anne M. Frank*

*Dearest Kitty,*

TUESDAY, APRIL 25, 1944

For the last ten days Dussel hasn't been on speaking terms with Mr. van Daan, and all because of the new security measures since the break-in. One of these was that he's no longer allowed to go downstairs in the evenings. Peter and Mr. van Daan make the last round every night at nine-thirty, and after that no one may go downstairs. We can't flush the toilet anymore after eight at night or after eight in the morning. The windows may be opened only in the morning when the lights go on in Mr. Kugler's office, and they can no longer be propped open with a stick at night. This last measure is the reason for Dussel's sulking. He claims that Mr. van Daan bawled him out, but he has only himself to blame. He says he'd rather live without food than without air, and that they simply must figure out a way to keep the windows open.

"I'll have to speak to Mr. Kugler about this," he said to me.

I replied that we never discussed matters of this sort with Mr. Kugler, only within the group.

"Everything's always happening behind my back. I'll have to talk to your father about that."

He's also not allowed to sit in Mr. Kugler's office anymore on Saturday afternoons or Sundays, because the manager of Keg's might hear him if he happens to be next door. Dussel promptly went and sat there anyway. Mr. van Daan was furious, and Father went downstairs to talk to Dussel, who came up with some flimsy excuse, but even Father didn't fall for it this time. Now Father's keeping his dealings with Dussel to a minimum because Dussel insulted him. Not one of us knows what he said, but it must have been pretty awful.

And to think that that miserable man has his birthday next week. How can you celebrate your birthday when you've got the sulks, how can you accept gifts from people you won't even talk to?

\*    \*    \*

Mr. Voskuijl is going downhill rapidly. For more than ten days he's had a temperature of almost a hundred and four. The doctor said his condition is hopeless; they think the cancer has spread to his lungs. The poor man, we'd so like to help him, but only God can help him now!

I've written an amusing story called "Blurry the Explorer," which was a big hit with my three listeners.

I still have a bad cold and have passed it on to Margot, as well as Mother and Father. If only Peter doesn't get it. He insisted on a kiss, and called me his El Dorado. You can't call a person that, silly boy! But he's sweet anyway!

                                                            *Yours, Anne M. Frank*

*Dearest Kitty,*                              THURSDAY, APRIL 27, 1944

Mrs. van D. was in a bad mood this morning. All she did was complain, first about her cold, not being able to get cough drops and the agony of having to blow her nose all the time. Next she grumbled that the sun wasn't shining, the invasion hadn't started, we weren't allowed to look out the windows, etc., etc. We couldn't help but laugh at her, and it couldn't have been that bad, since she soon joined in.

Our recipe for potato kugel, modified due to lack of onions:

> Put peeled potatoes through a food mill and add a little dry government-issue flour and salt. Grease a mold or oven-proof dish with paraffin or stearin and bake for $2\frac{1}{2}$ hours. Serve with rotten strawberry compote. (Onions not available. Nor oil for mold or dough!)

At the moment I'm reading *Emperor Charles V*, written by a professor at the University of Göttingen; he's spent forty years working on this book. It took me five days to read fifty pages. I can't do any more than that. Since the book has 598 pages, you can figure out just how long it's going to take me. And that's not even counting the second volume. But . . . very interesting!

The things a schoolgirl has to do in the course of a single day! Take me, for example. First, I translated a passage on Nelson's last battle from Dutch into English. Then, I read more about the

Northern War (1700–21) involving Peter the Great, Charles XII, Augustus the Strong, Stanislaus Leczinsky, Mazeppa, von Görz, Brandenburg, Western Pomerania, Eastern Pomerania and Denmark, plus the usual dates. Next, I wound up in Brazil, where I read about Bahia tobacco, the abundance of coffee, the one and a half million inhabitants of Rio de Janeiro, Pernambuco and São Paulo and, last but not least, the Amazon River. Then about Negroes, mulattoes, mestizos, whites, the illiteracy rate – over 50 percent – and malaria. Since I had some time left, I glanced through a genealogical chart: John the Old, William Louis, Ernest Casimir I, Henry Casimir I, right up to little Margriet Franciska (born in 1943 in Ottawa).

Twelve o'clock: I resumed my studies in the attic, reading about deans, priests, ministers, popes and ... whew, it was one o'clock!

At two the poor child (ho hum) was back at work. Old World and New World monkeys were next. Kitty, tell me quickly, how many toes does a hippopotamus have?

Then came the Bible, Noah's Ark, Shem, Ham and Japheth. After that, Charles V. Then, with Peter, Thackeray's book about the colonel, in English. A French test, and then a comparison between the Mississippi and the Missouri!

Enough for today. Adieu!

*Yours, Anne M. Frank*

FRIDAY, APRIL 28, 1944
*Dearest Kitty,*

I've never forgotten my dream of Peter Schiff (see the beginning of January). Even now I can still feel his cheek against mine, and that wonderful glow that made up for all the rest. Once in a while I'd had the same feeling with this Peter, but never so intensely ... until last night. We were sitting on the divan, as usual, in each other's arms. Suddenly the everyday Anne slipped away and the second Anne took her place. The second Anne, who's never overconfident or amusing, but wants only to love and be gentle.

I sat pressed against him and felt a wave of emotion come over me. Tears rushed to my eyes; those from the left fell on his overalls, while those from the right trickled down my nose and into the air and landed beside the first. Did he notice? He made no movement to show that he had. Did he feel the same way I did? He hardly said a word. Did he realize he had two Annes at his side? My questions went unanswered.

At eight-thirty I stood up and went to the window, where we always say good-bye. I was still trembling, I was still Anne number two. He came over to me, and I threw my arms around his neck and kissed him on his left cheek. I was about to kiss the other cheek when my mouth met his, and we pressed our lips together. In a daze, we embraced, over and over again, never to stop, oh!

Peter needs tenderness. For the first time in his life he's discovered a girl; for the first time he's seen that even the biggest pests also have an inner self and a heart, and are transformed as soon as they're alone with you. For the first time in his life he's given himself and his friendship to another person. He's never had a friend before, boy or girl. Now we've found each other. I, for that matter, didn't know him either, had never had someone I could confide in, and it's led to this . . .

The same question keeps nagging me: "Is it right?" Is it right for me to yield so soon, for me to be so passionate, to be filled with as much passion and desire as Peter? Can I, a girl, allow myself to go that far?

There's only one possible answer: "I'm longing so much . . . and have for such a long time. I'm so lonely and now I've found comfort!"

In the mornings we act normally, in the afternoons too, except now and then. But in the evenings the suppressed longing of the entire day, the happiness and the bliss of all the times before come rushing to the surface, and all we can think about is each other. Every night, after our last kiss, I feel like running away and never looking him in the eyes again. Away, far away into the darkness and alone!

And what awaits me at the bottom of those fourteen stairs? Bright lights, questions and laughter. I have to act normally and hope they don't notice anything.

My heart is still too tender to be able to recover so quickly from a shock like the one I had last night. The gentle Anne makes infrequent appearances, and she's not about to let herself be shoved out the door so soon after she's arrived. Peter's reached a part of me that no one has ever reached before, except in my dream! He's taken hold of me and turned me inside out. Doesn't everyone need a little quiet time to put themselves to rights again? Oh, Peter, what have you done to me? What do you want from me?

Where will this lead? Oh, now I understand Bep. Now, now that I'm going through it myself, I understand her doubts; if I were older and he wanted to marry me, what would my answer be? Anne, be honest! You wouldn't be able to marry him. But it's so hard to let go. Peter still has too little character, too little willpower, too little courage and strength. He's still a child, emotionally no older than I am; all he wants is happiness and peace of mind. Am I really only fourteen? Am I really just a silly schoolgirl? Am I really so inexperienced in everything? I have more experience than most; I've experienced something almost no one my age ever has.

I'm afraid of myself, afraid my longing is making me yield too soon. How can it ever go right with other boys later on? Oh, it's so hard, the eternal struggle between heart and mind. There's a time and a place for both, but how can I be sure that I've chosen the right time?

Yours, *Anne M. Frank*

TUESDAY, MAY 2, 1944

*Dearest Kitty,*

Saturday night I asked Peter whether he thinks I should tell Father about us. After we'd discussed it, he said he thought I should. I was glad; it shows he's sensible, and sensitive. As soon as I came downstairs, I went with Father to get some water. While we were on the stairs, I said, "Father, I'm sure you've gathered that when Peter and I are together, we don't exactly sit at opposite ends of the room. Do you think that's wrong?"

Father paused before answering: "No, I don't think it's wrong. But Anne, when you're living so close together, as we do, you have to be careful." He said some other words to that effect, and then we went upstairs.

Sunday morning he called me to him and said, "Anne, I've been thinking about what you said." (Oh, oh, I knew what was coming!) "Here in the Annex it's not such a good idea. I thought you were just friends. Is Peter in love with you?"

"Of course not," I answered.

"Well, you know I understand both of you. But you must be the one to show restraint; don't go upstairs so often, don't encourage him more than you can help. In matters like these, it's always the man who takes the active role, and it's up to the woman to set the limits. Outside, where you're free, things are quite different. You see other boys and girls, you can go outdoors, take part in sports and all kinds of activities. But here, if you're together too much and want to get away, you can't. You see each other every hour of the day – all the time, in fact. Be careful, Anne, and don't take it too seriously!"

"I don't, Father, but Peter's a decent boy, a nice boy!"

"Yes, but he doesn't have much strength of character. He can easily be influenced to do good, but also to do bad. I hope for his sake that he stays good, because he's basically a good person."

We talked some more and agreed that Father would speak to him too.

Sunday afternoon when we were in the front attic, Peter asked, "Have you talked to your Father yet, Anne?"

"Yes," I replied, "I'll tell you all about it. He doesn't think it's wrong, but he says that here, where we're in such close quarters, it could lead to conflicts."

"We've already agreed not to quarrel, and I plan to keep my promise."

"Me too, Peter. But Father didn't think we were serious, he thought we were just friends. Do you think we still can be?"

"Yes, I do. How about you?"

"Me too. I also told Father that I trust you. I do trust you, Peter, just as much as I do Father. And I think you're worthy of my trust. You are, aren't you?"

"I hope so." (He was very shy, and blushing.)

"I believe in you, Peter," I continued. "I believe you have a good character and that you'll get ahead in this world."

After that we talked about other things. Later I said, "If we ever get out of here, I know you won't give me another thought."

He got all fired up. "That's not true, Anne. Oh no, I won't let you even think that about me!"

Just then somebody called us.

Father did talk to him, he told me Monday. "Your Father thought our friendship might turn into love," he said. "But I told him we'd keep ourselves under control."

Father wants me to stop going upstairs so often, but I don't want to. Not just because I like being with Peter, but because I've said I trust him. I do trust him, and I want to prove it to him, but I'll never be able to if I stay downstairs out of distrust.

No, I'm going!

In the meantime, the Dussel drama has been resolved. Saturday evening at dinner he apologized in beautiful Dutch. Mr. van Daan was immediately reconciled. Dussel must have spent all day practicing his speech.

Sunday, his birthday, passed without incident. We gave him a bottle of good wine from 1919, the van Daans (who can now give their gift after all) presented him with a jar of piccalilli and a package of razor blades, and Mr. Kugler gave him a jar of lemon syrup (to make lemonade), Miep a book, *Little Martin*, and Bep a plant. He treated everyone to an egg.

*Yours, Anne M. Frank*

*Dearest Kitty,*

WEDNESDAY, MAY 3, 1944

First the weekly news! We're having a vacation from politics. There's nothing, and I mean absolutely nothing, to report. I'm also gradually starting to believe that the invasion will come. After all, they can't let the Russians do all the dirty work; actually, the Russians aren't doing anything at the moment either.

Mr. Kleiman comes to the office every morning now. He got a new set of springs for Peter's divan, so Peter will have to get to work reupholstering it. Not surprisingly, he isn't at all in the mood. Mr. Kleiman also brought some flea powder for the cats.

Have I told you that our Boche has disappeared? We haven't
seen hide nor hair of her since last Thursday. She's probably
already in cat heaven, while some animal lover has turned her
into a tasty dish. Perhaps some girl who can afford it will be wearing a cap made of Boche's fur. Peter is heartbroken.

For the last two weeks we've been eating lunch at eleven-
thirty on Saturdays; in the mornings we have to make do with a
cup of hot cereal. Starting tomorrow it'll be like this every day;
that saves us a meal. Vegetables are still very hard to come by.
This afternoon we had rotten boiled lettuce. Ordinary lettuce,
spinach and boiled lettuce, that's all there is. Add to that rotten
potatoes, and you have a meal fit for a king!

I hadn't had my period for more than two months, but it
finally started last Sunday. Despite the mess and bother, I'm glad
it hasn't deserted me.

As you can no doubt imagine, we often say in despair, "What's
the point of the war? Why, oh, why can't people live together
peacefully? Why all this destruction?"

The question is understandable, but up to now no one has
come up with a satisfactory answer. Why is England manufactur-
ing bigger and better airplanes and bombs and at the same time
churning out new houses for reconstruction? Why are millions
spent on the war each day, while not a penny is available for medical science, artists or the poor? Why do people have to starve
when mountains of food are rotting away in other parts of the
world? Oh, why are people so crazy?

I don't believe the war is simply the work of politicians and
capitalists. Oh no, the common man is every bit as guilty; otherwise, people and nations would have rebelled long ago! There's
a destructive urge in people, the urge to rage, murder and kill.
And until all of humanity, without exception, undergoes a meta-
morphosis, wars will continue to be waged, and everything that
has been carefully built up, cultivated and grown will be cut
down and destroyed, only to start all over again!

I've often been down in the dumps, but never desperate. I look
upon our life in hiding as an interesting adventure, full of danger

and romance, and every privation as an amusing addition to my diary. I've made up my mind to lead a different life from other girls, and not to become an ordinary housewife later on. What I'm experiencing here is a good beginning to an interesting life, and that's the reason – the only reason – why I have to laugh at the humorous side of the most dangerous moments.

I'm young and have many hidden qualities; I'm young and strong and living through a big adventure; I'm right in the middle of it and can't spend all day complaining because it's impossible to have any fun! I'm blessed with many things: happiness, a cheerful disposition and strength. Every day I feel myself maturing, I feel liberation drawing near, I feel the beauty of nature and the goodness of the people around me. Every day I think what a fascinating and amusing adventure this is! With all that, why should I despair?

Yours, Anne M. Frank

FRIDAY, MAY 5, 1944

*Dear Kitty,*

Father's unhappy with me. After our talk on Sunday he thought I'd stop going upstairs every evening. He won't have any of that "*Knutscherei*"* going on. I can't stand that word. Talking about it was bad enough – why does he have to make me feel bad too! I'll have a word with him today. Margot gave me some good advice. Here's more or less what I'd like to say:

I think you expect an explanation from me, Father, so I'll give you one. You're disappointed in me, you expected more restraint from me, you no doubt want me to act the way a fourteen-year-old is supposed to. But that's where you're wrong!

Since we've been here, from July 1942 until a few weeks ago, I haven't had an easy time. If only you knew how much I used to cry at night, how unhappy and despondent I was, how lonely I felt, you'd understand my wanting to go upstairs! I've now reached the point where I don't need the support of Mother or anyone else. It didn't happen overnight. I've struggled long and hard and shed many tears to

*Necking.

become as independent as I am now. You can laugh and refuse to believe me, but I don't care. I know I'm an independent person, and I don't feel I need to account to you for my actions. I'm only telling you this because I don't want you to think I'm doing things behind your back. But there's only one person I'm accountable to, and that's me.

When I was having problems, everyone – and that includes you – closed their eyes and ears and didn't help me. On the contrary, all I ever got were admonitions not to be so noisy. I was noisy only to keep myself from being miserable all the time. I was overconfident to keep from having to listen to the voice inside me. I've been putting on an act for the last year and a half, day in, day out. I've never complained or dropped my mask, nothing of the kind, and now . . . now the battle is over. I've won! I'm independent, in both body and mind. I don't need a mother anymore, and I've emerged from the struggle a stronger person.

Now that it's over, now that I know the battle has been won, I want to go my own way, to follow the path that seems right to me. Don't think of me as a fourteen-year-old, since all these troubles have made me older; I won't regret my actions, I'll behave the way I think I should!

Gentle persuasion won't keep me from going upstairs. You'll either have to forbid it, or trust me through thick and thin. Whatever you do, just leave me alone!

Yours, Anne M. Frank

SATURDAY, MAY 6, 1944

Dearest Kitty,

Last night before dinner I tucked the letter I'd written into Father's pocket. According to Margot, he read it and was upset for the rest of the evening. (I was upstairs doing the dishes!) Poor Pim, I might have known what the effect of such an epistle would be. He's so sensitive! I immediately told Peter not to ask any questions or say anything more. Pim's said nothing else to me about the matter. Is he going to?

Everything here is more or less back to normal. We can hardly believe what Jan, Mr. Kugler and Mr. Kleiman tell us about the prices and the people on the outside; half a pound of tea costs

350.00 guilders, half a pound of coffee 80.00 guilders, a pound of butter 35.00 guilders, one egg 1.45 guilders. People are paying 14.00 guilders an ounce for Bulgarian tobacco! Everyone's trading on the black market; every errand boy has something to offer. The delivery boy from the bakery has supplied us with darning thread – 90 cents for one measly skein – the milkman can get hold of ration books, an undertaker delivers cheese. Break-ins, murders and thefts are daily occurrences. Even the police and night watchmen are getting in on the act. Everyone wants to put food in their stomachs, and since salaries have been frozen, people have had to resort to swindling. The police have their hands full trying to track down the many girls of fifteen, sixteen, seventeen and older who are reported missing every day.

I want to try to finish my story about Ellen, the fairy. Just for fun, I can give it to Father on his birthday, together with all the copyrights.

See you later! (Actually, that's not the right phrase. In the German program broadcast from England they always close with "*Auf wiederhören.*" * So I guess I should say, "Until we write again.")

*Yours, Anne M. Frank*

SUNDAY MORNING, MAY 7, 1944

*Dearest Kitty,*

Father and I had a long talk yesterday afternoon. I cried my eyes out, and he cried too. Do you know what he said to me, Kitty?

"I've received many letters in my lifetime, but none as hurtful as this. You, who have had so much love from your parents. You, whose parents have always been ready to help you, who have always defended you, no matter what. You talk of not having to account to us for your actions! You feel you've been wronged and left to your own devices. No, Anne, you've done us a great injustice!

"Perhaps you didn't mean it that way, but that's what you wrote. No, Anne, we have done nothing to deserve such a reproach!"

* Until we speak again.

Oh, I've failed miserably. This is the worst thing I've ever done in my entire life. I used my tears to show off, to make myself seem important so he'd respect me. I've certainly had my share of unhappiness, and everything I said about Mother is true. But to accuse Pim, who's so good and who's done everything for me – no, that was too cruel for words.

It's good that somebody has finally cut me down to size, has broken my pride, because I've been far too smug. Not everything Mistress Anne does is good! Anyone who deliberately causes such pain to someone they say they love is despicable, the lowest of the low!

What I'm most ashamed of is the way Father has forgiven me; he said he's going to throw the letter in the stove, and he's being so nice to me now, as if *he* were the one who'd done something wrong. Well, Anne, you still have a lot to learn. It's time you made a beginning, instead of looking down at other people and always blaming them!

I've known a lot of sorrow, but who hasn't at my age? I've been putting on an act, but was hardly even aware of it. I've felt lonely, but never desperate! Not like Father, who once ran out into the street with a knife so he could put an end to it all. I've never gone that far.

I should be deeply ashamed of myself, and I am. What's done can't be undone, but at least you can keep it from happening again. I'd like to start all over, and that shouldn't be difficult, now that I have Peter. With him supporting me, I *know* I can do it! I'm not alone anymore. He loves me, I love him, I have my books, my writing and my diary. I'm not all that ugly, or that stupid, I have a sunny disposition, and I want to develop a good character!

Yes, Anne, you knew full well that your letter was unkind and untrue, but you were actually proud of it! I'll take Father as my example once again, and I *will* improve myself.

*Yours, Anne M. Frank*

*Dearest Kitty,*

MONDAY, MAY 8, 1944

Have I ever told you anything about our family? I don't think I have, so let me begin. Father was born in Frankfurt am Main to very wealthy parents: Michael Frank owned a bank and became a millionaire, and Alice Stern's parents were prominent and well-to-do. Michael Frank didn't start out rich; he was a self-made man. In his youth Father led the life of a rich man's son. Parties every week, balls, banquets, beautiful girls, waltzing, dinners, a huge house, etc. After Grandpa died, most of the money was lost, and after the Great War and inflation there was nothing left at all. Up until the war there were still quite a few rich relatives. So Father was extremely well-bred, and he had to laugh yesterday because for the first time in his fifty-five years, he scraped out the frying pan at the table.

Mother's family wasn't as wealthy, but still fairly well-off, and we've listened openmouthed to stories of private balls, dinners and engagement parties with 250 guests.

We're far from rich now, but I've pinned all my hopes on after the war. I can assure you, I'm not so set on a bourgeois life as Mother and Margot. I'd like to spend a year in Paris and London learning the languages and studying art history. Compare that with Margot, who wants to nurse newborns in Palestine. I still have visions of gorgeous dresses and fascinating people. As I've told you many times before, I want to see the world and do all kinds of exciting things, and a little money won't hurt!

This morning Miep told us about her cousin's engagement party, which she went to on Saturday. The cousin's parents are rich, and the groom's are even richer. Miep made our mouths water telling us about the food that was served: vegetable soup with meatballs, cheese, rolls with sliced meat, hors d'oeuvres made with eggs and roast beef, rolls with cheese, genoise, wine and cigarettes, and you could eat as much as you wanted.

Miep drank ten schnapps and smoked three cigarettes – could this be our temperance advocate? If Miep drank all those, I wonder how many her spouse managed to toss down? Everyone at the party was a little tipsy, of course. There were also two officers from the Homicide Squad, who took photographs of the wedding couple. You can see we're never far from Miep's thoughts, since she promptly noted their names and addresses in case anything should happen and we needed contacts with good Dutch people.

Our mouths were watering so much. We, who'd had nothing

but two spoonfuls of hot cereal for breakfast and were absolutely famished; we, who get nothing but half-cooked spinach (for the vitamins!) and rotten potatoes day after day; we, who fill our empty stomachs with nothing but boiled lettuce, raw lettuce, spinach, spinach and more spinach. Maybe we'll end up being as strong as Popeye, though up to now I've seen no sign of it!

If Miep had taken us along to the party, there wouldn't have been any rolls left over for the other guests. If we'd been there, we'd have snatched up everything in sight, including the furniture. I tell you, we were practically pulling the words right out of her mouth. We were gathered around her as if we'd never in all our lives heard of delicious food or elegant people! And these are the granddaughters of the distinguished millionaire. The world is a crazy place!

Yours, Anne M. Frank

TUESDAY, MAY 9, 1944

*Dearest Kitty,*

I've finished my story about Ellen, the fairy. I've copied it out on nice notepaper, decorated it with red ink and sewn the pages together. The whole thing looks quite pretty, but I don't know if it's enough of a birthday present. Margot and Mother have both written poems.

Mr. Kugler came upstairs this afternoon with the news that starting Monday, Mrs. Broks would like to spend two hours in the office every afternoon. Just imagine! The office staff won't be able to come upstairs, the potatoes can't be delivered, Bep won't get her dinner, we can't go to the bathroom, we won't be able to move and all sorts of other inconveniences! We proposed a variety of ways to get rid of her. Mr. van Daan thought a good laxative in her coffee might do the trick. "No," Mr. Kleiman answered, "please don't, or we'll never get her off the can!"

A roar of laughter. "The can?" Mrs. van D. asked. "What does that mean?" An explanation was given. "Is it all right to use that word?" she asked in perfect innocence.

"Just imagine," Bep giggled, "there you are shopping at The Bijenkorf and you ask the way to the can. They wouldn't even know what you were talking about!" Dussel now sits on the "can," to borrow the expression, every day at twelve-thirty on the dot. This afternoon I boldly took a piece of pink paper and wrote:

*Mr. Dussel's Toilet Timetable*

Mornings from 7:15 to 7:30 a.m.
Afternoons after 1 p.m.
Otherwise, only as needed!

I tacked this to the green bathroom door while he was still inside. I might well have added "Transgressors will be subject to confinement!" Because our bathroom can be locked from both the inside and the outside.

Mr. van Daan's latest joke:

After a Bible lesson about Adam and Eve, a thirteen-year-old boy asked his father, "Tell me, Father, how did I get born?"

"Well," the father replied, "the stork plucked you out of the ocean, set you down in Mother's bed and bit her in the leg, hard. It bled so much she had to stay in bed for a week."

Not fully satisfied, the boy went to his mother. "Tell me, Mother," he asked, "how did you get born and how did I get born?"

His mother told him the very same story. Finally, hoping to hear the fine points, he went to his grandfather. "Tell me, Grandfather," he said, "how did you get born and how did your daughter get born?" And for the third time he was told exactly the same story.

That night he wrote in his diary: "After careful inquiry, I must conclude that there has been no sexual intercourse in our family for the last three generations!"

I still have work to do; it's already three o'clock.

*Yours, Anne M. Frank*

PS. Since I think I've mentioned the new cleaning lady, I just want to note that she's married, sixty years old and hard of hearing! Very convenient, in view of all the noise that eight people in hiding are capable of making.

Oh, Kit, it's such lovely weather. If only I could go outside!

*Dearest Kitty,*                          WEDNESDAY, MAY 10, 1944

We were sitting in the attic yesterday afternoon working on our French when suddenly I heard the splatter of water behind me. I asked Peter what it might be. Without pausing to reply, he dashed up to the loft – the scene of the disaster – and shoved Mouschi who was squatting beside her soggy litter box, back to the right place. This was followed by shouts and squeals, and then Mouschi, who by that time had finished peeing, took off downstairs. In search of something similar to her box, Mouschi had found herself a pile of wood shavings, right over a crack in the floor. The puddle immediately trickled down to the attic and, as luck would have it, landed in and next to the potato barrel. The ceiling was dripping, and since the attic floor has also got its share of cracks, little yellow drops were leaking through the ceiling and onto the dining table, between a pile of stockings and books.

I was doubled up with laughter, it was such a funny sight. There was Mouschi crouched under a chair, Peter armed with water, powdered bleach and a cloth, and Mr. van Daan trying to calm everyone down. The room was soon set to rights, but it's a well-known fact that cat puddles stink to high heaven. The potatoes proved that all too well, as did the wood shavings, which Father collected in a bucket and brought downstairs to burn.

Poor Mouschi! How were you to know it's impossible to get peat for your box?

*Anne*

*Dearest Kitty,*                          THURSDAY, MAY 11, 1944

A new sketch to make you laugh:

Peter's hair had to be cut, and as usual his mother was to be the hairdresser. At seven twenty-five Peter vanished into his room, and reappeared at the stroke of seven-thirty, stripped down to his blue swimming trunks and a pair of tennis shoes.

"Are you coming?" he asked his mother.

"Yes, I'll be up in a minute, but I can't find the scissors!"

Peter helped her look, rummaging around in her cosmetics drawer. "Don't make such a mess, Peter," she grumbled.

I didn't catch Peter's reply, but it must have been insolent, because she cuffed him on the arm. He cuffed her back, she punched him with all her might, and Peter pulled his arm away with a look of mock horror on his face. "Come on, old girl!"

Mrs. van D. stayed put. Peter grabbed her by the wrists and pulled her all around the room. She laughed, cried, scolded and kicked, but nothing helped. Peter led his prisoner as far as the attic stairs, where he was obliged to let go of her. Mrs. van D. came back to the room and collapsed into a chair with a loud sigh.

"*Die Entführung der Mutter*," * I joked.

"Yes, but he hurt me."

I went to have a look and cooled her hot, red wrists with water. Peter, still by the stairs and growing impatient again, strode into the room with his belt in his hand, like a lion tamer. Mrs. van D. didn't move, but stayed by her writing desk, looking for a handkerchief. "You've got to apologize first."

"All right, I hereby offer my apologies, but only because if I don't, we'll be here till midnight."

Mrs. van D. had to laugh in spite of herself. She got up and went toward the door, where she felt obliged to give us an explanation. (By us I mean Father, Mother and me; we were busy doing the dishes.) "He wasn't like this at home," she said. "I'd have belted him so hard he'd have gone flying down the stairs [!]. He's never been so insolent. This isn't the first time he's deserved a good hiding. That's what you get with a modern upbringing, modern children. I'd never have grabbed my mother like that. Did you treat your mother that way, Mr. Frank?" She was very upset, pacing back and forth, saying whatever came into her head, and she still hadn't gone upstairs. Finally, at long last, she made her exit.

Less than five minutes later she stormed back down the stairs, with her cheeks all puffed out, and flung her apron on a chair. When I asked if she was through, she replied that she was going downstairs. She tore down the stairs like a tornado, probably straight into the arms of her Putti.

She didn't come up again until eight, this time with her

* *The Abduction of Mother*, a possible reference to Mozart's opera *The Abduction from the Seraglio*.

husband. Peter was dragged from the attic, given a merciless scolding and showered with abuse: ill-mannered brat, no-good bum, bad example, Anne this, Margot that, I couldn't hear the rest.

Everything seems to have calmed down again today!

*Yours, Anne M. Frank*

PS. Tuesday and Wednesday evening our beloved Queen addressed the country. She's taking a vacation so she'll be in good health for her return to the Netherlands. She used words like "soon, when I'm back in Holland," "a swift liberation," "heroism" and "heavy burdens."

This was followed by a speech by Prime Minister Gerbrandy. He has such a squeaky little child's voice that Mother instinctively said, "Oooh." A clergyman, who must have borrowed his voice from Mr. Edel, concluded by asking God to take care of the Jews, all those in concentration camps and prisons and everyone working in Germany.

*Dearest Kitty,*                              THURSDAY, MAY 11, 1944

Since I've left my entire "junk box" – including my fountain pen – upstairs and I'm not allowed to disturb the grown-ups during their nap time (until two-thirty), you'll have to make do with a letter in pencil.

I'm terribly busy at the moment, and strange as it may sound, I don't have enough time to get through my pile of work. Shall I tell you briefly what I've got to do? Well then, before tomorrow I have to finish reading the first volume of a biography of Galileo Galilei, since it has to be returned to the library. I started reading it yesterday and have gotten up to page 220 out of 320 pages, so I'll manage it. Next week I have to read *Palestine at the Crossroads* and the second volume of Galilei. Besides that, I finished the first volume of a biography of Emperor Charles V yesterday, and I still have to work out the many genealogical charts I've collected and the notes I've taken. Next I have three pages of foreign words from my various books, all of which have to be written down, memorized and read aloud. Number four: my movie stars are in a terrible disarray and are dying to be straightened out, but since it'll take several days to do that and Professor Anne is, as she's already said, up to her ears in work, they'll have to put up with the chaos a while longer. Then there're Theseus, Oedipus, Peleus, Orpheus, Jason and Hercules all waiting to be untangled, since their various deeds are running crisscross through my mind like multicolored threads in a dress. Myron and Phidias are also urgently in need of attention, or else I'll forget entirely how they fit into the picture. The same applies, for example, to the Seven Years' War and the Nine Years' War. Now I'm getting everything all mixed up. Well, what can you do with a memory like mine! Just imagine how forgetful I'll be when I'm eighty!

Oh, one more thing. The Bible. How long is it going to take before I come to the story of the bathing Susanna? And what do they mean by Sodom and Gomorrah? Oh, there's still so much to find out and learn. And in the meantime, I've left Charlotte of the Palatine in the lurch.

You can see, can't you, Kitty, that I'm full to bursting?

And now something else. You've known for a long time that my greatest wish is to be a journalist, and later on, a famous writer. We'll have to wait and see if these grand illusions (or delusions!) will ever come true, but up to now I've had no lack of topics. In any case, after the war I'd like to publish a book called *The Secret Annex*. It remains to be seen whether I'll succeed, but my diary can serve as the basis.

I also need to finish "Cady's Life." I've thought up the rest of the plot. After being cured in the sanatorium, Cady goes back home and continues writing to Hans. It's 1941, and it doesn't take her long to discover Hans's Nazi sympathies, and since Cady is deeply concerned with the plight of the Jews and of her friend Marianne, they begin drifting apart. They meet and get back together, but break up when Hans takes up with another girl. Cady is shattered, and because she wants to have a good job, she studies nursing. After graduation she accepts a position, at the urging of her father's friends, as a nurse in a TB sanatorium in Switzerland. During her first vacation she goes to Lake Como, where she runs into Hans. He tells her that two years earlier he'd married Cady's successor, but that his wife took her life in a fit of depression. Now that he's seen his little Cady again, he realizes how much he loves her, and once more asks for her hand in marriage. Cady refuses, even though, in spite of herself, she loves him as much as ever. But her pride holds her back. Hans goes away, and years later Cady learns that he's wound up in England, where he's struggling with ill health.

When she's twenty-seven, Cady marries a well-to-do man from the country, named Simon. She grows to love him, but not as much as Hans. She has two daughters and a son, Lilian, Judith and Nico. She and Simon are happy together, but Hans is always in the back of her mind until one night she dreams of him and says farewell.

It's not sentimental nonsense: it's based on the story of Father's life.

*Yours, Anne M. Frank*

SATURDAY, MAY 13, 1944

*My dearest Kitty,*

Yesterday was Father's birthday, Father and Mother's nineteenth wedding anniversary, a day without the cleaning lady . . . and the sun was shining as it's never shone before in 1944. Our chestnut tree is in full bloom. It's covered with leaves and is even more beautiful than last year.

Father received a biography of Linnaeus from Mr. Kleiman, a book on nature from Mr. Kugler, *The Canals of Amsterdam* from Dussel, a huge box from the van Daans (wrapped so beautifully it might have been done by a professional), containing three eggs, a bottle of beer, a jar of yogurt and a green tie. It made our jar of molasses seem rather paltry. My roses smelled wonderful compared to Miep and Bep's red carnations. He was thoroughly spoiled. Fifty petits fours arrived from Siemons' Bakery, delicious! Father also treated us to spice cake, the men to beer and the ladies to yogurt. Everything was scrumptious!

*Yours, Anne M. Frank*

TUESDAY, MAY 16, 1944

*My dearest Kitty,*

Just for a change (since we haven't had one of these in so long) I'll recount a little discussion between Mr. and Mrs. van D. last night:

Mrs. van. D.: "The Germans have had plenty of time to fortify the Atlantic Wall, and they'll certainly do everything within their power to hold back the British. It's amazing how strong the Germans are!"

Mr. van D.: "Oh, yes, amazing!"

Mrs. van D.: "It is!"

Mr. van D.: "So strong they're bound to win the war in the end, is that what you mean?"

Mrs. van D.: "They might. I'm not convinced that they won't."

Mr. van D.: "I won't even answer that."

Mrs. van D.: "You always wind up answering. You let yourself get carried away, every single time."

Mr. van D.: "No, I don't. I always keep my answers to the bare minimum."

Mrs. van D.: "But you always do have an answer and you always have to be right! Your predictions hardly ever come true, you know!"

Mr. van D.: "So far they have."

Mrs. van D.: "No they haven't. You said the invasion was going to start last year, the Finns were supposed to have been out of the war by now, the Italian campaign ought to have been over by last winter, and the Russians should already have captured Lemberg. Oh no, I don't set much store by your predictions."

Mr. van D. (leaping to his feet): "Why don't you shut your trap for a change? I'll show you who's right; someday you'll get tired of needling me. I can't stand your bellyaching a minute longer. Just wait, one day I'll make you eat your words!" (End of Act One.)

Actually, I couldn't help giggling. Mother couldn't either, and even Peter was biting his lips to keep from laughing. Oh, those stupid grown-ups. They need to learn a few things first before they start making so many remarks about the younger generation!

Since Friday we've been keeping the windows open again at night.

*Yours, Anne M. Frank*

## What Our Annex Family Is Interested In
### (*A Systematic Survey of Courses and Reading Matter*)

*Mr. van Daan.* No courses; looks up many things in Knaur's Encyclopedia and Lexicon; likes to read detective stories, medical books and love stories, exciting or trivial.

*Mrs. van Daan.* A correspondence course in English; likes to read biographical novels and occasionally other kinds of novels.

*Mr. Frank.* Is learning English (Dickens!) and a bit of Latin; never reads novels, but likes serious, rather dry descriptions of people and places.

*Mrs. Frank.* A correspondence course in English; reads everything except detective stories.

*Mr. Dussel.* Is learning English, Spanish and Dutch with no noticeable results; reads everything; goes along with the opinion of the majority.

*Peter van Daan.* Is learning English, French (correspondence course), shorthand in Dutch, English and German, commercial correspondence in English, woodworking, economics and sometimes math; seldom reads, sometimes geography.

*Margot Frank.* Correspondence courses in English, French and Latin, shorthand in English, German and Dutch, trigonometry, solid geometry, mechanics, physics, chemistry, algebra, geometry, English literature, French literature, German literature, Dutch literature, bookkeeping, geography, modern history, biology, economics; reads everything, preferably on religion and medicine.

*Anne Frank.* Shorthand in French, English, German and Dutch, geometry, algebra, history, geography, art history, mythology, biology, Bible history, Dutch literature; likes to read biographies, dull or exciting, and history books (sometimes novels and light reading).

*Dearest Kitty,* FRIDAY, MAY 19, 1944

I felt rotten yesterday. Vomiting (me of all people!), headache, stomachache and anything else you can imagine. I'm feeling better today. I'm famished, but I think I'll skip the beans we're having for dinner.

Everything's going fine between Peter and me. The poor boy has an even greater need for tenderness than I do. He still blushes every evening when he gets his good-night kiss, and then begs for another one. Am I merely a better substitute for Boche? I don't mind. He's so happy just knowing somebody loves him.

After my laborious conquest, I've distanced myself a little from the situation, but you mustn't think my love has cooled. Peter's a sweetheart, but I've slammed the door to my inner self; if he ever wants to force the lock again, he'll have to use a harder crowbar!

*Yours, Anne M. Frank*

*Dearest Kitty,*

SATURDAY, MAY 20, 1944

Last night when I came down from the attic, I noticed, the moment I entered the room, that the lovely vase of carnations had fallen over. Mother was down on her hands and knees mopping up the water and Margot was fishing my papers off the floor. "What happened?" I asked with anxious foreboding, and before they could reply, I assessed the damage from across the room. My entire genealogy file, my notebooks, my books, everything was afloat. I nearly cried, and I was so upset I started speaking German. I can't remember a word, but according to Margot I babbled something about "*unübersehbarer Schaden, schrecklich, entsetzlich, nie zu ersetzen*"* and much more. Father burst out laughing and Mother and Margot joined in, but I felt like crying because all my work and elaborate notes were lost.

I took a closer look and, luckily, the "incalculable loss" wasn't as bad as I'd expected. Up in the attic I carefully peeled apart the sheets of paper that were stuck together and then hung them on the clothesline to dry. It was such a funny sight, even I had to laugh. Maria de' Medici alongside Charles V, William of Orange and Marie Antoinette.

"It's *Rassenschande*,"† Mr. van Daan joked.

After entrusting my papers to Peter's care, I went back downstairs.

---

*Incalculable loss, terrible, awful, irreplaceable.
†An affront to racial purity.

"Which books are ruined?" I asked Margot, who was going through them.

"Algebra," Margot said.

But as luck would have it, my algebra book wasn't entirely ruined. I wish it had fallen right in the vase. I've never loathed any book as much as that one. Inside the front cover are the names of at least twenty girls who had it before I did. It's old, yellowed, full of scribbles, crossed-out words and revisions. The next time I'm in a wicked mood, I'm going to tear the darned thing to pieces!

*Yours, Anne M. Frank*

*Dearest Kitty,*                            MONDAY, MAY 22, 1944

On May 20, Father lost his bet and had to give five jars of yogurt to Mrs. van Daan: the invasion still hasn't begun. I can safely say that all of Amsterdam, all of Holland, in fact the entire western coast of Europe, all the way down to Spain, are talking about the invasion day and night, debating, making bets and . . . hoping.

The suspense is rising to fever pitch; by no means has everyone we think of as "good" Dutch people kept their faith in the English, not everyone thinks the English bluff is a masterful strategical move. Oh no, people want deeds – great, heroic deeds.

No one can see farther than the end of their nose, no one gives a thought to the fact that the British are fighting for their own country and their own people; everyone thinks it's England's duty to save Holland, as quickly as possible. What obligations do the English have toward us? What have the Dutch done to deserve the generous help they so clearly expect? Oh no, the Dutch are very much mistaken. The English, despite their bluff, are certainly no more to blame for the war than all the other countries, large and small, that are now occupied by the Germans. The British are not about to offer their excuses; true, they were sleeping during the years Germany was rearming itself, but all the other countries, especially those bordering on Germany, were asleep too. England and the rest of the world have discovered that burying your head in the sand doesn't work, and now each of them, especially England, is having to pay a heavy price for its ostrich policy.

No country sacrifices its men without reason, and certainly not in the interests of another, and England is no exception. The invasion, liberation and freedom will come someday; yet England, not the occupied territories, will choose the moment.

To our great sorrow and dismay, we've heard that many people have changed their attitude toward us Jews. We've been told that anti-Semitism has cropped up in circles where once it would have been unthinkable. This fact has affected us all very, very deeply. The reason for the hatred is understandable, maybe even human, but that doesn't make it right. According to the Christians, the Jews are blabbing their secrets to the Germans, denouncing their helpers and causing them to suffer the dreadful fate and punishments that have already been meted out to so many. All of this is true. But as with everything, they should look at the matter from both sides: would Christians act any differently if they were in our place? Could anyone, regardless of whether they're Jews or Christians, remain silent in the face of German pressure? Everyone knows it's practically impossible, so why do they ask the impossible of the Jews?

It's being said in underground circles that the German Jews who immigrated to Holland before the war and have now been sent to Poland shouldn't be allowed to return here. They were granted the right to asylum in Holland, but once Hitler is gone, they should go back to Germany.

When you hear that, you begin to wonder why we're fighting this long and difficult war. We're always being told that we're fighting for freedom, truth and justice! The war isn't even over, and already there's dissension and Jews are regarded as lesser beings. Oh, it's sad, very sad that the old adage has been confirmed for the umpteenth time: "What one Christian does is his own responsibility, what one Jew does reflects on all Jews."

To be honest, I can't understand how the Dutch, a nation of good, honest, upright people, can sit in judgment on us the way they do. On *us* – the most oppressed, unfortunate and pitiable people in all the world.

I have only one hope: that this anti-Semitism is just a passing thing, that the Dutch will show their true colors, that they'll never waver from what they know in their hearts to be just, for this is unjust!

And if they ever carry out this terrible threat, the meager handful of Jews still left in Holland will have to go. We too will have to shoulder our bundles and move on, away from this beautiful country, which once so kindly took us in and now turns its back on us.

I love Holland. Once I hoped it would become a fatherland to me, since I had lost my own. And I hope so still!

*Yours, Anne M. Frank*

THURSDAY, MAY 25, 1944

*Dearest Kitty,*

Bep's engaged! The news isn't much of a surprise, though none of us are particularly pleased. Bertus may be a nice, steady, athletic young man, but Bep doesn't love him, and to me that's enough reason to advise her against marrying him.

Bep's trying to get ahead in the world, and Bertus is pulling her back; he's a laborer, without any interests or any desire to make something of himself, and I don't think that'll make Bep happy. I can understand Bep's wanting to put an end to her indecision; four weeks ago she decided to write him off, but then she felt even worse. So she wrote him a letter, and now she's engaged.

There are several factors involved in this engagement. First, Bep's sick father, who likes Bertus very much. Second, she's the oldest of the Voskuijl girls and her mother teases her about being an old maid. Third, she's just turned twenty-four, and that matters a great deal to Bep.

Mother said it would have been better if Bep had simply had an affair with Bertus. I don't know, I feel sorry for Bep and can understand her loneliness. In any case, they can get married only after the war, since Bertus is in hiding, or at any rate has gone underground. Besides, they don't have a penny to their name and nothing in the way of a hope chest. What a sorry prospect for Bep, for whom we all wish the best. I only hope Bertus improves under her influence, or that Bep finds another man, one who knows how to appreciate her!

*Yours, Anne M. Frank*

THE SAME DAY

There's something happening every day. This morning Mr. van Hoeven was arrested. He was hiding two Jews in his house. It's a heavy blow for us, not only because those poor Jews are once again balancing on the edge of an abyss, but also because it's terrible for Mr. van Hoeven.

The world's been turned upside down. The most decent people are being sent to concentration camps, prisons and lonely cells, while the lowest of the low rule over young and old, rich and poor. One gets caught for black marketeering, another for hiding Jews or other unfortunate souls. Unless you're a Nazi, you don't know what's going to happen to you from one day to the next.

Mr. van Hoeven is a great loss to us too. Bep can't possibly lug such huge amounts of potatoes all the way here, nor should she have to, so our only choice is to eat fewer of them. I'll tell you what we have in mind, but it's certainly not going to make life here any more agreeable. Mother says we'll skip breakfast, eat hot cereal and bread for lunch and fried potatoes for dinner and, if possible, vegetables or lettuce once or twice a week. That's all there is. We're going to be hungry, but nothing's worse than being caught.

*Yours, Anne M. Frank*

FRIDAY, MAY 26, 1944

*My dearest Kitty,*

At long, long last, I can sit quietly at my table before the crack in the window frame and write you everything, everything I want to say.

I feel more miserable than I have in months. Even after the break-in I didn't feel so utterly broken, inside and out. On the one hand, there's the news about Mr. van Hoeven, the Jewish question (which is discussed in detail by everyone in the house), the invasion (which is so long in coming), the awful food, the tension, the miserable atmosphere, my disappointment in Peter. On the other hand, there's Bep's engagement, the Pentecost reception, the flowers, Mr. Kugler's birthday, cakes and stories about cabarets, movies and concerts. That gap, that enormous gap, is always there. One day we're laughing at the comical side of life in hiding, and the next day (and there are many such days), we're frightened, and the fear, tension and despair can be read on our faces.

Miep and Mr. Kugler bear the greatest burden for us, and for all those in hiding – Miep in everything she does and Mr. Kugler through his enormous responsibility for the eight of us, which is sometimes so overwhelming that he can hardly speak from the pent-up tension and strain. Mr. Kleiman and Bep also take very good care of us, but they're able to put the Annex out of their minds, even if it's only for a few hours or a few days. They have their own worries, Mr. Kleiman with his health and Bep with her engagement, which isn't looking very promising at the moment. But they also have their outings, their visits with friends, their everyday lives as ordinary people, so that the tension is sometimes relieved, if only for a short while, while ours never is, never has been, not once in the two years we've been here. How much longer will this increasingly oppressive, unbearable weight press down on us?

The drains are clogged again. We can't run the water, or if we do, only a trickle; we can't flush the toilet, so we have to use a toilet brush; and we've been putting our dirty water into a big earthenware jar. We can manage for today, but what will happen if the plumber can't fix it on his own? The Sanitation Department can't come until Tuesday.

Miep sent us a raisin bread with "Happy Pentecost" written on top. It's almost as if she were mocking us, since our moods and cares are far from "happy."

We've all become more frightened since the van Hoeven business. Once again you hear "shh" from all sides, and we're doing everything more quietly. The police forced the door there; they could just as easily do that here too! What will we do if we're ever . . . no, I mustn't write that down. But the question won't let itself be pushed to the back of my mind today; on the contrary, all the fear I've ever felt is looming before me in all its horror.

I had to go downstairs alone at eight this evening to use the bathroom. There was no one down there, since they were all listening to the radio. I wanted to be brave, but it was hard.

I always feel safer upstairs than in that huge, silent house; when I'm alone with those mysterious muffled sounds from upstairs and the honking of horns in the street, I have to hurry and remind myself where I am to keep from getting the shivers.

Miep has been acting much nicer toward us since her talk with Father. But I haven't told you about that yet. Miep came up one afternoon all flushed and asked Father straight out if we thought they too were infected with the current anti-Semitism. Father was stunned and quickly talked her out of the idea, but some of Miep's suspicion has lingered on. They're doing more errands for us now and showing more of an interest in our troubles, though we certainly shouldn't bother them with our woes. Oh, they're such good, noble people!

I've asked myself again and again whether it wouldn't have been better if we hadn't gone into hiding, if we were dead now and didn't have to go through this misery, especially so that the others could be spared the burden. But we all shrink from this thought. We still love life, we haven't yet forgotten the voice of nature, and we keep hoping, hoping for . . . everything.

Let something happen soon, even an air raid. Nothing can be more crushing than this anxiety. Let the end come, however cruel; at least then we'll know whether we are to be the victors or the vanquished.

Yours, Anne M. Frank

WEDNESDAY, MAY 31, 1944
Dearest Kitty,

Saturday, Sunday, Monday and Tuesday it was too hot to hold my fountain pen, which is why I couldn't write to you. Friday the drains were clogged, Saturday they were fixed. Mrs. Kleiman came for a visit in the afternoon and told us a lot about Jopie; she and Jacque van Maarsen are in the same hockey club. Sunday Bep dropped by to make sure there hadn't been a break-in and stayed for breakfast. Monday (a holiday because of Pentecost), Mr. Gies served as the Annex watchman, and Tuesday we were finally allowed to open the windows. We've seldom had a Pentecost weekend that was so beautiful and warm. Or maybe "hot" is a better word. Hot weather is horrible in the Annex. To give you an idea of the numerous complaints, I'll briefly describe these sweltering days.

Saturday: "Wonderful, what fantastic weather," we all said in the morning. "If only it weren't quite so hot," we said in the afternoon, when the windows had to be shut.

Sunday: "The heat's unbearable, the butter's melting, there's not a cool spot anywhere in the house, the bread's drying out, the milk's going sour, the windows can't be opened. We poor outcasts are suffocating while everyone else is enjoying their Pentecost." (According to Mrs. van D.)

Monday: "My feet hurt, I have nothing cool to wear, I can't do the dishes in this heat!" Grumbling from early in the morning to late at night. It was awful.

I can't stand the heat. I'm glad the wind's come up today, but that the sun's still shining.

*Yours, Anne M. Frank*

FRIDAY, JUNE 2, 1944

*Dear Kitty,*

"If you're going to the attic, take an umbrella with you, preferably a large one!" This is to protect you from "household showers." There's a Dutch proverb: "High and dry, safe and sound," but it obviously doesn't apply to wartime (guns!) and to people in hiding (cat box!). Mouschi's gotten into the habit of relieving herself on some newspapers or between the cracks in the floorboards, so we have good reason to fear the splatters and, even worse, the stench. The new Moortje in the warehouse has the same problem. Anyone who's ever had a cat that's not house-broken can imagine the smells, other than pepper and thyme, that permeate this house.

I also have a brand-new prescription for gunfire jitters: When the shooting gets loud, proceed to the nearest wooden staircase. Run up and down a few times, making sure to stumble at least once. What with the scratches and the noise of running and falling, you won't even be able to hear the shooting, much less worry about it. Yours truly has put this magic formula to use, with great success!

*Yours, Anne M. Frank*

MONDAY, JUNE 5, 1944

*Dearest Kitty,*

New problems in the Annex. A quarrel between Dussel and the Franks over the division of butter. Capitulation on the part of Dussel. Close friendship between the latter and Mrs. van Daan, flirtations, kisses and friendly little smiles. Dussel is beginning to long for female companionship.

The van Daans don't see why we should bake a spice cake for Mr. Kugler's birthday when we can't have one ourselves. All very petty. Mood upstairs: bad. Mrs. van D. has a cold. Dussel caught with brewer's yeast tablets, while we've got none.

The Fifth Army has taken Rome. The city neither destroyed nor bombed. Great propaganda for Hitler.

Very few potatoes and vegetables. One loaf of bread was moldy.

Scharminkeltje (name of new warehouse cat) can't stand pepper. She sleeps in the cat box and does her business in the wood shavings. Impossible to keep her.

Bad weather. Continuous bombing of Pas de Calais and the west coast of France.

No one buying dollars. Gold even less interesting. The bottom of our black moneybox is in sight. What are we going to live on next month?

*Yours, Anne M. Frank*

TUESDAY, JUNE 6, 1944

*My dearest Kitty,*

"This is D Day," the BBC announced at twelve. "This is *the* day." The invasion has begun!

This morning at eight the British reported heavy bombing of Calais, Boulogne, Le Havre and Cherbourg, as well as Pas de Calais (as usual). Further, as a precautionary measure for those in the occupied territories, everyone living within a zone of twenty miles from the coast was warned to prepare for bombardments. Where possible, the British will drop pamphlets an hour ahead of time.

According to the German news, British paratroopers have landed on the coast of France. "British landing craft are engaged in combat with German naval units," according to the BBC.

Conclusion reached by the Annex while breakfasting at nine: this is a trial landing, like the one two years ago in Dieppe.

BBC broadcast in German, Dutch, French and other languages at ten: The invasion has begun! So this is the "real" invasion. BBC broadcast in German at eleven: speech by Supreme Commander General Dwight Eisenhower.

BBC broadcast in English: "This is D Day." General Eisenhower said to the French people: "Stiff fighting will come now, but after this the victory. The year 1944 is the year of complete victory. Good luck!"

BBC broadcast in English at one: 11,000 planes are shuttling back and forth or standing by to land troops and bomb behind enemy lines; 4,000 landing craft and small boats are continually arriving in the area between Cherbourg and Le Havre. English and American troops are already engaged in heavy combat. Speeches by Gerbrandy, the Prime Minister of Belgium, King Haakon of Norway, de Gaulle of France, the King of England and, last but not least, Churchill.

A huge commotion in the Annex! Is this really the beginning of the long-awaited liberation? The liberation we've all talked so much about, which still seems too good, too much of a fairy tale ever to come true? Will this year, 1944, bring us victory? We don't know yet. But where there's hope, there's life. It fills us with fresh courage and makes us strong again. We'll need to be brave to endure the many fears and hardships and the suffering yet to come. It's now a matter of remaining calm and steadfast, of gritting our teeth and keeping a stiff upper lip! France, Russia, Italy, and even Germany, can cry out in agony, but we don't yet have that right!

Oh, Kitty, the best part about the invasion is that I have the feeling that friends are on the way. Those terrible Germans have oppressed and threatened us for so long that the thought of friends and salvation means everything to us! Now it's not just the Jews, but Holland and all of occupied Europe. Maybe, Margot says, I can even go back to school in September or October.

*Yours, Anne M. Frank*

PS. I'll keep you informed of the latest news!

This morning and last night, dummies made of straw and rubber were dropped from the air behind German lines, and they exploded the minute they hit the ground. Many paratroopers, their faces blackened so they couldn't be seen in the dark, landed as well. The French coast was bombarded with 5,500 tons of bombs during the night, and then, at six in the morning, the first landing craft came ashore. Today there were 20,000 airplanes in action. The German coastal batteries were destroyed even before the landing; a small bridgehead has already been formed. Everything's going well, despite the bad weather. The army and the people are "one will and one hope."

*Dearest Kitty,*                                    FRIDAY, JUNE 9, 1944

Great news of the invasion! The Allies have taken Bayeux, a village on the coast of France, and are now fighting for Caen. They're clearly intending to cut off the peninsula where Cherbourg is located. Every evening the war correspondents report on the difficulties, the courage and the fighting spirit of the army. To get their stories, they pull off the most amazing feats. A few of the wounded who are already back in England also spoke on the radio. Despite the miserable weather, the planes are flying diligently back and forth. We heard over the BBC that Churchill wanted to land along with the troops on D Day, but Eisenhower and the other generals managed to talk him out of it. Just imagine, so much courage for such an old man – he must be at least seventy!

The excitement here has died down somewhat; still, we're all hoping that the war will finally be over by the end of the year. It's about time! Mrs. van Daan's constant griping is unbearable; now that she can no longer drive us crazy with the invasion, she moans and groans all day about the bad weather. If only we could plunk her down in the loft in a bucket of cold water!

Everyone in the Annex except Mr. van Daan and Peter has read the *Hungarian Rhapsody* trilogy, a biography of the composer, piano virtuoso and child prodigy Franz Liszt. It's very interesting, though in my opinion there's a bit too much emphasis on women; Liszt was not only the greatest and most famous pianist

of his time, he was also the biggest womanizer, even at the age
of seventy. He had an affair with Countess Marie d'Agoult, Princess Carolyne Sayn-Wittgenstein, the dancer Lola Montez, the
pianist Agnes Kingworth, the pianist Sophie Menter, the
Circassian princess Olga Janina, Baroness Olga Meyendorff, act-
ress Lilla what's-her-name, etc., etc., and there's no end to it.
Those parts of the book dealing with music and the other arts
are much more interesting. Some of the people mentioned are
Schumann, Clara Wieck, Hector Berlioz, Johannes Brahms,
Beethoven, Joachim, Richard Wagner, Hans von Bülow, Anton
Rubinstein, Frédéric Chopin, Victor Hugo, Honoré de Balzac,
Hiller, Hummel, Czerny, Rossini, Cherubini, Paganini, Men-
delssohn, etc., etc.

Liszt appears to have been a decent man, very generous and
modest, though exceptionally vain. He helped others, put art
above all else, was extremely fond of cognac and women,
couldn't bear the sight of tears, was a gentleman, couldn't refuse
anyone a favor, wasn't interested in money and cared about religious freedom and the world.

*Yours, Anne M. Frank*

TUESDAY, JUNE 13, 1944

*Dearest Kit,*

Another birthday has gone by, so I'm now fifteen. I received
quite a few gifts: Springer's five-volume art history book, a set
of underwear, two belts, a handkerchief, two jars of yogurt, a jar
of jam, two honey cookies (small), a botany book from Father
and Mother, a gold bracelet from Margot, a sticker album from
the van Daans, Biomalt and sweet peas from Dussel, candy from
Miep, candy and notebooks from Bep, and the high point: the
book *Maria Theresa* and three slices of full-cream cheese from Mr.
Kugler. Peter gave me a lovely bouquet of peonies; the poor boy
had put a lot of effort into finding a present, but nothing quite
worked out.

The invasion is still going splendidly, in spite of the miserable
weather – pouring rains, gale winds and high seas.

Yesterday Churchill, Smuts, Eisenhower and Arnold visited
the French villages that the British have captured and liberated.

Churchill was on a torpedo boat that shelled the coast. Like many men, he doesn't seem to know what fear is – an enviable trait!

From our position here in Fort Annex, it's difficult to gauge the mood of the Dutch. No doubt many people are glad the idle (!) British have finally rolled up their sleeves and gotten down to work. Those who keep claiming they don't want to be occupied by the British don't realize how unfair they're being. Their line of reasoning boils down to this: England must fight, struggle and sacrifice its sons to liberate Holland and the other occupied countries. After that the British shouldn't remain in Holland: they should offer their most abject apologies to all the occupied countries, restore the Dutch East Indies to its rightful owner and then return, weakened and impoverished, to England. What a bunch of idiots. And yet, as I've already said, many Dutch people can be counted among their ranks. What would have become of Holland and its neighbors if England had signed a peace treaty with Germany, as it's had ample opportunity to do? Holland would have become German, and that would have been the end of that!

All those Dutch people who still look down on the British, scoff at England and its government of aging lords, call the English cowards, yet hate the Germans, should be given a good shaking, the way you'd plump up a pillow. Maybe that would straighten out their jumbled brains!

Wishes, thoughts, accusations and reproaches are swirling around in my head. I'm not really as conceited as many people think; I know my various faults and shortcomings better than anyone else, but there's one difference: I also know that I want to change, will change and already have changed greatly!

Why is it, I often ask myself, that everyone still thinks I'm so pushy and such a know-it-all? Am I really so arrogant? Am *I* the one who's so arrogant, or are they? It sounds crazy, I know, but I'm not going to cross out that last sentence, because it's not as crazy as it seems. Mrs. van Daan and Dussel, my two chief accusers, are known to be totally unintelligent and, not to put too fine a point on it, just plain "stupid"! Stupid people usually can't bear it when others do something better than they do; the best examples of this are those two dummies, Mrs. van Daan and Dussel. Mrs. van D. thinks I'm stupid because I don't suffer so much from this ailment as she does, she thinks I'm pushy because she's even pushier, she thinks my dresses are too short because hers are even shorter, and she thinks I'm such a know-it-all because she talks twice as much as I do about topics she knows nothing about. The same goes for Dussel. But one of my favorite sayings is "Where there's smoke there's fire," and I readily admit I'm a know-it-all.

What's so difficult about my personality is that I scold and curse myself much more than anyone else does; if Mother adds her advice, the pile of sermons becomes so thick that I despair of ever getting through them. Then I talk back and start contradicting everyone until the old familiar Anne refrain inevitably crops up again: "No one understands me!"

This phrase is part of me, and as unlikely as it may seem, there's a kernel of truth in it. Sometimes I'm so deeply buried under self-reproaches that I long for a word of comfort to help me dig myself out again. If only I had someone who took my feelings seriously. Alas, I haven't yet found that person, so the search must go on.

I know you're wondering about Peter, aren't you, Kit? It's true, Peter loves me, not as a girlfriend, but as a friend. His affection grows day by day, but some mysterious force is holding us back, and I don't know what it is.

Sometimes I think my terrible longing for him was over-exaggerated. But that's not true, because if I'm unable to go to his room for a day or two, I long for him as desperately as I ever did. Peter is kind and good, and yet I can't deny that he's disappointed me in many ways. I especially don't care for his dislike of religion, his talk of food and various things of that nature. Still, I'm firmly convinced that we'll stick to our agreement never to quarrel. Peter is peace-loving, tolerant and extremely easygoing. He lets me say a lot of things to him that he'd never accept from his mother. He's making a determined effort to remove the blots from his copybook and keep his affairs in order. Yet why does he hide his innermost self and never allow me access? Of course, he's much more closed than I am, but I know from experience (even though I'm constantly being accused of knowing all there is to know in theory, but not in practice) that in time, even the most uncommunicative types will long as much, or even more, for someone to confide in.

Peter and I have both spent our contemplative years in the Annex. We often discuss the future, the past and the present, but as I've already told you, I miss the real thing, and yet I know it exists!

Is it because I haven't been outdoors for so long that I've become so smitten with nature? I remember a time when a magnificent blue sky, chirping birds, moonlight and budding blossoms wouldn't have captivated me. Things have changed since I came here. One night during the Pentecost holiday, for instance, when it was so hot, I struggled to keep my eyes open until eleven-thirty so I could get a good look at the moon, all on my own for once. Alas, my sacrifice was in vain, since there was too much glare and I couldn't risk opening a window. Another time, several months ago, I happened to be upstairs one night when the window was open. I didn't go back down until it had to be closed again. The dark, rainy evening, the wind, the racing clouds, had me spellbound; it was the first time in a year and a half that I'd seen the night face-to-face. After that evening my longing to see it again was even greater than my fear of burglars, a dark rat-infested house or police raids. I went downstairs all by myself and looked out the windows in the kitchen and private office. Many people think nature is beautiful, many people sleep from time to time under the starry sky, and many people in hospitals and prisons long for the day when they'll be free to enjoy what nature has to offer. But few are as isolated and cut off as we are from the joys of nature, which can be shared by rich and poor alike.

It's not just my imagination — looking at the sky, the clouds, the moon and the stars really does make me feel calm and hopeful. It's much better medicine than valerian or bromide. Nature makes me feel humble and ready to face every blow with courage!

As luck would have it, I'm only able — except for a few rare occasions – to view nature through dusty curtains tacked over dirt-caked windows; it takes the pleasure out of looking. Nature is the one thing for which there is no substitute!

One of the many questions that have often bothered me is why women have been, and still are, thought to be so inferior to men. It's easy to say it's unfair, but that's not enough for me; I'd really like to know the reason for this great injustice!

Men presumably dominated women from the very beginning because of their greater physical strength; it's men who earn a living, beget children and do as they please ... Until recently, women silently went along with this, which was stupid, since the longer it's kept up, the more deeply entrenched it becomes. Fortunately, education, work and progress have opened women's eyes. In many countries they've been granted equal rights; many people, mainly women, but also men, now realize how wrong it was to tolerate this state of affairs for so long. Modern women want the right to be completely independent!

But that's not all. Women should be respected as well! Generally speaking, men are held in great esteem in all parts of the world, so why shouldn't women have their share? Soldiers and war heroes are honored and commemorated, explorers are granted immortal fame, martyrs are revered, but how many people look upon women too as soldiers?

In the book *Men Against Death* I was greatly struck by the fact that in childbirth alone, women commonly suffer more pain, illness and misery than any war hero ever does. And what's her reward for enduring all that pain? She gets pushed aside when she's disfigured by birth, her children soon leave, her beauty is gone. Women, who struggle and suffer pain to ensure the continuation of the human race, make much tougher and more courageous soldiers than all those big-mouthed freedom-fighting heroes put together!

I don't mean to imply that women should stop having children; on the contrary, nature intended them to, and that's the way it should be. What I condemn are our system of values and the men who don't acknowledge how great, difficult, but ultimately beautiful women's share in society is.

I agree completely with Paul de Kruif, the author of this book, when he says that men must learn that birth is no longer thought of as inevitable and unavoidable in those parts of the world we consider civilized. It's easy for men to talk – they don't and never will have to bear the woes that women do!

I believe that in the course of the next century the notion that it's a woman's duty to have children will change and make way for the respect and admiration of all women, who bear their burdens without complaint or a lot of pompous words!

*Yours, Anne M. Frank*

FRIDAY, JUNE 16, 1944

*Dearest Kitty,*

New problems: Mrs. van D. is at her wits' end. She's talking about getting shot, being thrown in prison, being hanged and suicide. She's jealous that Peter confides in me and not in her, offended that Dussel doesn't respond sufficiently to her flirtations and afraid her husband's going to squander all the fur-coat money on tobacco. She quarrels, curses, cries, feels sorry for herself, laughs and starts all over again.

What on earth can you do with such a silly, sniveling specimen of humanity? Nobody takes her seriously, she has no strength of character, she complains to one and all, and you should see how she walks around: *von hinten Lyzeum, von vorne Museum.** Even worse, Peter's becoming insolent, Mr. van Daan irritable and Mother cynical. Yes, everyone's in quite a state! There's only one rule you need to remember: laugh at everything and forget everybody else! It sounds egotistical, but it's actually the only cure for those suffering from self-pity.

Mr. Kugler's supposed to spend four weeks in Alkmaar on a work detail. He's trying to get out of it with a doctor's certificate and a letter from Opekta. Mr. Kleiman's hoping his stomach will be operated on soon. Starting at eleven last night, all private phones were cut off.

*Yours, Anne M. Frank*

---

*Acts like a schoolgirl, looks like a frump.

*Dearest Kitty,*                           FRIDAY, JUNE 23, 1944

Nothing special going on here. The British have begun their all-out attack on Cherbourg. According to Pim and Mr. van Daan, we're sure to be liberated before October 10. The Russians are taking part in the campaign; yesterday they started their offensive near Vitebsk, exactly three years to the day that the Germans invaded Russia.

Bep's spirits have sunk lower than ever. We're nearly out of potatoes; from now on, we're going to count them out for each person, then everyone can do what they want with them. Starting Monday, Miep's taking a week of vacation. Mr. Kleiman's doctors haven't found anything on the X rays. He's torn between having an operation and letting matters take their course.

*Yours, Anne M. Frank*


*My dearest Kitty,*                        TUESDAY, JUNE 27, 1944

The mood has changed, everything's going enormously well. Cherbourg, Vitebsk and Zhlobin fell today. They're sure to have captured lots of men and equipment. Five German generals were killed near Cherbourg and two taken captive. Now that they've got a harbor, the British can bring whatever they want on shore. The whole Cotentin Peninsula has been captured just three weeks after the invasion! What a feat!

In the three weeks since D Day there hasn't been a day without rain and storms, neither here nor in France, but this bad luck hasn't kept the British and the Americans from displaying their might. And how! Of course, the Germans have launched their wonder weapon, but a little firecracker like that won't hardly make a dent, except maybe minor damage in England and screaming headlines in the Kraut newspapers. Anyway, when they realize in "Krautland" that the Bolsheviks really are getting closer, they'll be shaking in their boots.

All German women who aren't working for the military are being evacuated, together with their children, from the coastal regions to the provinces of Groningen, Friesland and Gelderland.

Mussert* has announced that if the invasion reaches Holland, he'll enlist. Is that fat pig planning to fight? He could have done that in Russia long before now. Finland turned down a peace offer some time ago, and now the negotiations have been broken off again. Those numskulls, they'll be sorry!

How far do you think we'll be on July 27?

*Yours, Anne M. Frank*

FRIDAY, JUNE 30, 1944

*Dearest Kitty,*

*Bad weather from one at a stretch to the thirty June.*† Don't I say that well? Oh yes, I already know a little English; just to prove it I'm reading *An Ideal Husband* with the help of a dictionary! War's going wonderfully: Bobruysk, Mogilev and Orsha have fallen, lots of prisoners.

Everything's all right here. Spirits are improving, our super-optimists are triumphant, the van Daans are doing disappearing acts with the sugar, Bep's changed her hair, and Miep has a week off. That's the latest news!

I've been having really ghastly root-canal work done on one of my front teeth. It's been terribly painful. It was so bad Dussel thought I was going to faint, and I nearly did. Mrs. van D. promptly got a toothache as well!

*Yours, Anne M. Frank*

P S. We've heard from Basel that Bernd† played the part of the innkeeper in *Minna von Barnhelm*. He has "artistic leanings," says Mother.

THURSDAY, JULY 6, 1944

*Dearest Kitty,*

My blood runs cold when Peter talks about becoming a criminal or a speculator; of course, he's joking, but I still have the feeling he's afraid of his own weakness. Margot and Peter are always saying to me, "If I had your spunk and your strength, if I had your drive and unflagging energy, I could . . . !"

Is it really such an admirable trait not to let myself be influenced by others? Am I right in following my own conscience?

* The leader of the Dutch National Socialist (Nazi) Party.
† Anne's English.
‡ Cousin Bernhard (Buddy) Elias.

To be honest, I can't imagine how anyone could say "I'm weak" and then stay that way. If you know that about yourself, why not fight it, why not develop your character? Their answer has always been: "Because it's much easier not to!" This reply leaves me feeling rather discouraged. Easy? Does that mean a life of deceit and laziness is easy too? Oh no, that can't be true. It can't be true that people are so readily tempted by ease . . . and money. I've given a lot of thought to what my answer should be, to how I should get Peter to believe in himself and, most of all, to change himself for the better. I don't know whether I'm on the right track.

I've often imagined how nice it would be if someone were to confide everything to me. But now that it's reached that point, I realize how difficult it is to put yourself in someone else's shoes and find the *right* answer. Especially since "easy" and "money" are new and completely alien concepts to me.

Peter's beginning to lean on me and I don't want that, not under any circumstances. It's hard enough standing on your own two feet, but when you also have to remain true to your character and soul, it's harder still.

I've been drifting around at sea, have spent days searching for an effective antidote to that terrible word "easy." How can I make it clear to him that, while it may seem easy and wonderful, it will drag him down to the depths, to a place where he'll no longer find friends, support or beauty, so far down that he may never rise to the surface again?

We're all alive, but we don't know why or what for; we're all searching for happiness; we're all leading lives that are different and yet the same. We three have been raised in good families, we have the opportunity to get an education and make something of ourselves. We have many reasons to hope for great happiness, but . . . we have to earn it. And that's something you can't achieve by taking the easy way out. Earning happiness means doing good and working, not speculating and being lazy. Laziness may *look* inviting, but only work gives you *true* satisfaction.

I can't understand people who don't like to work, but that isn't Peter's problem either. He just doesn't have a goal, plus he thinks he's too stupid and inferior to ever achieve anything. Poor boy, he's never known how it feels to make someone else happy, and I'm afraid I can't teach him. He isn't religious, scoffs at Jesus Christ and takes the Lord's name in vain, and though I'm not Orthodox either, it hurts me every time to see him so lonely, so scornful, so wretched.

People who are religious should be glad, since not everyone is blessed with the ability to believe in a higher order. You don't even have to live in fear of eternal punishment; the concepts of purgatory, heaven and hell are difficult for many people to accept, yet religion itself, any religion, keeps a person on the right path. Not the fear of God, but upholding your own sense of honor and obeying your own conscience. How noble and good everyone could be if, at the end of each day, they were to review their own behavior and weigh up the rights and wrongs. They would automatically try to do better at the start of each new day and, after a while, would certainly accomplish a great deal. Everyone is welcome to this prescription; it costs nothing and is definitely useful. Those who don't know will have to find out by experience that "a quiet conscience gives you strength!"

*Yours, Anne M. Frank*

*Dearest Kitty,*

Mr. Broks was in Beverwijk and managed to get hold of strawberries at the produce auction. They arrived here dusty and full of sand, but in large quantities. No less than twenty-four crates for the office and us. That very same evening we canned the first six jars and made eight jars of jam. The next morning Miep started making jam for the office.

At twelve-thirty the outside door was locked, crates were lugged into the kitchen, with Peter, Father and Mr. van Daan stumbling up the stairs. Anne got hot water from the water heater, Margot went for a bucket, all hands on deck! With a funny feeling in my stomach, I entered the overcrowded office kitchen. Miep, Bep, Mr. Kleiman, Jan, Father, Peter: the Annex contingent and the Supply Corps all mixed up together, and that in the middle of the day! Curtains and windows open, loud voices, banging doors – I was trembling with excitement. I kept thinking, "Are we really in hiding?" This must be how it feels when you can finally go out into the world again. The pan was full, so I dashed upstairs, where the rest of the family was hulling strawberries around the kitchen table. At least that's what they were supposed to be doing, but more was going into their mouths than into the buckets. They were bound to need another bucket soon. Peter went back downstairs, but then the doorbell rang twice. Leaving the bucket where it was, Peter raced upstairs and shut the bookcase behind him. We sat kicking our heels impatiently; the strawberries were waiting to be rinsed, but we stuck to the house rule: "No running water when strangers are downstairs – they might hear the drains."

Jan came up at one to tell us it had been the mailman. Peter hurried downstairs again. Ding-dong . . . the doorbell, about-face. I listened to hear if anyone was coming, standing first at the bookcase, then at the top of the stairs. Finally Peter and I leaned over the banister, straining our ears like a couple of burglars to hear the sounds from downstairs. No unfamiliar voices. Peter tiptoed halfway down the stairs and called out, "Bep!" Once more: "Bep!" His voice was drowned out by the racket in the kitchen. So he ran down to the kitchen while I nervously kept watch from above.

"Go upstairs at once, Peter, the accountant's here, you've got to leave!" It was Mr. Kugler's voice. Sighing, Peter came upstairs and closed the bookcase.

Mr. Kugler finally came up at one-thirty. "My gosh, the whole world's turned to strawberries. I had strawberries for breakfast, Jan's having them for lunch, Kleiman's eating them as a snack, Miep's boiling them, Bep's hulling them, and I can smell them everywhere I go. I come upstairs to get away from all that red and what do I see? People washing strawberries!"

The rest of the strawberries were canned. That evening: two jars came unsealed. Father quickly turned them into jam. The next morning: two more lids popped up; and that afternoon: four lids. Mr. van Daan hadn't gotten the jars hot enough when he was sterilizing them, so Father ended up making jam every evening. We ate hot cereal with strawberries, buttermilk with strawberries, bread with strawberries, strawberries for dessert, strawberries with sugar, strawberries with sand. For two days there was nothing but strawberries, strawberries, strawberries, and then our supply was either exhausted or in jars, safely under lock and key.

"Hey, Anne," Margot called out one day, "Mrs. van Hoeven has let us have some peas, twenty pounds!"

"That's nice of her," I replied. And it certainly was, but it's so much work . . . ugh!

"On Saturday, you've all got to shell peas," Mother announced at the table.

And sure enough, this morning after breakfast our biggest enamel pan appeared on the table, filled to the brim with peas. If you think shelling peas is boring work, you ought to try removing the inner linings. I don't think many people realize that once you've pulled out the linings, the pods are soft, delicious and rich in vitamins. But an even greater advantage is that you get nearly three times as much as when you eat just the peas.

Stripping pods is a precise and meticulous job that might be suited to pedantic dentists or finicky spice experts, but it's a horror for an impatient teenager like me. We started work at nine-thirty; I sat down at ten-thirty, got up again at eleven, sat down again at eleven-thirty. My ears were humming with the following refrain: snap the end, strip the pod, pull the string, pod in the pan, snap the end, strip the pod, pull the string, pod in the pan, etc., etc. My eyes were swimming: green, green, worm, string, rotten pod, green, green. To fight the boredom and have something to do, I chattered all morning, saying whatever came into my head and making everyone laugh. The monotony was killing me. Every string I pulled made me more certain that I never, ever, want to be just a housewife!

At twelve we finally ate breakfast, but from twelve-thirty to one-fifteen we had to strip pods again. When I stopped, I felt a bit seasick, and so did the others. I napped until four, still in a daze because of those wretched peas.

*Yours, Anne M. Frank*

*Dearest Kitty,*                          SATURDAY, JULY 15, 1944

We've received a book from the library with the challenging title *What Do You Think of the Modern Young Girl?* I'd like to discuss this subject today.

The writer criticizes "today's youth" from head to toe, though without dismissing them all as "hopeless cases." On the contrary, she believes they have it within their power to build a bigger, better and more beautiful world, but that they occupy themselves with superficial things, without giving a thought to true beauty.

In some passages I had the strong feeling that the writer was directing her disapproval at me, which is why I finally want to bare my soul to you and defend myself against this attack.

I have one outstanding character trait that must be obvious to anyone who's known me for any length of time: I have a great deal of self-knowledge. In everything I do, I can watch myself as if I were a stranger. I can stand across from the everyday Anne and, without being biased or making excuses, watch what she's doing, both the good and the bad. This self-awareness never leaves me, and every time I open my mouth, I think, "You should have said that differently" or "That's fine the way it is." I condemn myself in so many ways that I'm beginning to realize the truth of Father's adage: "Every child has to raise itself." Parents can only advise their children or point them in the right direction. Ultimately, people shape their own characters. In addition, I face life with an extraordinary amount of courage. I feel so strong and capable of bearing burdens, so young and free! When I first realized this, I was glad, because it means I can more easily withstand the blows life has in store.

But I've talked about these things so often. Now I'd like to turn to the chapter "Father and Mother Don't Understand Me." My parents have always spoiled me rotten, treated me kindly, defended me against the van Daans and done all that parents can. And yet for the longest time I've felt extremely lonely, left out, neglected and misunderstood. Father did everything he could to curb my rebellious spirit, but it was no use. I've cured myself by holding my behavior up to the light and looking at what I was doing wrong.

Why didn't Father support me in my struggle? Why did he fall short when he tried to offer me a helping hand? The answer is: he used the wrong methods. He always talked to me as if I were a child going through a difficult phase. It sounds crazy, since Father's the only one who's given me a sense of confidence and made me feel as if I'm a sensible person. But he overlooked one thing: he failed to see that this struggle to triumph over my difficulties was more important to me than anything else. I didn't want to hear about "typical adolescent problems," or "other girls," or "you'll grow out of it." I didn't want to be treated the same as all-the-other-girls, but as Anne-in-her-own-right, and Pim didn't understand that. Besides, I can't confide in anyone unless they tell me a lot about themselves, and because I know very little about him, I can't get on a more intimate footing. Pim always acts like the elderly father who once had the same fleeting impulses, but who can no longer relate to me as a friend, no matter how hard he tries. As a result, I've never shared my out-look on life or my long-pondered theories with anyone but my diary and, once in a while, Margot. I've hid anything having to do with me from Father, never shared my ideals with him, deliberately alienated myself from him.

I couldn't have done it any other way. I've let myself be guided entirely by my feelings. It was egotistical, but I've done what was best for my own peace of mind. I would lose that, plus the self-confidence I've worked so hard to achieve, if I were to be subjected to criticism halfway through the job. It may sound hard-hearted, but I can't take criticism from Pim either, because not only do I never share my innermost thoughts with him, but I've pushed him even further away by being irritable.

This is a point I think about quite often: why is it that Pim annoys me so much sometimes? I can hardly bear to have him tutor me, and his affection seems forced. I want to be left alone, and I'd rather he ignored me for a while until I'm more sure of myself when I'm talking to him! I'm still torn with guilt about the mean letter I wrote him when I was so upset. Oh, it's hard to be strong and brave in every way!

*    *    *

Still, this hasn't been my greatest disappointment. No, I think about Peter much more than I do Father. I know very well that he was my conquest, and not the other way around. I created an image of him in my mind, pictured him as a quiet, sweet, sensitive boy badly in need of friendship and love! I needed to pour out my heart to a living person. I wanted a friend who would help me find my way again. I accomplished what I set out to do and drew him, slowly but surely, toward me. When I finally got him to be my friend, it automatically developed into an intimacy that, when I think about it now, seems outrageous. We talked about the most private things, but we haven't yet touched upon the things closest to my heart. I still can't make head or tail of Peter. Is he superficial, or is it shyness that holds him back, even with me? But putting all that aside, I made one mistake: I used intimacy to get closer to him, and in doing so, I ruled out other forms of friendship. He longs to be loved, and I can see he's beginning to like me more with each passing day. Our time together leaves him feeling satisfied, but just makes me want to start all over again. I never broach the subjects I long to bring out into the open. I forced Peter, more than he realizes, to get close to me, and now he's holding on for dear life. I honestly don't see any effective way of shaking him off and getting him back on his own two feet. I soon realized he could never be a kindred spirit, but still tried to help him break out of his narrow world and expand his youthful horizons.

"Deep down, the young are lonelier than the old." I read this in a book somewhere and it's stuck in my mind. As far as I can tell, it's true.

So if you're wondering whether it's harder for the adults here than for the children, the answer is no, it's certainly not. Older people have an opinion about everything and are sure of themselves and their actions. It's twice as hard for us young people to hold on to our opinions at a time when ideals are being shattered and destroyed, when the worst side of human nature predominates, when everyone has come to doubt truth, justice and God.

Anyone who claims that the older folks have a more difficult time in the Annex doesn't realize that the problems have a far greater impact on us. We're much too young to deal with these problems, but they keep thrusting themselves on us until, finally, we're forced to think up a solution, though most of the time our solutions crumble when faced with the facts. It's difficult in times like these: ideals, dreams and cherished hopes rise within us, only to be crushed by grim reality. It's a wonder I haven't abandoned all my ideals, they seem so absurd and impractical. Yet I cling to them because I still believe, in spite of everything, that people are truly good at heart.

It's utterly impossible for me to build my life on a foundation of chaos, suffering and death. I see the world being slowly transformed into a wilderness, I hear the approaching thunder that, one day, will destroy us too, I feel the suffering of millions. And yet, when I look up at the sky, I somehow feel that everything will change for the better, that this cruelty too will end, that peace and tranquility will return once more. In the meantime, I must hold on to my ideals. Perhaps the day will come when I'll be able to realize them!

Yours, Anne M. Frank

Dearest Kitty,
FRIDAY, JULY 21, 1944

I'm finally getting optimistic. Now, at last, things are going well! They really are! Great news! An assassination attempt has been made on Hitler's life, and for once not by Jewish Communists or English capitalists, but by a German general who's not only a count, but young as well. The Führer owes his life to "Divine Providence": he escaped, unfortunately, with only a few minor burns and scratches. A number of the officers and generals who were nearby were killed or wounded. The head of the conspiracy has been shot.

This is the best proof we've had so far that many officers and generals are fed up with the war and would like to see Hitler sink into a bottomless pit, so they can establish a military dictatorship, make peace with the Allies, rearm themselves and, after a few decades, start a new war. Perhaps Providence is deliberately biding its time getting rid of Hitler, since it's much easier, and cheaper, for the Allies to let the impeccable Germans kill each other off. It's less work for the Russians and the British, and it allows them to start rebuilding their own cities all that much sooner. But we haven't reached that point yet, and I'd hate to anticipate the glorious event. Still, you've probably noticed that I'm telling the truth, the whole truth and nothing but the truth. For once, I'm not rattling on about high ideals.

Furthermore, Hitler has been so kind as to announce to his loyal, devoted people that as of today all military personnel are under orders of the Gestapo, and that any soldier who knows that one of his superiors was involved in this cowardly attempt on the Führer's life may shoot him on sight!

A fine kettle of fish that will be. Little Johnny's feet are sore after a long march and his commanding officer bawls him out. Johnny grabs his rifle, shouts, "You, you tried to kill the Führer. Take that!" One shot, and the snooty officer who dared to reprimand him passes into eternal life (or is it eternal death?). Eventually, every time an officer sees a soldier or gives an order, he'll be practically wetting his pants, because the soldiers have more say-so than he does.

Were you able to follow that, or have I been skipping from one subject to another again? I can't help it, the prospect of going back to school in October is making me too happy to be logical! Oh dear, didn't I just get through telling you I didn't want to anticipate events? Forgive me, Kitty, they don't call me a bundle of contradictions for nothing!

*Yours, Anne M. Frank*

TUESDAY, AUGUST 1, 1944
*Dearest Kitty,*

"A bundle of contradictions" was the end of my previous letter and is the beginning of this one. Can you please tell me exactly what "a bundle of contradictions" is? What does "contradiction" mean? Like so many words, it can be interpreted in two ways: a contradiction imposed from without and one imposed from within. The former means not accepting other people's opinions, always knowing best, having the last word; in short, all those unpleasant traits for which I'm known. The latter, for which I'm not known, is my own secret.

As I've told you many times, I'm split in two. One side contains my exuberant cheerfulness, my flippancy, my joy in life and, above all, my ability to appreciate the lighter side of things. By that I mean not finding anything wrong with flirtations, a kiss, an embrace, an off-color joke. This side of me is usually lying in wait to ambush the other one, which is much purer, deeper and finer. No one knows Anne's better side, and that's why most people can't stand me. Oh, I can be an amusing clown for an afternoon, but after that everyone's had enough of me to last a month. Actually, I'm what a romantic movie is to a profound thinker – a mere diversion, a comic interlude, something that is soon forgotten: not bad, but not particularly good either. I hate having to tell you this, but why shouldn't I admit it when I know it's true? My lighter, more superficial side will always steal a march on the deeper side and therefore always win. You can't imagine how often I've tried to push away this Anne, which is only half of what is known as Anne – to beat her down, hide her. But it doesn't work, and I know why.

I'm afraid that people who know me as I usually am will discover I have another side, a better and finer side. I'm afraid they'll mock me, think I'm ridiculous and sentimental and not take me seriously. I'm used to not being taken seriously, but only the "lighthearted" Anne is used to it and can put up with it; the "deeper" Anne is too weak. If I force the good Anne into the spotlight for even fifteen minutes, she shuts up like a clam the moment she's called upon to speak, and lets Anne number one do the talking. Before I realize it, she's disappeared.

So the nice Anne is never seen in company. She's never made a single appearance, though she almost always takes the stage when I'm alone. I know exactly how I'd like to be, how I am . . . on the inside. But unfortunately I'm only like that with myself. And perhaps that's why – no, I'm sure that's the reason why – I think of myself as happy on the inside and other people think I'm happy on the outside. I'm guided by the pure Anne within, but on the outside I'm nothing but a frolicsome little goat tugging at its tether.

As I've told you, what I say is not what I feel, which is why I have a reputation for being boy-crazy as well as a flirt, a smart aleck and a reader of romances. The happy-go-lucky Anne laughs, gives a flippant reply, shrugs her shoulders and pretends she doesn't give a darn. The quiet Anne reacts in just the opposite way. If I'm being completely honest, I'll have to admit that it does matter to me, that I'm trying very hard to change myself, but that I'm always up against a more powerful enemy.

A voice within me is sobbing, "You see, that's what's become of you. You're surrounded by negative opinions, dismayed looks and mocking faces, people who dislike you, and all because you don't listen to the advice of your own better half." Believe me, I'd like to listen, but it doesn't work, because if I'm quiet and serious, everyone thinks I'm putting on a new act and I have to save myself with a joke, and then I'm not even talking about my own family, who assume I must be sick, stuff me with aspirins and sedatives, feel my neck and forehead to see if I have a temperature, ask about my bowel movements and berate me for being in a bad mood, until I just can't keep it up anymore, because when everybody starts hovering over me, I get cross, then sad, and finally end up turning my heart inside out, the bad part on the outside and the good part on the inside, and keep trying to find a way to become what I'd like to be and what I could be if . . . if only there were no other people in the world.

*Yours, Anne M. Frank*

ANNE'S DIARY ENDS HERE.

# AFTERWORD

ON THE MORNING of August 4, 1944, sometime between ten and ten-thirty, a car pulled up at 263 Prinsengracht. Several figures emerged: an SS sergeant, Karl Josef Silberbauer, in full uniform, and at least three Dutch members of the Security Police, armed but in civilian clothes. Someone must have tipped them off.

They arrested the eight people hiding in the Annex, as well as two of their helpers, Victor Kugler and Johannes Kleiman — though not Miep Gies and Elisabeth (Bep) Voskuijl — and took all the valuables and cash they could find in the Annex.

After the arrest, Kugler and Kleiman were taken to a prison in Amsterdam. On September 11, 1944, they were transferred, without benefit of a trial, to a camp in Amersfoort (Holland). Kleiman, because of his poor health, was released on September 18, 1944. He remained in Amsterdam until his death in 1959.

Kugler managed to escape his imprisonment on March 28, 1945, when he and his fellow prisoners were being sent to Germany as forced laborers. He immigrated to Canada in 1955 and died in Toronto in 1989.

Elisabeth (Bep) Voskuijl Wijk died in Amsterdam in 1983.

Miep Santrouschitz Gies died in Amsterdam in January 2010; her husband Jan died in 1993.

Upon their arrest, the eight residents of the Annex were first brought to a prison in Amsterdam and then transferred to Westerbork, the transit camp for Jews in the north of Holland. They were deported on September 3, 1944, in the last transport to leave Westerbork, and arrived three days later in Auschwitz (Poland).

Hermann van Pels (van Daan) was, according to the testimony of Otto Frank, gassed to death in Auschwitz in October or November 1944, shortly before the gas chambers were dismantled.

Auguste van Pels (Petronella van Daan) was transported from Auschwitz to Bergen-Belsen, from there to Buchenwald, then to Theresienstadt on April 9, 1945, and apparently to another concentration camp after that. It is certain that she did not survive, though the date of her death is unknown.

Peter van Pels (van Daan) was forced to take part in the January 16, 1945 "death march" from Auschwitz to Mauthausen (Austria), where he died on May 5, 1945, three days before the camp was liberated.

Fritz Pfeffer (Albert Dussel) died on December 20, 1944, in the Neuengamme concentration camp, where he had been transferred from either Buchenwald or Sachsenhausen.

Edith Frank died in Auschwitz-Birkenau on January 6, 1945, from hunger and exhaustion.

Margot and Anne Frank were transported from Auschwitz at the end of October and brought to Bergen-Belsen, a concentration camp near Hannover (Germany). The typhus epidemic that broke out in the winter of 1944–1945, as a result of the horrendous hygienic conditions, killed thousands of prisoners, including Margot and, a few days later, Anne. She must have died in late February or early March. The bodies of both girls were probably dumped in Bergen-Belsen's mass graves. The camp was liberated by British troops on April 12, 1945.

Otto Frank was the only one of the eight to survive the concentration camps. After Auschwitz was liberated by Russian troops, he was repatriated to Amsterdam by way of Odessa and Marseille. He arrived in Amsterdam on June 3, 1945, and stayed there until 1953, when he moved to Basel (Switzerland), where his sister and her family, and later his brother, lived. He married Elfriede Markovits Geiringer, originally from Vienna, who had survived Auschwitz and lost a husband and son in Mauthausen. Until his death on August 19, 1980, Otto Frank continued to live in Birsfelden, outside Basel, where he devoted himself to sharing the message of his daughter's diary with people all over the world.